BY:

Jumping

Lightyears

Jumping Lightyears

The Evolution of Interstellar Travel

Dr.H

Copyright © 2002 by Dr.H.

Library of Congress Number: 2002091463

ISBN :   Softcover   1-4010-5454-4

All rights reserved. No part of this book may be reproduced or transmitted in any form or by any means, electronic or mechanical, including photocopying, recording, or by any information storage and retrieval system, without permission in writing from the copyright owner.

This book was printed in the United States of America.

To order additional copies of this book, contact:
Xlibris Corporation
1-888-795-4274
www.Xlibris.com
Orders@Xlibris.com

Contents

Overview 7
The Absence of Technology for Space Travel 15
Physics Without Paradox 23
Scientific Method 38
Psi Studies in China 49
Seven Reproducible Psi Facts 54
A Testable Theory of the Mind 73
Fermi's Paradox 85
A Science of Civilization 90
Seven True Ideals 95
Evidence 101
Liberty and the War-On-Drugs 116
Lady Justice 125
Catching Terrorists and Serial Killers 132
An Anthropologist's View of Morality 137
The Third Republic 144
Ending War Using Hierarchies of Community 151
Seeds of Hate 155
Urban Gridlock 159
Hubbert's Peak 166
The Beautiful City 170
Saving the Planet 176
A Social Safety Net 188
Learning Versus Indoctrination 199
Discrimination and Tribalism 208

Stability and Instability of Families	210
The Full Keynesian Economy	218
A Philosophical Breakthrough	223
Sophistry	228
Funetik English	234
Mysticism and Revelation; A Science?	242
Mysticism—A First Hand Account	248
Creation	252
The Problem of Evil	254
Animacy, Free Will, Challenge-And-Response	257
The Desert Religions	261
The Sayings of Jesus	271
A Kind of Autobiography	275
The Alphabet of Symbolic Elements	285
Mandalas in Music and Architecture	295
My Meditation Practices	311
The Seeker	314
Bibliography	333

Overview

Is interstellar travel possible? Yes. UFOs are interstellar travelers. And they jump hundreds of lightyears in an instant. Is there any scientific evidence for that? Yes, but some of the most important books are hard to find and not very well known. Aside from that, there is the difficulty that the subject of UFOs is controversial and divisive. People tend to have their minds already made up about the subject. Human beings are extraordinarily good at picking up the tribal mythology of their time, and the tribal mythology of our time is reduction. Scientific method is one thing, the religion of the scientists something else. We shall have to deal with those issues, but let us begin with the evidence.

An example of an important book for Ufologists is *The Humanoids*, edited by Charles Bowen. It is a collection of studies made by a variety of scholars of reports of landed UFOs, with aliens outside, seen by multiple witnesses, in broad daylight, and at close range. Each case was investigated. These are not anecdotal reports, like the odd things that Charles Fort found in local newspapers. No. The town was visited, the character and sobriety of the witnesses determined, and each witness independently queried. There is no motive for fraud in these cases. Their neighbors only made fun of them, and called them crazy. All witnesses remained anonymous. None became famous. None ever got on TV or had books written about them. This classic scientific study, *The Humanoids,* was published in 1969, and can only be obtained from *The Flying Saucer Review*, Snodland, Kent, ME6 5HJ, UK.

The observations are independent of one another, and so are the studies. Between 1947 and 1969, when these observations were made, there were no programs like "Encounters" or "Sightings" on TV to give a sympathetic treatment to UFO experience. The media were united with the authorities and academia in laughing off such reports. And the aliens in science fiction (then and now) were nothing like the real aliens. The fictional aliens are aggressive non-humanoid BEMs (Bug-Eyed Monsters) for the most part, like those in the movie "Aliens," or "Independence Day." Nor does the Starship Enterprise in any way resemble real space-craft. Figments of imagination tend to resemble those other figments of imagination found on TV or in movies and books.

Scientific method requires reproducibility and veridicality. The reproducibility lies in the rather astounding fact that all the aliens are humanoid. They range in height from 1 foot to 10 feet. They range in skin color from white to pink to brown to gray to a greenish color. Some have fur. Some are hairless. But they all have the classic hallmarks of the humanoid, which is to say, they are bipedal, binaural, binocular, bilateral, with two arms, 3 to 6 fingers, a head arranged like ours, with eyes above nostrils above mouth, a neck, shoulders, arms, trunk, legs, and feet with toes. Some cannot breath our atmosphere and wear spacesuits, but most do not. Many do wear black contact lenses, being unused to such strong sun light. That is true for most of the gray species, who probably come from K2 planetary systems. Let me explain what is meant by "K2."

Star brightness and longevity correlates with mass and is classified by letter. Our star is G2. The "2" indicates second generation (at least), containing many metals, products of earlier generations of stars which went through the main sequence quickly and exploded as a supernova. Elements heavier than helium are produced only in stars. Elements heavier than iron are only produced in a supernova. Even a star like our own will push much of its mass off into space, and produce what is called a planetary nebula. K2 are dimmer than G2, but will last longer. Red Dwarfs are class M, and are not expected to host planets with life, because the planet would have to orbit so closely to the star that tidal interactions would pull it apart. That is too bad, because 80% of the stars within 22 light-years of the Sun are class M. They can only be seen with powerful telescopes. On the other end of the scale, very bright short lived stars are class A. In order to have complex life forms, it is necessary to have an Earth-like planet in a stable orbit in the zone where water is mostly liquid. And the star must be long-lived. Our own G2 has a lifetime of 10 to 15 giga-yr, and is now middle-aged.

The veridicality of Charles Bowen's collection of studies lies in the fact that we can rule out fraud (how would these thousands of anonymous witnesses get together to concoct a story, considering that the studies are world wide and range over 20 years?). I think we can safely rule out Venus, swamp gas, aircraft, and pranks, and everything else you can think of. These are not mysterious lights in the night time sky, which might have any number of possible explanations. These humanoids couldn't be kids dressed up in alien suits, because many species are quite small, under 1 meter in height. They are not Jungian archetypal visions, like visions of Mother Mary. One citizen got into a wrestling match with a 35 pound humanoid covered with red fur, who had claws and glowing eyes. That is number 188 in Vallee's list. They are flesh and blood, just like us.

So the only remaining alternatives are beings from another dimension, or time travelers. They may very well pass through a fifth space-like dimension when they teleport across hundreds of light-years. But they don't live there. They live here, in this world, and can point out their home star to contactees. We will discuss this in more detail later, but there is no reason to think time travel is possible. Despite Einstein's Special Theory of Relativity, time does not function as a space-like dimension. In physics, it is imaginary time that functions as a space-like dimension, but we cannot travel in imaginary time. In any case, it seems very unlikely that so many different creatures could be part of Earth's future. It took 4.5 giga-yr to produce us, and a special set of circumstances at that.

Why is Ufology one of the forbidden sciences? As we shall see later, physics does not allow interstellar travel. And the religion of the scientists is "reduction to physics." That is why the scientists reject the possibility of UFOs, and assume that if there is ETI out there, it would be sending us radio signals. This is stupidity in search of stupidity, in my opinion. Why would any intelligent species send out a beacon saying "Here I am, a nice water-fat, oxygenated planet for the taking?" Even a primitive culture like ours could probably launch a solar sail ark before long, if we had a known destination. Could all the academics be wrong? After all, they are supposed to be smart. They have Ph.D.s. Well, so do I. It is well to remember that Galileo could not persuade a single one of his colleagues at the University of Padua to come look through his telescope. He wrote a letter about it to his fellow natural philosopher, Kepler.

"I think, my Kepler, we will laugh at the extraordinary stupidity of the multitude. What do you say of the leading philosophers here to whom I have offered a thousand times of my own accord to show my studies but who have never consented to look at the planets, moon, or telescope." Letter from Galileo to Kepler. (Koestler, p. 213). The "multitude" Galileo refers to are his own academic colleagues at the University of Padua. I think, my Kepler, that we shall also laugh at the extraordinary stupidity of our own leading philosophers and scientists. Intelligence is the ability to benefit from experience; stupidity is its opposite. Extraordinary stupidity is the refusal even to look.

Some people insist that physical and tangible evidence is required by scientific method. They are wrong. Bring me a quark. Bring me a supernova. I want it right here right now. And bring me a cosmic black hole while you are at it. It would be nice, of course, to have an actual UFO or parts of one. According to Colonel Corso (ret), two crashed UFOs were recovered near Roswell in 1947 (see bibliography), along with alien bodies, and they no doubt still exist somewhere in the labyrinth of pointless government secrecy. I wonder why. That is, I wonder why they keep it secret? Do they think we would be shocked? That we would be panic stricken? Knowing that UFO aliens are just anthropologists, and bring no weapons, why would be worried? We have real terrors to worry about, such as the possibility that the Al Qaeda terrorists possess nuclear weapons. I suspect it is actually a case of the Air Force keeping secrets from the Army and both keeping secrets from the Navy, and all of them keeping secrets from the civilian government. Incidentally, some UFO landings do have physical effects on the landing site. Not all UFOs leave a tangible trace, just as some UFOs can be tracked on radar, and some cannot.

So back to my original train of thought. Of course interstellar travel is possible. The UFOs do it all the time. And what they have done, we can do as well. After all, they are just humanoids like us. Most people who believe in UFOs think they just have a more advanced technology. Not so. That would not explain Fermi's paradox, nor would it explain the behavior of the UFO aliens.

What is Fermi's Paradox? Enrico Fermi was a famous Italian physicist of the 1940s and 1950s, who had much to do with the development of nuclear energy. He posed a simple question back in 1940. "If space traveling species are common, where are they?" Let me spell that out a little bit. For the past 1.5 giga-yr, the Earth has had oceans and oxygen and dry land. So why didn't any aliens come and colonize it? They didn't, you know, despite the disinformation given to contactees. Except for the occasional comet or asteroid, there is no evidence of any outside influence on the course of evolution on Earth.

It is a remarkable fact that the 57 species (according to one count, make it somewhere between 25 and 100) that have visited us have never wanted to make any official contact. For the early

Ufologists, this was the first puzzle. None of these visitors have landed on the White House Lawn, as in the movie "The Day the Earth Stood Still," and said "Take me to your leader." Nor will they ever do so. For that would violate the Prime Directive, absolutely the only thing that Star Trek got right.

This is apparently the code of all space-traveling species: "Thou shalt not interfere in the evolution of any planet." In any case, that would spoil the fun. They come not as conquerors, or traders, or diplomats. They come as anthropologists. And that is the explanation of the Fermi paradox.

We know that human anthropologists never want to disturb the primitive cultures they are studying. For one thing, anthropologists are all too cognizant of the hundreds of primitive cultures that have simply vanished on contact with more advanced civilizations. Any contact between primitive and advanced cultures is very dangerous to the primitive culture. That's us. We are the primitive culture, violent, greedy, raping and destroying the world without giving any thought for tomorrow. We may be extinct before the 21st Century is over. The aliens undoubtedly want to observe us while they still can. Do not look to them for salvation. We created this mess, and we must work our way out of it. Any interference by the Aliens would violate the Prime Directive.

So UFO aliens have never colonized the planet, and have taken some pains to hide their visits now. They accurately gauge the collective stupidity of the scientific establishment, so they don't have to try very hard. They just confine their landings to remote and largely uninhabited places. When they make contact with a human, they use disinformation as a disguise, knowing this "revelation" will be rejected by the larger society, with good reason.

So, to summarize my argument, (1) physics does not allow true interstellar travel, although it might allow some sort of slow exodus. (2) Since 1947, we have been frequently visited by interstellar travelers, so it must be possible. (3) If not by the powers of physics, UFOs must travel by the powers of the mind.

(4) In human experience, only spiritually advanced humans ever demonstrate spontaneous psychic powers. (5) The UFO aliens must also be spiritually advanced, since they have refrained from interfering in the evolution of life on Earth.

The obvious conclusion is that only spiritually evolved species can become space-travelers. So, the evolution of interstellar travel is really the social and mental evolution of mankind. A species that still has wars is not as evolved as one that doesn't. A species that can control its population growth and not be forced to emigrate is more evolved than one without such self-control. An anthropologist is more evolved than a missionary, a conquistador, a trader, or a colonist. An evolved species knows how to meet its material needs without taking over other planets, without using up non-renewable resources, without destroying ecological systems. We might reach such a state of advancement eventually. Indeed, if we don't, we are likely to become extinct, probably before the 21st Century is finished.

This book divides into 4 sections of varying length. First we look at space technology and modern physics. Standard stuff, but perhaps difficult reading. Then we take a philosophical and historical look at scientific method, because the rest of the book is not going to be standard stuff. If we are going to go against tribal mythology, and against the present worldview, we can only do so in the name of scientific method. The second section deals with the main discoveries of psychical research and a non-reductionist but testable theory of the Mind. Since the main thesis of this book is that spiritual evolution, not new technology, will take us to the stars, I revisit this concept of "spiritual evolution," and find that it means the evolution of civilization and of our spiritual life. And those two subjects make up the last two sections, which constitute the bulk of the book. So if you are not big on science and technology, you could skip to chapter 9 to look at some ideas on the future evolution of our civilization, or chapter 32 to see what I have to say about the developing spiritual life of mankind.

The Absence of Technology for Space Travel

It is impossible to get to the stars in any reasonable length of time by any means known to physics. Lawrence Krauss, a well-respected neutrino physicist, proved that in his careful analysis of *The Physics of Startrek*. He has done all the calculations, demonstrating the absurdity of everything about Startrek.

The stars are just too far away. This is a fortunate thing, since it provides a natural quarantine for nasty little cultures like us. Even if we could accelerate to near the speed of light, that would still be far too slow for interstellar exploration. Most of the familiar objects that we can see in the night time sky are hundreds or thousands of light-years away. That familiar constellation of the winter nights, the Pleiades (Seven Sisters), is over 350 light years away. A round trip at the speed of light would take over 700 years. It would be like leaving during the medieval Black Death and returning in the 21st Century. That is not exploration; it is exodus. That is assuming travel near the speed of light, which is itself impossible.

We are looking for G2 or K2 singlets and there are none really close. Multiple star systems could have planets, but would the orbits of these planets be stable? Would their orbits stay in the comfort zone where water is liquid? Probably not. The "2" indicates metal rich stars. Our own star is G2, what is called a yellow dwarf. K2 is the next sized smaller. Maybe we could call it an orange dwarf. Judging from the gray skin of many of our alien visitors, many come from K2s, which do not produce enough ultraviolet to cause sunburn. The smallest of stars, red dwarfs and brown dwarfs, are thought unlikely to have planets with life. For a red dwarf, a planet close enough to be warm enough to have liquid water would be so close as to be disrupted by tidal interaction. Red dwarfs are quite common, though they cannot be seen with the naked eye. A full eighty percent of the stars within about 22 light-years are red dwarfs. Brown dwarfs have recently been detected in the infrared, and may be quite common. In any case, they are too dim to give rise to life. So, how far do we have to go to find K2 or G2 singlets?

The nearest star system is Alpha Centauri, about 4.3 light-years away. This is a group of 3 stars, one of which is a G2. But another star is only 40 AU away, about as far away as the Kuiper belt is from our sun. Would planetary orbits be stable enough? Maybe, but Earth-like planets would likely be pounded by comets and asteroids disturbed by the second star in the system. Tau Ceti and Epsilon Eridani are sunlike stars, both about 10 light-years away. Both are smaller, fainter, younger and depleted in metals compared to our sun. There are many web sites about both. http://www.solstation.com/stars/ is a web site that has a lot of information on stars within 30 light-years.

Our sun appears to be the only high metal G2 singlet within about 22 light-years. But we find plenty of possible targets within about 100 light-years. Many of the nearby stars which are said to be "sun-like" are parts of multiple star systems, i.e., not singlets, and have low metallicity. Systems with low metallicity seem unlikely to have Earth-like planets, although both Tau Ceti and Epsilon Eridani appear to have planets of some sort. This theory is based on the absence of infrared in a 30 AU disk around these stars. This dark disk does not glow in the infrared because planets have swept up all the dust within this region.

The trouble with stars much larger and brighter than our own is that they will not survive long enough to evolve intelligence. There is a relationship between mass, brightness, color and longevity. A G star has a small enough mass to last a long time. Our star has already burned steadily for about 5 billion years, and should be good for another 5 billion years. Why is longevity so important? Because it takes 5 billion years to evolve intelligence and civilization. For several billion years, a star traveler would have found nothing more exciting on Earth than stromatolites, colonies of cyano-bacteria. It takes several billion years to generate enough oxygen to oxidate all the iron in the sea, and all the rocks on the shore. Only then can oxygen begin to build up in the seas and the atmosphere. Oxygen in the atmosphere is a sure sign of life. Complex cells, able to utilize oxygen, only appeared about 1.5 billion years ago at the very earliest.

For ninety percent of Earth's history, there has been no life on land. Mammals have existed for only the last one percent of our history. It just takes time to get to where we are now. And stars that are much more massive than our Sun will not last long enough for intelligence to evolve.

So we can ignore the few blue-white giants within 22 light years (the local neighborhood), because they will blow up as supernovas in only a few million years. Likewise, we can ignore the white dwarfs in the local neighborhood, old stars that have become red giants, destroying their planets, expelling most of their gas before sinking back to a dying ember. That will be the fate of our sun as well.

The fastest possible rocket would expel an ionized propellant. This rocket could conceivably reach 1/10th the speed of light. The limiting factor on this kind of rocket (impulse power to Trekkies) is a law of vanishing returns, not Einstein's speed limit. To go faster requires more propellant, which increases ones initial mass, thus making one accelerate slower. At about one-tenth the speed of light, simply adding more propellant does not increase the velocity one can reach. A better alternative would be a solar sail, since it could provide acceleration to leave home and deceleration when it approached its target star. The forces involved would be enormous, so some way would have to be found to allow the human body to withstand huge G forces, such as 14 G, if that is possible.

Even if we had a one-tenth C fusion powered rocket, it would still take 43 years to go to the G2 of Alpha Centauri, and 43 years to return. Primitive and dangerous cultures like ours could launch a one-way "Ark" which would take many generations to cross a few light-years. A primitive culture would probably only do this if it found some sort of radio or laser beacon, saying "here I am, a nice, fat, water-rich, oxygenated planet, ready to be conquered." It is for that reason that the SETI search is not a search for intelligent life. It is a search for stupidity.

An "Ark" is a self-contained ecological system, capable of renewing itself generation after generation, which would be born on the ark, reproduce, live to a ripe old age, and die. Such an Ark could be built by a primitive culture if the high-G force problem can be solved. By traveling at a lower speed, they wouldn't have to worry that interstellar dust grains would explode into the hull with the force of an H-bomb. It wouldn't really matter how long it took to cross interstellar space. It would eventually get there. It could carry nuclear generators to create electricity. It would not have to carry much propellant, just enough for maneuvering. It has the virtue that the same method used to propel it could also be used to stop it at the other end of the journey. For interstellar takeoff, it would maneuver as close to the sun as possible, point itself in the right direction, and unfurl an enormous solar sail. The reverse process would be used for deceleration at the end of the trip, many thousands of years later. This is the only technology of space travel proposed so far that might work, but only as a form of exodus.

What about those favorite tricks of science fiction writers: cryogenics and time warp? Time warp does not become noticeable until one reaches about 90% of the speed of light. Some hope to harness the ZPE in space to constantly accelerate half the trip, and decelerate the other half. But there is no ZPE in empty space. This fanciful idea is based on virtual particles, which imply an infinite energy for space, a *reductio ad absurdem* for virtual particles. Or at least, a theoretical puzzle to be solved.

For the voyagers themselves, relativistic effects could make the trip take far less of their time, if velocities close to C could be reached, and if they could deflect interstellar dust grains. Time and space are relative to the frame of reference, if two such frames have a velocity near the speed of light C with respect to one another. Some enthusiasts don't really care how long a voyage might take in Earth time, if it could be made speedily in spacecraft time. But I wouldn't call that exploring the universe. It would be an exodus, a one-way trip as far as one's civilization is concerned.

As far as cryogenics and similar ways of extending life indefinitely, they only work for species that have evolved those capabilities. For instance, some bacteria can dehydrate and crystallize and become a bacterial spore, which is viable for millions of years. Just add water. Such cryogenic travel, if it worked, would be even less like exploration.

What about hibernation? Even human beings can survive several hours of immersion in cold water because of the mammalian hibernation reflex. However, such hibernation cannot last for years and years. Mammals that regularly hibernate allow their temperature to fall to the ambient temperature, and the heart beats only occasionally. But such mammals have to wake up every few months, and rev up their metabolism. Why? Physiologists aren't sure, but think it is because of their need for sleep. By the way, there is no evidence that hibernation increases lifespan.

There are primitive species that can actually be frozen and revived. However, they have evolved that ability over millions of years, usually by dehydrating and filling their cells with glycol (anti-freeze). Such species cannot remain in a frozen state very long, certainly not for hundreds or thousands or millions of years. And again there is no evidence that being frozen part of ones life increases longevity.

When we consider the orders of magnitude of both space and time required for a space craft powered by physics, we can see why most scientists have no interest in putting people in space, and no interest in a Mars colony or a Moon colony, considering this is a dead end. It is not a jumping off point to Interstellar travel. No one is much interested in "space exploration" where a single round-trip voyage would take 2000 years or more with impulse power.

Judging from the entries in the guestbook on my web site at http://members.aol.com/thales97/index.htm I would predict that many technophiles will counter with an argument from analogy. "We went from the Wright brothers to walking on the Moon in less than a century," they will say. "Surely future technology will give us things we cannot imagine, things we could not yet understand, including perhaps the Starship Enterprise." We not only have a religion of science, we also have a kind of idolatry of technology. That is surely a religious attitude. Technology, the Golden Calf.

Civilizations always change, but the type of change does not remain constant. There was very little improvement in the speed of travel or communication from Alexander the Great to Thomas Jefferson. Since then, we have seen a complete transformation in that area, while our social structures have not changed at all. The Century of Voltaire and Thomas Jefferson saw radical social change. The 17th Century saw religious wars and the beginnings of science. The 16th Century saw the exploration of the globe. The 15th Century saw a revival of classical humanism and a Renaissance in art and architecture. The 21st Century might very well return to religious, social and artistic changes. Rapid technological change may soon come to an end, along with the rejection of the ideal of growth.

Technology cannot violate the laws of physics. And there is no theory in physics more firmly established than Special

Relativity, which says nothing can be accelerated past the speed of light, because its mass (and thus inertia) approaches infinity as we approach C, the speed of light. This theory is tested every time we turn on an atom smasher, which are designed according to the principles of Special Relativity, and would not work if this theory were wrong. Indeed, the point of colliders is not to increase speed, but to increase the mass and thus the energy of the particles to be collided. Those idiots on the Web who are constantly coming up with some FTL (Faster Than Light) scheme remind me of those other idiots in the past Century who wished to violate the Second Law of Thermodynamics, by building perpetual motion machines.

Some interstellar travel enthusiasts are working on alternative physics, hoping that the future progress of physics will provide some hope for the star traveler. In particular, they are looking for ways of using the supposed ZPE (Zero Point Energy of the vacuum) to allow unlimited acceleration. They still face the 0.1C speed limit imposed by propellant. The devotees of alternative physics are also looking for methods of propulsion that do not require a propellant. Maybe by warping space . . . However, Krauss, in his *Physics of Startrek* does the calculation to see how much energy would be required for Star Trek's warp one. It is more than the entire sum of energy that has been produced by the Sun, plus the entire amount that it will produce in its remaining lifetime. While we cannot foresee future discoveries in physics, we can be quite sure they won't contradict past discoveries . . . only show those past discoveries to be approximations. Nonetheless, on the off chance that physics offers some explanation of UFO propulsion, I have explored the fundamentals of 20th Century physics in the following chapter. I do so quite independently of the search for FTL loopholes. As a result I have created the first interpretation of Quantum Mechanics without paradox or any other quantum weirdness. Many people will be sorry to hear that, since quantum weirdness has been connected to Zen Buddhism and theories of consciousness. The ideas of modern physics (some of them) are used in my theory of the mind as a natural object. So you might find it worthwhile to skim through the following chapter, even though it provides no loopholes for FTL.

Physics Without Paradox

In this past Century, we learned how stars shine for billions of years and how the elements were formed. Our new technology of lasers and semiconductors is based on Quantum Mechanics, while our understanding of the Cosmos is based on General Relativity. Our view of the universe went from the Milky Way and an Earth a few million years old, to a vast structure of galactic clusters, quasars, pulsars, black holes, and Gamma Ray Bursts which has evolved over a period of time of roughly 15 giga-years. We can now measure the true age of rocks, and we can model the stages of a supernova. The adventure of ideas in physics and astronomy has been enormously exciting and mind-expanding.

Despite its many triumphs, the Standard Model is based on the acceptance of paradox, singularities, and the infinite energy of the vacuum. A paradox is a form of self-contradiction. Goedel proved that from a logical system which contains a contradiction, absolutely any proposition may be proven. Since Newton, physics has been mathematical physics, not just so we can crank out the numbers, but also to enable us to be consistent and to catch logical errors.

A singularity is a place where a variable goes to plus or minus infinity, and that is the meaning I use. We know there can be no actual infinities, because they would gobble up the rest of the universe. We know that the vacuum cannot have infinite energy, because energy is mass, and infinite mass would have folded up the universe long before the CMBR was released, long before atoms were formed, long before the first quasar or galaxy. After all, space is finite, because it has been expanding at a finite rate for a finite time. So infinite vacuum energy implies infinite energy density for the vacuum. This is an absurd and logically impossible idea. Yet just such views have been accepted as part of the Standard Model in the 20th Century, only because QED and QCD can crank out the right numbers. For some things. Physics has been quite unable to help with the mysteries of astronomy. There are many of these. Why do spiral galaxies have the shape they do? Why is the large scale structure of superclusters like that of soap bubbles? What is dark matter? And how can we possibly understand the Big Bang? If we compress all the matter in the universe into the space of a proton, it should create a black hole, not a universe. I suspect that physics has become useless to astronomy because the physicists have been content to get the numbers right, even if they are just adding deferents to epicycles. A deep understanding of nature does not exist.

All is not lost. It is not the equations that are wrong, but in some cases our use of them, for instance, applying Heisenberg's uncertainty rules to the vacuum, which results in the infinite energy of the vacuum. And in some cases, the problem is not the equations, but our interpretation of them. That is the problem with basic quantum mechanics.

A non-paradoxical interpretation of quantum mechanics is possible if we accept the fundamental reality of the de Broglie wave. All we have to do is show why particles sometimes have a wave-like behavior (while remaining particles) and why vibrations sometimes act like particles, (while remaining vibrations in a field). A thing cannot be simultaneously a particle and a wave. The scale of things doesn't change logic. Fortunately, we can avoid the wave-particle paradox with the de Broglie wave. It was Prince Louis de Broglie, a French aristocrat, who discovered this wave in 1923. His Ph.D. was in history, and he went on to a career as a civil servant. According to Fred Alan Wolf, in *Taking the Quantum Leap*, de Broglie regarded his wave as either a pilot wave or a matter wave. My view, however, is that it is neither. It is something real in and of itself, which we may call the de Broglie wave, and it is a possibility / probability wave. It shows us what is possible, and their probabilities.

The properties of the de Broglie wave are described by two equations:

$p = h / L$ and $W = C^{**}2 / v$ where p is momentum, L is the de Broglie wavelength, W is the velocity of the de Broglie wave, v is the ordinary velocity of the associated particle and h is Planck's constant ($6.6*10^{**}(-27)$ erg-sec), while C is the speed of light ($3*10^{**}10$ cm/sec).

The ideas of de Broglie excited immediate interest, because he could use his formula to calculate the orbits of atoms. Each orbit is determined by the standing waves (or resonances) of the de Broglie vibration. The ground state orbit will fit precisely one wavelength, the second orbit two wavelengths, and so forth to higher and higher overtones. These standing waves can themselves move, which indicates movement of their associated particle. This movement of the standing wave is never faster than the speed of light. Prince de Broglie's ideas are very similar to the theory of musical instruments, as he well knew.

There are actually several ways of deriving the orbits of atoms. Before de Broglie, Bohr, noticing that Planck's constant, h, has the units of angular momentum, found that he could calculate the orbits of the hydrogen atom by taking Planck's constant as the unit of angular momentum. The first orbit had an angular momentum of h, the second 2h and so on. And from this, he could calculate the energy levels of each orbit, and more importantly, the difference in energy given up in dropping from a higher orbit down to a lower orbit. Since 1905, scientists had known that for the photon, E=hf, to know the energy lost in a given transition is to know the resulting photon's frequency and thus its wavelength (since C=L*f). Much to Bohr's delight, his calculations agreed exactly with the Balmer series of the spectral lines emitted or absorbed by hydrogen.

A standing wave is sometimes called an Eigenstate, with a quantum number N=0,1,2,3 . . . , with an Eigenvalue E(N) associated with each value of the quantum number. In a musical instrument, the standing wave is the note produced by the instrument. In music, the Eigenvalue would be frequency and the quantum number would indicate the fundamental tone and its first, second, third, etc., overtones. This leads to the mature form of the de Broglie wave equation. If the de Broglie function is described by F(r,t), and H is the Hamiltonian differential operator, then H[F(r,t)] becomes the left half of a differential equation. We let E(n) be the eigenvalues, which for the Hamiltonian operator will be energy states, a different one in most cases for each value of n=0,1,2,3 . . . So the mature forms of the equation resemble:H[F(r,t)] = E(n)*F(r,t).

It was Erwin Schroedinger who took de Broglie's formulas and plugged them into the partial differential equation for a wave. He then imposed severe boundary conditions, which in effect made each solution of the equation a probability function. In this way, the 2-dimensional picture of orbits is transformed into a 3-dimensional picture of orbitals. There are s, p, d and f orbitals. All the s orbitals are spherical. The other orbitals can assume more complicated, multi-lobed shapes. There are 3 such shapes for the p orbitals, 5 for the d orbitals and 7 for the f orbitals. Knowing the size, shape, and energy level of each orbital, chemists can understand the periodic table of elements. This, in turn, provides an understanding of ionic bonds and valence bonds and the general behavior of all of the elements, alone or in combination. See *The Periodic Kingdom*, by P.W. Atkins, especially pages 112 and 113.

If you have trouble understanding resonances, think of musical instruments. Louis de Broglie's theory is similar to the theory of a musical instrument, as he well knew. For a trumpet with a given length of tubing, there is a lowest note, one where exactly one wavelength of sound will resonate in the tube. It is possible to make higher notes on a trumpet, by producing overtones, but impossible to make a lower note. The same is true of electrons in orbit around a nucleus, although this analogy is only a teaching device and doesn't really explain the behavior of atoms.

So far so good. This picture even allows us to see why the first orbit of electrons around a nucleus can only hold two electrons, one somewhere under the maxima of the de Broglie resonance, and the other opposite to it under the minima. These two electrons have slightly different energy, because in the up electron, its magnetic pole aligns with that of the nucleus, while the down electron has its magnetic pole alignment opposite to that of the nucleus. The picture even allows us to understand why we can never predict exactly where the electron is. The de Broglie wave is a probability wave. It shows us where the probability is greatest, but some of the time the electron will be anywhere its probability is non-zero.

What we must add to this picture are Heisenberg's uncertainty rules, and relativity, which gives us electron spin and antiparticles. I won't go into that. If Z is some observable, then we will indicate the spread of its probability function (its Heisenberg uncertainty) by putting a "d" in front of it, dZ. The Heisenberg rules describe a curious coupling of position with momentum, and energy with time. Heisenberg's rules are therefore: dP * dx = h, and dE * dt = h where P is momentum, x is position, E is energy, t is time, and h is Planck's constant ($6.6*10^{**}(-27)$)erg-sec). So if the positions are spread out, momenta will not be spread out. They will be "sharp." If the duration of an energy state has a large Heisenberg uncertainty, the energy will not. It will be "sharp." The product of the uncertainties is always Planck's constant, h. Sometimes Heisenberg's rules are written h/2pi, pronounced h-bar, but it is always possible to incorporate this geometric factor into the definition of a "spread."

Consider an electron in an excited orbit in the hydrogen atom.

It will remain in that state for a certain duration of time, t, and when it falls back into a lower orbit, it will release a quantum of electro-magnetic energy, where E=hf (f being the frequency). However, if we have a large number of hydrogen atoms making the same transition, both the energy E and the time t will vary a little. That is the "spread." There is a little probability curve that goes with each variable. The product of those spreads is Planck's constant h. Nature is fundamentally probabilistic on an atomic or sub-atomic level. Notice that the product of the spreads is an extremely small number, far smaller than experimental error. The real importance of Heisenberg's laws is that it is from them that we get virtual particles and the infinite energy of the vacuum. More on that later. Incidentally, Heisenberg's rules provide yet a third way of calculating the orbits of the electrons in an atom.

The paradoxical interpretation of QM arose at the Fifth Solvay conference in 1927, where the principals were Bohr, Einstein, de Broglie, Born, and Schroedinger. Schroedinger had plugged in de Broglie's equation for the wavelength into the standard partial differential equation for moving particles, and produced the Schroedinger equation for calculating wave packets. The problem is that these Schroedinger packets steadily spread out in time, unlike the de Broglie wave. Heisenberg suggested that the act of observation collapsed the Schroedinger wave function, so it was once again localized. Thus, reality is created by our observation of it. Some people like mystery. Schroedinger was that sort of person, even before he produced his equation. So it became part of the standard interpretation of QM which is still accepted. Not by me.

Years later, in 1952, David Bohm argued that the underlying assumptions of Heisenberg's uncertainty rules could be contradicted by an unknown underlying level of reality. This is known as the hidden variables theory. In the 1960s, John Bell proved that hidden variables would be non-local. In other words, a change in a hidden variable might simultaneously and instantaneously change an observable variable light-years away, if the two events were "entangled." Bell's theorem has become famous. It does not exclude hidden variables. But they must be non-local, which would be an even stranger idea than quantum mechanics.

I should emphasize that I do not believe in hidden variables. I don't accept Bohm's objections to quantum mechanics, nor those of Einstein. It doesn't bother me in the slightest that sub-atomic reality is fundamentally probabilistic, and is in many ways different from the macroscopic reality we directly observe. All I am saying is that our theories about sub-atomic reality cannot be paradoxical or allow logical impossibilities.

If we assume that the de Broglie wave is not a mathematical fiction, we can make all the quantum paradoxes and all the quantum weirdness go away. The electron does not go through both slits in the famous two-slit interferometer experiment. But its de Broglie wave does, and produces the diffraction patterns on the far side. The electron goes through one slit or the other; we just don't know which, since the de Broglie wave intensity is equal at the two slits. The electron is always in one place or another. It does not have a ghostly presence in each of the places it could be. Thus, observing an electron does not "collapse the wave function," nor does it pick out one among an infinity of universes.

The de Broglie functions describe the experiment, such as the 2-slit interferometer. It describes what is possible, and their probabilities. For the detector on the 2-slit interferometer, we use wave theory and positive and negative interference to produce a curve of the intensity of the de Broglie wave at the plane of the detector. This will be a curve with two humps. Now suppose we feed our electrons through one at a time. It might land on the right, or it might land on the left. What has collapsed? Nothing. The function for this apparatus remains the same. And if we keep on feeding electrons through it, the results will more and more closely match the two humped probability wave of de Broglie. We do not change it by observing it.

Incidentally, the 2-slit experiment has now been done with atoms, molecules, and even a 60 carbon atom bucky-ball (Arndt, M. et al. (1999) Letters to *Nature*, vol 401, October 14, 1999 pg 680). This implies that one can calculate the de Broglie wave of an entire object, such as the Bucky-ball, as if it were a single simple thing having a particular mass, velocity, and location. This is somewhat like the Center of Mass theorem in Newtonian physics. Of course, someone is sure to repeat the mantra of QM, which is that the position and velocity of an object cannot be known simultaneously. But this is not what the Heisenberg Uncertainty relationship says. It says we can simultaneously know each of these quantities to 13 significant digits! I am sure any experimenter would be very happy with that.

The de Broglie vibration explains the sometimes wavelike behavior of electrons. When a beam of electrons is reflected off a crystal, it forms diffraction patterns. This is because the de Broglie wave associated with the electron goes before, (since its velocity is always greater than that of the electron), and bounces off each atom on the surface of the crystal. The result is a whole series of reflected de Broglie waves, which add or subtract, producing a diffraction pattern. The probability of an electron hitting the detector screen in a particular place is proportional to the intensity of its de Broglie wave there.

Photons: recall that the velocity of the de Broglie wave for an object traveling at velocity V is W = C**2 / V but V for photons is C, thus W = C. We also know from textbooks on quantum mechanics that the de Broglie frequency of any particle is f = E / h, or E = f * h, the familiar Planck formula for the energy of a photon (Rojansky, p. 236), thus the de Broglie wave acts just like the classical electro-magnetic wave, with positive and negative interference. In other words, the de Broglie frequency and velocity are the same as the electro-magnetic frequency and velocity. Since photons are Bosons, any number can be in the quantum state, and the de Broglie pattern for all of them will contribute to the interference pattern, which provides the probability pattern for any and all. This suggests that we cannot draw a classical ray trace for individual photons.

The problem of photons is quite different from the problem of atoms. In atoms, we have resonances of the de Broglie wave, which determine the orbits of the electrons. With EM radiation, the de Broglie wave does not form a resonance. It just spreads out like ripples in a pond, in three-dimensions, and has positive and negative interference with all the other de Broglie waves from other photons in the same quantum state. As usual, where the de Broglie wave is strongest, that is where you are most likely to find a photon. What does a photon look like?

I believe it looks like a packet of waves, tapered to a point at each end, except we must imagine a second wave packet at right angles to the first one. The first wave is in the electric field, and the one perpendicular to it is in the magnetic field. I think photons are highly localized in space. They probably all have the same size. However, one can get fewer long wavelength waves into a packet than you can with shorter wavelengths, which would explain why E=hf, that is, the energy of a photon is proportional do the number of waves of electrical and magnetic energy one can get into a photon.

I should remind everybody that there is no new physics here. I'm not changing the equations. This is just an interpretation of the equations, i.e., a word picture and a mental picture. This interpretation avoids the weirdness of later quantum mechanics, such as the wave-particle paradox, multiple universes, instantaneous action at a distance, the collapse of the wave-function and the entanglement of observer with observed, which crept in with Schroedinger, Heisenberg, and Bohr. This non-paradoxical interpretation is consistent with observation. We cannot ask more of an interpretation. I would make a stronger statement. Physics cannot simply accept paradox, any more than it can just accept singularities. To do so is the end of physics as a rational enterprise, because absolutely any proposition can be derived from a system of ideas which allows logical impossibilities.

The infinite energy of the vacuum (which would curl the whole universe up faster than I can type this sentence) arises from the theory of virtual particles. The entire theory of virtual particles arises from applying Heisenberg's rule of dE*dt=h to the vacuum. Remember, dt is the spread in duration, and dE is the spread in energy. If we make dt very sharp, dE becomes very broad, so broad in fact, that the formation of a particle and an anti-particle has non-zero probability, although this pair will exist for the minute fraction of time allowed it by dt. This is the origin of the theory of virtual particles, which has the unfortunate consequence that the energy of the vacuum is infinite.

It is possible to prevent infinity by cutting off the possible wavelengths when they are small enough to enter the realm of quantum gravity. But that *ad hoc* device still gives us a vacuum energy 120 orders of magnitude greater than the energy contained in all the matter in the universe! According to Lawrence Krauss, a well-respected neutrino physicist, "[This] discrepancy between theory and observation is the most perplexing quantitative puzzle in physics today (*Scientific American*, Jan. 1999, "Cosmological Antigravity," p. 55)." I am glad that Lawrence Krauss agrees with me. Some would say that if the vacuum has any energy density, it would be infinite if the universe is spatially infinite. But space is not infinite. The universe (including space-time) has been expanding from a Hawking no-boundary beginning for a finite time, about 15 billion years. So it cannot be spatially infinite, though it could still be unbounded.

Guth's inflation theory does not change this. Guth's theory goes very well with one idea about the Big Bang. The universe could be a zero energy quantum fluctuation in the primordial chaos which produces a bubble of false vacuum, much smaller than a proton, which expands 50 orders of magnitude to the size of a marble, before the false vacuum freezes out into a storm of energy and particles. If it has zero energy, it can have infinite duration. A charming idea, but totally untestable. Incidentally, it could have zero energy because all the gravitational potential energy is negative, which might just balance out all kinds of positive energy. Another interesting consequence arises if the universe someday collapses into a Big Crunch. This is possible, you know. The acceleration of Hubble expansion is probably due to the anti-gravity of the anti-particles that collect in cosmic voids. But as time goes by, some mixing occurs, the anti-particles are annhilated, and gravity may take over again. If this happens, and pulls the universe back into a Big Crunch, it will not explode into another Big Bang, because the universe as a whole has zero energy, remember? As it collapses, the energy balances will be canceled out, and the universe just quietly vanishes back into the primordial chaos. But no doubt other universes are constantly being started with zero energy quantum fluctuations producing tiny bubbles of false vacuum.

Fortunately, it is possible to get rid of virtual particles, simply by saying that it is appropriate to apply Heisenberg's rules only when we can calculate a de Broglie wave. There is no de Broglie wave for the vacuum. So how then do we explain Casimir's force and other apparent confirmations of this idea? By applying de Broglie theory to the Electro-Magnetic field, which extends through all of space. As we bring two plates closer together, we begin limiting the wavelengths of photons that can exist between them. This draws the plates together. At least, that is one idea. Better than accepting an absurdity such as infinite energy for the vacuum. If there are no virtual particles, then the vacuum goes back to what it was in Newton's time. Nothing. It is just empty space. Those people who are planning space-ships which will extract energy from the ZPE are just wasting their time.

I have now eliminated the paradox from Quantum Mechanics. I would like to begin my discussion of cosmology with an observation about anti-particles.

It was Richard Feynman who suggested that anti-particles are like ordinary particles moving backwards in time. If that is true, anti-particles should have anti-gravity, a conjecture which has never been tested, although there is evidence for it.

Newsweek (*Newsweek*, May 12, 1997, "Fountain of Annihilation") and Discover magazines have reported a fountain of anti-electrons spouting from the center of our own galaxy, which is suspected of harboring an old quasar, also known as a giant black hole. Giant jets of particles and energy have been seen erupting from many galactic centers. Wouldn't it be interesting if all such jets start out as anti-particles? This is exactly what we would expect if anti-particles have anti-gravity. When particle and anti-particle pairs are formed inside the intense gravitational field of a black hole or quasar, the anti-particle seems to shoot out one pole or the other, producing the jet. This implies that quasars and black holes gradually evaporate, which is why there are no quasars left in recent times. Ordinary stellar black holes could very well have a limited lifetime as well.

Think about this and you see that there is no singularity inside a black hole. First, we must assume that all black holes are spinning, and the unseen particles inside the black hole are orbiting the center as well. Instead of a singularity at the heart of a black hole, let us say that the zero point in our system of coordinates is a Hawking no-boundary zero point in imaginary time. Any particle plunging down its throat would steadily pick up energy, and continuously split into particles and anti-particles. The anti-particles zoom away with enormous acceleration out the poles. Why out the poles? Because in any other direction, it will meet particles, and annihilate. This process would continue until all the remaining particles inside the black hole are in stable orbits around the Hawking zero point.

Recent observations show that the universe is not only expanding, it has been accelerating at some point. The evaporation of black holes and quasars could explain this, since it produces anti-matter. The proportion of anti-matter to matter should increase (up to a point), and so should the repulsive force produced by anti-matter. The force of repulsion will decline as quasars and black holes disappear, since the anti-matter will gradually be annihilated. The acceleration phase may already be passing, since there have been no quasars in the last billion years. There has been just enough acceleration to make the universe old enough to hold the oldest stars. If the universe is closed, it will repeatedly return to the Hartle-Hawking no-boundary and explode outward again, all its laws of nature unchanged. There is no need for Guth's Inflation theory. Fiddling with Einstein's Cosmic Constant is unnecessary. It is zero, and to make it anything else would be hopelessly ad hoc. Quintessence is not required. There is no ZPE. A mathematically consistent theory of physics might be a good start towards understanding the mysteries of astronomy.

If anti-particles have anti-gravity, they would not clump. Indeed, they would produce the soap bubble large scale structure of the universe that we in fact observe. The anti-matter particles would try to stay as far away from every other particle as possible. Thus, we must imagine the voids inside the soap-bubbles filled with anti-matter, pushing out the walls of matter (both normal and "dark") until the walls collide. It is along these collisions between bubbles that we see matter become dense enough to form galaxies, clusters and super-clusters. Anti-matter still has inertia, in other words, positive mass. The mass density of the universe has on average been close to the critical value needed to make the universe flat, and anti-particles with anti-gravity filling the vast voids between super-clusters of galaxies must comprise a large, but variable, component.

And now a few thoughts about the graviton. First, an analogy. Existing quantum theory was developed entirely by observation of the interaction between photons and electrons. The theory of the photon could not be derived from the field theory of Electro-Magnetism, i.e. Maxwell's equations. It required new evidence. So it shall be with the graviton. The field theory, General Relativity, is predicting gravitons of tiny energy, which can be absorbed by tiny objects. But no one has been able to detect such gravitons. If the field theory is wrong, we must develop quantum gravity by observing the absorption and emission of gravitons.

We have been looking at the absorption and emission of gravitons for 30 years, but not recognizing it as such. This is based on a little noted experiment, reported in *Scientific American* back in 1970 by Mansinha and Smylie, which shows that the Earth experiences abrupt changes of spin vector speed on the order of 10 milli-arc-seconds per second. Or changes in direction on the order of 10 milli-arc-seconds. These abrupt changes look exactly like the absorption or emission of gravitational quanta, and thus could be the beginning of a theory of quantum gravity.

There is nothing in geology that could explain this.

Magma movements are too slow, and the flow of currents in the liquid metal outer core of the earth cause continuous rather than discontinuous movements in the magnetic pole, with no associated change in the spin vector. The jumps in the spin vector are not caused by earthquakes. Mansinha & Smylie's observations are a mystery . . . unless they represent the absorption or emission of gravitons of enormous energy.

The field theory of gravity (Einstein's general theory of relativity) gives us misleading advice about the graviton, just as the field theory of EM gave misleading advice about the photon. Einstein's theory predicts that a graviton carries an extremely small amount of energy. So that is the kind of graviton being looked for, and not being found. And it is assumed in classical gravitational theory that a relatively small object can absorb a graviton, which is also not true. It takes a planetary sized object to absorb or emit a graviton. Add to this Bode's Law and we have the beginning of a theory.

Bode's law takes the series 0,3,6,12,24, each time doubling the previous number, adds 4 and divides by 10. The result is the mean distance of each planet's orbit expressed in units of AU (which is one for the Earth). Bode's law very accurately describes the orbits of all the planets (and the asteroid belt) except the outer two, Neptune and Pluto. And we know that Pluto is not really a planet, but just a planetesimal captured by Neptune and put into a 2:3 gravitational resonance. It is also out of the plane of the ecliptic by about 17 degrees. We know that in the early years of the formation of the Solar System, the outermost planet would be busy throwing out planetesimals, and each time, moving in a little closer to the sun. So it is easy to imagine that Neptune formed at 38.8 AU, but gradually moved inward to 30.1 AU as a result of tossing out planetesimals. No one has ever come up with an explanation of Bode's law. I suggest it makes our solar system resemble an atom, and we know that an atom's orbits are determined by the theory of photons. Likewise, it seems reasonable that a solar system should be explained by the theory of gravitons, with a touch of chaos thrown in. By the way, this means our Solar System is typical, and the ones currently being found in the year 2001 are atypical. This increases the odds of finding life and intelligence in the universe.

In conclusion, I turn out to be a conservative. I uphold mathematical rigor and consistency in physics. I reject paradox, singularity and infinity. I like to think that Galileo and Newton would approve, and would agree with me that physics has somewhat gone off the tracks of normal scientific method since 1927 and the Fifth Solvay Conference. I offer no new equations, although I do offer some overlooked evidence pertaining to the graviton and to quantum gravity. I strongly suggest that anti-matter has anti-gravity. The evidence for this lies in the fountain of anti-matter erupting from the black hole at the center of our own galaxy.

On the Web, there are News Groups and Yahoo Groups totally dedicated to a kind of mathematical alchemy trying to find a way around the Einsteinian speed limit. They will fail. There is no theory better established or more free of mathematical problems than that of Einstein's Special Relativity, which makes the speed of light the absolute limit for anything traveling through ordinary space and time. I completely agree with this. No future discovery in physics is ever going to overturn this result. Thus, UFOs cannot travel by physics. Yet they are here. It is on that paradox that this entire book hinges.

Scientific Method

Galileo talked a little bit about scientific method, but since then, scientists generally have not. They generally agree that what academic philosophers call the Philosophy of Science, with its inductive logic, is ludicrous and all wrong. I agree. Scientists will generally tell you there is nothing that complicated about scientific method. Again, I agree. Scientists learn it by example. But it would help if we also had it written down. If we had a verbal statement which scientists could accept, the intellectual history of the West might be quite different. So, I am going to attempt it, before we study the informal but controlled experiments in apportation made by the Chinese. Scientific method should include everything we know to be a reliable method of finding the truth, and no more. The psi-cops wish to restrict it, so that it only includes the existing sciences.

Scientific method is just the common sense of the West, used by shadetree mechanics, mothers with crying babies, gardeners, and even the master detective himself, Sherlock Holmes. If the baby is crying, we first see if it is wet. No. Hungry? No. Is a pin or other object sticking the baby? No. Needs to burp? No. Maybe the baby is bored. Get out the stroller, take the baby for a walk in the park. The crying stops and the baby takes a nap. Problem solved. The key thing is to see scientific method as problem solving. The problems may be varied and abstract. Newton solved all sorts of problems, having to do with the tides, and the trade winds, the flight of cannon balls, the working of pendulum clocks, and indeed, the motion of everything in the heavens and on Earth.

The genius and humanity of science lives in a certain kind of curiosity. Thousands of people over thousands of generations must have walked past cliffs showing geological unconformities, without thinking about it, without wondering about it, without caring about it. But in the 18th Century, a Scotchman named James Hutton wandered past just such cliff, and stopped to wonder, to question, and to imagine what might have happened. The top formation showed layers of marine limestone and shale. These layers were horizontal. Hutton and others before him thought these horizontal layers must have been laid down in some ancient ocean or shallow sea by the processes of sedimentation going on at the present. Below this was a formation where the layers were nearly vertical. This is what geologists now call an uncomformity. Hutton realized a huge gap in time must be missing. The second formation must also have been laid down in horizontal layers by sedimentation, then uplifted in a mountain range, which was then worn away by erosion and eventually found itself on the bottom of the ocean again, to receive the top formation, which was once again raised up as mountains, which must have in turn been worn down by erosion into the gentle hills of Scotland.

Below the second formation was a third, in which the layers were sharply folded, and the minerals changed. Hutton thought that both the folding and the transformation of sedimentary rocks into other kinds of rock could only have happened in great heat, deep within the Earth. These are the pictures conjured up in Hutton's imagination by looking at a cliff. Sometimes being a scientist is just being curious about things which other people take for granted.

Scientific method in general does not require math, laboratories, or even explanation. We have a problem. We try to solve it, whether it is a car that won't start, a crying baby, a wilting plant, or an unsolved string of crimes. Scientific method requires reproducibility, veridical details, and rigorous tests to rule out all the known alternatives. A theory that survives alone amidst continued rigorous testing and expansion of its range of application is called "well-established." It is theory which allows us to apply past experience to the present problem.

Scientific method for particular sciences may very well require math, laboratories, or explanation. Mathematical physics should not only use math, but it should abide by the logical rules of math. If it had done so, physics might not have wandered off the path in 1927 into paradox, singularity, and infinity. Many sciences are best done in the field. That is true of psychical research, for instance. J. B. Rhine did not make the field more scientific by bringing it into the laboratory. Quite the contrary, since his kind of parapsychology does not seem to be reproducible. So, it appears that undergraduates who wander in off the street do not possess ESP or PK. It did not help that J. B. Rhine simply ignored all the studies of apparitions and poltergeists that had already been done in the previous 40 years of work by the Society for Psychical Research.

Part of scientific method is what some call Occam's razor, but really should be called Newton's razor. Every explanation is in terms which are not explained. In Newtonian theory, this was gravity. When asked to explain gravity, he loftily replied, in my translation of 17th Century English, "I make no untestable speculations." So add that to your list of rules of scientific method. Don't make assertions that are unsupported by evidence, and don't put forward "theories" which cannot be tested, even if at some future date, testable hypotheses about it may be possible. It is this last rule which is mostly ignored in academic physics and entirely ignored in alternative or exotic physics.

When Sherlock is examining a crime scene, he is not making deductions. He is making up hypotheses to account for this smudge of boot black on the mantel, the sailor's knots holding the damsel in distress, the bit of candle wax on the carpet, and the three glasses of port, one of which has no dregs. These things mean nothing to the police, but Sherlock is dreaming up fantastic theories involving a sailor in collusion with the said damsel. And he knows of ways to check this hypothesis. That's where the deduction comes in. Sometimes more than one theory will fit the facts, and he has to rule out alternatives. Sometimes he fails to come up with the correct hypothesis until more crimes are committed or more facts emerge.

"When you have ruled out the alternatives, whatever remains, no matter how improbable, must be the truth." This is often quoted by scientists. Ian Stevenson ruled out the alternatives, leaving reincarnation as the only explanation for the young children who spontaneously recall former lifetimes, in the concluding chapter of his book, *Twenty Cases Suggestive of Reincarnation*. Improbable, perhaps, given our current worldview. But, if we call ourselves scientists, we must either redo the studies, or accept these improbable results, and reject reductionism.

Scientific method requires reproducibility, to catch fraud, incompetence and "gremlins." And there have been many follow-up studies of reincarnation children, published in the *JSPR* over the years. Anyone can repeat the studies. By contrast, cold fusion never seemed able to produce results when visiting scholars were around. Similarly, Stephen Hawking discovered that the more rigorous the controls in Parapsychology, the less the Psi observed. He is probably right about parapsychology (lab investigations), which is to be distinguished from psychical research (field investigation). Perhaps the biggest difference is that Parapsychologists generally come into the field from psychology, while psychical researchers are generally MDs or physicists. However, we must remember that psi events depend on human psychology. People are not machines, and do not respond well to being treated like machines. A true test of any phenomenon cannot be designed in such a way as to prevent the phenomenon.

For instance, in one of the psi-cop's appearances on the Discovery Science channel I saw a "test" of staring at someone until they notice and turn around. But they put the two people in different rooms! How can that be a test of the phenomenon? Similarly, it always seemed to me that J. B. Rhine's ESP tests were designed to prevent any ESP, since they consist in deadly dull and repetitious guesses, with no positive feedback, involving cards which have absolutely no symbolic or emotive significance. In other words, J. B. Rhine seemed to treat his "subjects" like machines. I am leery of any science which depends on statistical wizardry to get any results. Not only is it easy to lie with statistics, there is also the problem of a very faint signal lost in the noise, and a single mistake in conducting the test could easily produce a false positive or false negative result. Stevenson's studies do not depend on statistics.

Remember that our facts must be both reproducible and veridical. "Veridical" means "details which cannot be explained away, which are found to be true." In the Chinese tests of apportation, girls known to have this talent were asked to "remove the cigarettes" from a sealed box. Every time one of the girls said she had done so, the investigators would open up the box and count the cigarettes. And there would be one fewer. Cigarettes do not spontaneously disappear. The girls did not touch the box, which remained in plain sight of everybody throughout the test. What alternative could there be, other than an apport?

The "psi-cops" (members of CSICOP, who often publish in *The Skeptical Inquirer*) use Hume's rule that "extraordinary claims require extraordinary proofs," such as proof that fraud could not possibly have occurred, a proof that can be given neither for traditional scientific studies nor for those of the new sciences. Hume's rule is not part of scientific method. Suppose Hume's rule had been applied in the time of Galileo and Kepler? They made discoveries as extraordinary and upsetting in their day as UFOs and Psi are today. If Hume's rule had been invoked, we would still be burning witches and heretics and still living in Ptolemy's crystalline spheres.

The "psi-cops" do use Hume's rule. I will give you an example. When Martin Gardner heard about the demonstrations of dermo-optical vision through a blind, before the Soviet Academy of Sciences, Gardner immediately "debunked" it on the grounds that this could be duplicated by a stage illusionist (Gardner, 1966). Of course that is true, if the stage illusionist gets to "set the stage," and use her own blind. I'm sure the Soviet Scientists thought of that. According to the psi-cops, all famous psychics, like Uri Geller, are master illusionists, despite the total lack of evidence that they have any training in that art, or any of the equipment necessary. Stage "psychics" or "mentalists" are illusionists, but they would never submit to the controlled experiments inflicted on the Russian psychics or on Uri Geller. Remember, the appearance of anything can be duplicated by the illusionist's apparatus and skill. Every scientific discovery reported in *Nature* could also have been faked. But we don't make such charges without grounds.

Mystical experiences are reproducible. They are the same in all cultures, under all religions. Symbolic interpretation is reproducible, at least in the hands of experts like Carl Jung or Joseph Campbell. They find the same lessons in folk-tales, mythology, dreams and religious ritual. The seven pillars of wisdom in Psychical Research are reproducible (see the chapter "Seven Psi Facts"). Anyone with the time and money can reproduce any of these studies.

If all this is true, why isn't Psychical Research and Ufology widely accepted? More than anyone, academics have a vested interest in their store of knowledge. What if that store of "medieval scholasticism" should suddenly be shown to be worthless? It is especially difficult to get their attention when it is their worldview which is called into question.

Science is universal and non-sectarian. Even at the height of the Cold War, Soviet and Western physicists were friends and went to the same conferences, even those scientists who had built the H-bombs for each side. Every truly scientific theory has testable consequences, and thus we can decide between competing ideas by rigorous experimentation. It is not just that.

Only a theory with empirical consequences is of any use to the scientists. That is why Creationism is ignored. It is not out of any prejudice against Christianity. It is just that Creationism provides no help to the scientist in trying to figure out where to look for what.

Scientists can get just as opinionated and hot-headed about their favorite theories as anyone else. Every new idea is challenged, which is good, because it forces its originator to go back and examine new possibilities. Sometimes the new result turns out to be just an artifact, something not reproducible. But when the dust settles, and an idea is tested in lots of different ways, the issue is settled peaceably. This is what I love about science, that and the adventure of ideas.

On the other hand, the existing sciences are very narrow in their scope, and leave out most of the really interesting questions. The existing sciences restrict themselves to a narrow band on the spectrum of reproducible experience, namely, the visible and tangible.

The trouble is, mystical experience is not visible and tangible. It does not register on photographic equipment. And neither do most of the things investigated by Psi researchers. Poltergeist phenomena can be photographed, and even haunts show up on infrared cameras, but apparitions (which are far more common) do not register on photographic equipment. Nor is the mind itself visible or tangible. Yet it can be seen by powers inherent to the mind, and these observations can be tested, and they are reproducible. To restrict science to the visible and tangible is to build assumptions about the nature of reality into Science. And if we do that, how is Science any different from Religion?

The existing sciences also restrict themselves to a particular kind of problem, that of explanation and prediction. But we do not always want explanations, particularly not those of a reductionist kind. One of many Utopian problems is to find ways to prevent thermonuclear war. What good would it do to be able to predict it, even assuming that this is possible?

My goal is the Aristotelian task of separating the essence from the accidents. I say the essence of scientific method is problem solving, and for every kind of problem, there is a relevant realm of reproducible experience. All we need to do is find the equivalent of a fact, an experiment, and a theory. The concept of "well-established" is the same for all sciences, those accepted, those forbidden, those newly created, and any future ones. A "fact-equivalent" or a "theory-equivalent" is well-established if we can empirically rule out the alternatives.

I say that the independent experiences of numerous witnesses should be taken seriously as evidence of the truth of their experience. Every time scientists have deviated from this rule, they have turned out to be wrong. For instance, over the centuries many people have seen rocks falling from the sky, and picked them up, still hot. They have seen meteorites, in other words. Yet scientists refused to accept the reality of meteorites for several hundred years. It wasn't until scientists themselves saw meteorites land, coupled with the discovery of the asteroid belt, that the scientists changed their minds, and decided that "shooting stars" were meteorites burning up in the atmosphere.

Similarly with gorillas. For centuries, travelers to remote jungles of Africa came back with reports of an unknown primate, as large as a human when standing up. Again, blank rejection, which lasted until specimens were brought back to the lab or zoo. At the present time, the Yeti, also known as the Sasquatch, or Bigfoot has been repeatedly seen by numerous observers, yet not accepted as a reality by scientists. On one occasion, fur with hair roots from the Yeti were found, scratched off on a tree branch along a Yeti track of footprints, brought back to the lab, where a DNA analysis showed that this was indeed a primate, but not any known to science. In my opinion, the reality of the Yeti is thereby proven, and it is not necessary to capture or kill one of these rare creatures.

The independent testimony of numerous witnesses becomes especially important in the study of Near Death Experiences

(NDEs). The best evidence for NDEs probably comes from Raymond Moody's original book, *Life After Life*, which became a bestseller, since it may be hard to find independent witnesses today. It is only the first part of the experience, which resembles an ordinary Out-Of-Body-Experience (OOBE), that produces details which could be verified by someone who is not a clairvoyant. A physician would have to work fast to verify the details seen by the patient in an OOBE state, since they are usually just trivial details about who came in, who went out, what they did, what they said, things like that. And clairvoyants are rare, and it would be most improbable to find one in an Emergency Room (ER). So we have skimpy veridicality, yet we do have independent testimony from numerous people, all of whom swear that it was real, not any kind of dream or hallucination, a claim which is born out by the reproducibility of NDEs. In other words, they have characteristic features. The experiences also have lasting effects on those who have them. Hallucinations are not reproducible. They have no common features.

The psi-cops have an explanation of these common features, attributing the tunnel with the light at the end to hypoxia, and the feelings of love and well-being to a rush of endorphins in the dying brain. There are two things wrong with this debunking. It explains too much. Not every NDE involves a tunnel with light at the end. George Rodonaia initially experienced pure darkness. It was only after saying "let there be light," that he began to experience typical NDE features. There are many different ways people experience "crossing over." They might climb stairs, or take a boat across a river, or walk up a beautifully paneled corridor.

The other problem is that when people die, not only does the heart stop, and breathing stops, but so does the brain. If there is an EEG hooked up, it will go flatline at the same time as the EKG. Deprived of a steady flow of glucose and oxygen, brain cells quit working. There is no evidence of any rush of endorphins or any brain activity at all in those pronounced dead, as was

George Rodonaia, Dannion Brinkley, and most of the others who have had NDEs. Besides, hypoxia happens while the heart, lungs and brain are still working. Dead people do not have hypoxia, which refers to a reduction (not cessation) of oxygen to the brain.

There are a lot of things known by personal experience, which are not part of science. But there are also entire sciences which have not made it into the textbooks, or into *Scientific American*, discoveries which are not yet part of common knowledge. Indeed, reduction is a litmus test applied to everyone who wants to become a professional scientist. If a scientist believes in UFOs or Psi, he had better look for another line of work. Yet these forbidden sciences follow the same methods as every other science.

Are there any special rules when applying scientific method to UFOs? I don't think so. As usual, we look for "best evidence," that which has veridical details which rule out alternative interpretations of the experience. That is why I ignore night-time sightings of UFOs, although there are some very good ones, especially the experience of the talk radio guru Art Bell. He and his wife saw a huge black triangle silently float overhead, visible in the moonlight, blotting out stars. In general, however, there are almost always other possible explanations for mysterious lights in the night time sky, such as aerial formations of ultra-light aircraft, carrying bright lights, flying high and slow. Or flares dropped by distant military aircraft, which turned out to be the ultimate explanation of the large triangular craft seen over Phoenix.

I draw all major conclusions about UFOs from observations of UFOs on the ground, with aliens standing around, seen in broad daylight, at close range, by multiple witnesses. I have restricted myself to cases before 1969, because there had been no serious treatment of real UFOs in movies or TV at that time, so there can be no "rational" explanation for the common features of all the observations collected by Bowen in *The Humanoids*, other than the fact that these people were seeing real interstellar spacecraft and aliens from distant stars. How could people independently dream up the same things, very different from the aliens of fiction? Even today, what Hollywood mostly gives us are "Alien" slime monsters, hideous, evil and aggressive, while the real aliens are none of those things.

When it comes to applying scientific method to Psi research, the only special rule is to treat these people with dignity and respect. Treat them as human beings, not machines. If you change the psychological atmosphere, behavior will change as well. The rigid controls demanded by the psi-cops are really designed to prevent the phenomenon, rather than to test it.

Psi Studies in China

Levitation is the movement of objects by the powers of mind alone, without touching them or using any physical mechanism. Teleportation is the popular term for the instantaneous transfer of an object from one place to another, without being moved along in-between. The term used by psi researchers is "apport" from the Latin *apportare* (to carry to a place).

In this chapter, I describe some of the writings of Zhu Yi Yi, of Shanghai, a biology graduate of the Shanghai Fu Dan University, and staff writer for Ziran Zazhi (Nature Journal). A translation and summary of her work is found in *Incredible Tales of the Paranormal* edited by Alexander Imich, Ph.D. Despite the somewhat sensational title of this book, this is a scholarly collection of Psi research outside the English speaking world. The studies come from Italy, Iceland, Brazil, Poland, Russia and China. These Chinese studies start around 1980.

The Chinese cases especially appeal to me, because, (1) they are all done under normal lighting conditions, (2) there is no medium and no "spirits" involved, (3) the psychics are all amateurs, mostly young girls 12-19, who are able to do what they do with little or no practice, (4) the principal investigators are usually professors of physics or other sciences, and (5) these are contemporary studies, begun about 1980 and on-going. The Chinese seem quite open to the investigation of Psi phenomena, and place no mental limitations on what is possible or impossible.

All sorts of psi phenomena are represented. I better insert a note about terminology here. I do not use the term "ESP." I prefer the term "apparitional powers" since everything we know about telepathy and precognition comes from the study of apparitions. I don't use the term "telepathy" either, since it suggests the telephone, telegraph or television, all of which involve a serial, bit by bit stream of communications, which is not the case with apparitions. "ESP" should not be confused with "HSP," (Higher Sense Perception), a term coined by Shafica Karagulla. HSP allows one to see either physical or psychonic matter (such as auras), even in the dark, and it allows one to focus on successive internal layers of either physical or psychonic matter, which is a power something like Superman's X-ray vision. This is not a work of fiction. Such powers really exist. The term "psychonic" has the root "psyche," which means "mind" in Greek. Be sure to clearly pronounce the "n!" "Physical" and "psychonic" are mutually exclusive. Matter, for instance, can be one or the other, but not both. "Psychical" and "physical" are also mutually exclusive. I define "Psychical Research" as the study of the Mind, which we know to be completely independent from the Brain, as a result of Professor Ian Stevenson's studies of reincarnation. "Psi" is short for "psychical."

The first psi phenomenon to catch Zhu Yi Yi's attention were cases of HSP perception. Young girls could read pieces of paper put inside various objects. Some of these girls had the same kind of "x-ray" vision exhibited by Karagulla's "Diane." In other words, they could look inside a person's body. On one occasion Professors Xu Xinfang and Xia Xugan brought a 12 year old girl named Hu Lian to see Mr. Yao, a member of the Science Committee of Xuan Chen city. Mr. Yao had a piece of shrapnel left in his body from the war. The girl correctly pointed out the position of this piece of shrapnel and accurately drew its shape. This was verified by Mr. Yao's x-ray films, which he had in his house. Few people knew about Mr. Yao's shrapnel, although it is always possible that this young girl had heard about it.

The next kind of HSP perception was reading with the ear.

Yes, that's what I wrote, "reading with the ear." Words or phrases were written down, usually in Chinese characters, balled up and placed in the psychic's ears. After a few minutes, they could read the phrases, or describe the shapes if unfamiliar. Beijing Professors trained 10 year olds, and found that 60 percent of them could be trained to read with their ears. Shanghai investigators were similarly able to train juveniles in this art. This is very reminiscent of the Russian success at training juveniles in dermo-optic vision. Eventually, it was discovered that the psychic children could read with the ball under their foot or in their armpit, or by chewing it up.

Next, a boy was discovered who exhibited HSP control over mechanical watches. He could make them run fast or slow. If several watches were put on him, some would run fast, and some would run slow. In the terms of my theory of the mind as a natural object, this boy was "pushing the probabilities" that affect surface friction between mechanical parts, such as the escapement. By reducing the friction, the watch would run fast. Increase the friction and the watch would run slow. He had no effect on electronic watches. All this was quite unconscious. The boy had these abilities with no training.

Professors Zheng Tianming, Luo Xing, and Zhu Mingling of the University of Yun Nan devised a test for simple Psycho-Kinesis (PK), the same general phenomenon that is exhibited in levitation. They took the watches apart, so that the face with its hands was separated from the mechanism. They found several juveniles who could make the watch hands move rapidly without touching them. This is a good screening test for children who have PK ability. The watch hands are very light, and it would take very little force to make them move.

Finally, we come to apports. The first case brought to Zhu Yi Yi's attention was that of a young girl named Yang Li who could "remove the cigarettes." Ms. Zhu herself counted the cigarettes which were put inside a cardboard box with a lid. After awhile, Yang Li said "one had been removed." The box was opened, the cigarettes counted, and sure enough, one was missing. Where it went to is unknown.

There were also children who could apport something into a closed container. In this case, the containers were teacups with lids on them and the objects apported into the cups were flowers and flower buds. The source of one of the Jasmine buds was discovered. It came from a Jasmine plant growing in a pot on Mr. Yang's balcony. This incident took place at the home of Yang Li, mentioned above (in Chinese the Surname comes first) in the town of Kun Ming, famous for its flowers. Zhu Yi Yi invited two 12 year old girls trained for two years under Professors Luo Xinfun and Zheng Tianming, who also came along for the test. There were four young girls in all, and all were able to apport flowers and buds into the teacups, although none of them had tried this particular experiment before.

The Chinese studies suggest that young children, about 10 or 12, are more likely than adults to exhibit psi abilities spontaneously. They are also more trainable, and their abilities improve with practice. They were rewarded only with the delight and amazement their successes evoked from the adults. This is the way psi research should be done, quite the opposite from the boring card guessing or dice rolling of J.B. Rhine and the Parapsychologists. Psi is, after all, a mental ability, not something that can be done by machines. Social and psychological factors have to be relevant.

Today, China may be in the forefront of Psi research, largely because of the chilling effect of CSICOP (the psi-cops) on the West. The Chinese investigators have no pre-set notions of what is possible or impossible. Instead of treating their subjects like frauds when they exhibit psi abilities, they treat them like the special and advanced human beings they are. A psychic meets nothing but discouragement and disparagement in the West, and widespread approval and delight in China.

Zhu Yi Yi does not expect anyone to believe in psi abilities just from reading about it. It follows that the key to universal acceptance is the training of children to exhibit psi abilities, so that sooner or later, everyone witnesses examples of it for themselves. Thus, I do not expect this chapter or the "Seven Facts" chapter to convince everyone. As you see from my "Autobiography" I have been fortunate enough to witness macro psychokinesis, in the form of table-tipping.

There is a way all this might change. My theory of the mind, a testable non-reductionist theory based on 20th Century physics, a theory which explains all the major phenomena of Psychical Research, has as a consequence some tests which physicists can perform in the laboratory. If my theory is right, these will be reproducible, produce-on-demand psi events, measurable with physical equipment. If I can persuade any physicist to perform these tests, and if the theory passes muster, our Western attitudes toward psi phenomena would change very rapidly.

Seven Reproducible Psi Facts

The first successful project of the infant SPR back in 1882 was the study of apparitions. G.N.M. Tyrrell's book *Apparitions*, first published in 1942, is the classic summary and theory of the primary phenomenon of apparitions. This is a volume to go on the shelf of history's great books, along with *Twenty Cases, The Principia,* and *The Origin of Species.*

Tyrrell first shows us that apparitions are constructed by the collective unconscious of the recipients, because no physical change in the environment occurs. Yet, we cannot call them hallucinations. There is no such thing as a collective hallucination. Any experience which is shared by a number of people must be considered reality, although this is not our ordinary physical reality. The study of NDEs casts further light on this subject, and shows us that there is such a thing as apparitional reality, and it can engage the mental equivalents of all five senses. Furthermore, the "heavens and hells" experienced in NDEs are enduring realities, since comparison of NDEs show that some of them go to the same place. So, my view is that there is an apparitional reality as well as a physical reality. In some cultures, the two are combined.

We may experience apparitions and not realize it, so realistic are some apparitions. Sometimes an apparition is "found out" only when the recipient discovers that the person seen is dead. An apparition can include live people and inanimate objects, one more reason for putting it in the general category of "mental constructs of the recipient."

Apparitions vary in the "fullness" of their reality. They may be seen but not felt, or vice versa. Apparitions seldom frighten the recipient because it is usually a friend or relative that is seen, looking and acting just as if really present. Collective apparitions are seen by several people in the correct perspective for each percipient (Tyrrell, 1969, p. 76).

Unconscious levels of all the Minds present must create collective apparitions. Do they also create normal perception of reality? (Tyrrell, 1969, p. 121). This is an astounding idea, if true, the most important discovery ever made about psychology, one totally unknown to psychologists, the most "extraordinarily stupid" academics of all.

A brief mention of secondary effects: Sometimes physical effects do accompany apparitions, but this only happens when an Out-Of-Body person visits the percipient, tries to make himself visible (producing the apparition), and also tries to effect some physical change in the environs. Apparently, they are sometimes successful.

Most crisis apparitions contain veridical information. By that I mean detailed, unknown, (usually quite trivial) information conveyed by the sender to the recipient, which can be checked. The most usual information conveyed in crisis apparitions is simply the sender's own body-image (including clothing) at the moment of the crisis (usually the death of the sender), accompanied by reassurance of the recipient. The rest is unconsciously made up by the recipient.

Crisis apparitions sometimes happen up to 12 hours before or after the actual crisis event. Thus, apparition studies provide us with reproducible evidence for time-displacement (precognition, postcognition) of apparitional signals. Crisis apparitions are rare and spontaneous events, seldom time displaced by more than 12 hours. Thus, this evidence provides no support for fortune-tellers. If we assume that each apparition is triggered by a single message, then such messages are complex entities, conveying everything on the sender's Mind, or at least a complex thought or intent, including the sender's self-body-image, not single bits of information. This agrees with other kinds of Psi. This is why I don't like the term "telepathy," which suggests the "telephone," or the "telegraph," both of which send information one bit at a time, in a serial fashion. I don't use the term "ESP," either. I prefer "apparitional powers," since the data comes from the study of apparitions.

"ESP" is not to be confused with "HSP" (Higher Sensory Powers), which refer to completely different phenomena, such as the ability to see auras and other psychonic matter, as well as seeing physical matter, even in the dark. With HSP, one can focus on successive internal planes of either physical or psychonic matter, like Superman's X-ray vision. Such powers really exist. I use the term "Psychonic" (root "psyche," Greek for "mind") for anything that has to do with the psyche, including its substance, "psychonic matter."

The power to create or observe apparitional reality is one of the two conscious powers of mind, which spring to life automatically when one goes Out-Of-Body, in an OOBE or NDE, or at death. HSP is the other one. In an NDE, it is by HSP that we see our own body and other physical reality, but the rest is apparitional.

OOBEs and NDEs belong together. People can go Out-Of-Body spontaneously, during anesthesia or during flying dreams. Some people practice "lucid dreaming" to induce an OOBE. Lucid dreaming is knowing that one is dreaming while in the dream. Once self-aware in the dream, the dream can be changed. And from that state, some people find it easy to slip into an Out-Of-Body state. The OOBer may first float up to the ceiling. He can then turn over and see his body asleep below. Physical objects are seen much as they normally appear. OOBErs have difficulty recognizing or remembering signs, such as numbers or words, just as in a dream state. This skill must reside in the brain. So words or numbers do not make a good research target for investigating OOBEs. Use a red shoe or similar small object.

In the OOB state, one can fly any place just by wishing it. Flying dreams sometimes become OOBEs.

A Near Death Experience begins much like an OOBE. Upon being pronounced dead, the subject may roam around in the "earth plane" for a time. Eventually, the Nearly Dead go through a void, tunnel, hole, vortex, climb some stairs or take a boat ride to a white light, experience a total recall of one's life, and meet dead relatives and friends. At some point the Nearly Dead are told they must go back, otherwise, they become the Completely Dead. They seldom want to go back.

An NDE may last seconds, minutes, hours, or even days, if we are to believe the account of the soldier Er in Book X of Plato's *Republic*. Dannion Brinckley (see bibliography) was dead for 28 minutes, had been pronounced dead, covered with a sheet, put on a gurney and wheeled out to the elevator to be taken to the morgue, before forced to return to his body, which was agony. He was paralyzed and burning as if on fire (he had been struck by lightning), but was able to blow on the sheet, and the motion of the sheet caught someone's attention. A "dead" Vietnam soldier roamed around Out-Of-Body all day, and only re-entered his body as the embalmer made his cut in the femoral artery to drain the body's blood (Moody, 1975). He still has the scar to show it, which Moody examined. George Rodonaia was pronounced dead, sent to the morgue, put in one of those drawers and left for three days, during which time he has enjoying a most marvelous NDE. He came back to his body only when the incision was made to begin an autopsy, when his eyes fluttered open and his eyes moved. See http://www.near-death.com/rodonaia.html for all the details. Really "near death experience" is a misleading expression. In the cases above, we have clear examples of clinical death followed some time later by an amazing return to life.

I present an example of a "veridical" detail, the kind of fact which would rule out "brain hallucinations." Sabom presents the case of a retired air force pilot who had suffered a cardiac arrest 5 years earlier. He described the defibrillator. He said it had a meter on the face which was square and had two needles, one fixed, and one moving. The moving needle came up rather slowly. His description of a 1973 defibrillator is perfect. Later defibrillators are different, so he could not have gotten the information by going into an ER and studying one in 1978. Or consider the detailed description of the equipment and personnel in the NDE of an elderly woman blind since childhood. This case was recorded by Fred Schoonmaker, a cardiologist in Denver, Colorado, who claims to have three such cases among his former patients, including one congenitally blind person. He described these cases in detail to Kenneth Ring (Blackmore, 1993, p. 133). It is such veridical details that must be tracked down and checked. It is the veridical detail which cannot be explained away by the debunkers.

Professor Blackmore challenges all verifications of veridical details. She rejects the Sabom case for lack of details. For instance, do we have any proof that a defribillator was used on him? She throws out Schoonmaker's work simply because he never published it; he only conveyed it by phone to a well known NDE researcher, Kenneth Ring. There are a number of NDE cases with veridical details. Most of the best ones are published by Professor Blackmore. For instance, there is the "shoe on the roof case," reported by a social worker named Kimberly Clark. A woman named Maria was brought into a hospital in Seattle after a severe heart attack and then suffered a cardiac arrest. She later told Clark that she had been Out-Of-Body and noticed a tennis shoe on the third floor ledge at the north end of the building. It was a tennis shoe with a worn patch by the little toe and the lace stuck under the heel. Kimberly Clark looked out of various patient's windows until she found the shoe and retrieved. It was exactly as Maria described. (Blackmore, 1993, p. 128).

Yet Blackmore rejects the shoe story, because she was unable to get any further information. Well, what more does she need to know? How likely is something like this to happen by chance? Or does she simply think both Kimberly and Maria are liars?

I don't believe Blackmore is willing to accept any such case, no matter how good, because she has an alternative theory to explain NDEs and OOBEs. Blackmore has a theory of reality and self which is bizarre in the extreme, yet common among psychologists.

She thinks nothing is real but brain models (analogous to computer simulations), including one brain model which calls itself Professor Susan Blackmore. The world does not exist. You and I do not exist. None of the things discovered by science exist.

There is only the world of the brain model. And she has an ingenious theory to explain the feelings of well-being (endorphins in the temporal lobe), the black tunnel and growing light (hypoxia) and even a way of explaining the Out Of Body experience. Her book, Dying To Live is well-worth reading, by believers and skeptics alike. The main thing wrong with her theory is that she explains too much. According to her theory, everyone who has a cardiac arrest and nearly dies should have a NDE, but only a small percentage do. Furthermore, all those having NDEs should be transported to the light by a black and featureless tunnel, but that isn't true either. Some climb stairs, some are wafted away by angels, some get in a boat and cross a river, some walk up a corridor richly paved and paneled, and some just fall through a void to a distant point of light. There is another difficulty with her theory. It is self-contradictory! If reality doesn't exist, then neither do neurons, or endorphins or temporal lobes of brains. All that exist are brain models, and the only one of those Blackmore can be sure exists is the one arbitrarily labeled "Susan Blackmore." She has fallen into the classic trap of solipsism.

What is a person who calls herself a scientist who will never accept any data contrary to her own theories, no matter how good it is, data that everyone else accepts as valid? We call such a person "extraordinarily stupid" in Galileo's sense, a "High Priestess" of reduction, not a scientist at all.

There is a second way of checking the validity of NDEs. Some of them come back with prophecies about the future. For instance, Dannion Brinkley, in a book called *Saved By The Light*, describes 13 visions of the future shown to him in 1975. He was shown an enormous increase in the national debt, the election of Ronald Reagan, the destruction of the Chernobyl nuclear plant, the collapse of the Soviet Union, and the Desert Storm war in 1990. He was shown many more images which I shall not relate, and told that it was up to us whether these things came true or not.

Both OOBEs and NDEs involve the two kinds of conscious perception which come into action automatically when the Mind goes OOB. One of these is HSP and the other is the apparitional sense. HSP allows the percipient to see physical reality. It is not the same as normal vision, however, because the percipient can see in perfect darkness, see auras and other Mindstuff structures, focus on successive internal layers of both physical and Mindstuff structures, and can see in a 360 degree arc. An OOBEr may be aware of having an astral body, or he may not. If he is, it may be a duplicate of his physical body, complete with pajamas or whatever, in which case he is creating an apparitional self-image, one which might be visible to others. It he sees himself as a glowing blob, he is using his HSP to see himself "as he really is" to a physicist. It would be wonderful if we had a number of people as good at HSP as Karagulla's Diane. In that case, we could have "Diane" observe various people going out of body. It would be interesting to see if all of the mind goes OOB, or just a specific part of it, or none of it! In the third case, my theories would have to go back to the drawing board.

The apparitional sense in passive mode receives the collective apparitional creations of the sentient beings present. These can have all the attributes known to our five physical senses. In the active mode, one can create such apparitional realities, as Lady

Alexandra David-Neel did during her travels in Tibet. See *Magic and Mystery in Tibet*.

The later stages of either an OOBE or NDE use apparitional perception. An HSP sensitive may perceive a disembodied person as a glowing blob about a yard across. An apparitional sensitive will see a disembodied person as that person's body-image, younger or older than in life, lacking any handicaps, but automatically recognized.

Apparitional reality is a collective vision or hallucination created by all the sentient beings present. The passageway to death varies because it is an apparitional reality. Its character depends on those waiting on the other side, and perhaps on ones own unconscious expectations. If no one is waiting, and the percipient expects oblivion, the crossing may be a fall through a void towards a distant light. The apparitional sounds which accompany the experience also vary for the same reason, from an irritating buzz, to gongs, to beautiful ethereal music.

Why don't in-the-body individuals at the death scene also see the tunnel, the light, the dead friends and relatives? They sometimes do, if present at the transition, as in the movie "Ghost." Unfortunately, people today die anonymously and alone, in a highly drugged or comatose state, in hospitals, with no friends or relatives present. That is too bad, because death is usually a wonderful experience, which the living can sometimes share.

Finally, we must discuss the connection between NDEs and physical processes or chemicals. I refer to Ketamine, an animal tranquilizer, which can induce an NDE in humans, and electrical stimulation of the temporal lobe, which can also induce NDEs. Doesn't this show the NDE is really an illusion? No, it merely shows that physical events can precipate an NDE. Why should that surprise us?

As Morse himself points out in *Closer to the Light*, there is ample evidence that something really does leave the body, since NDErs (as well as OOBErs) can obtain information which they could not acquire even if their physical senses were working normally. This may include a view of who is out in the waiting room and what they are doing or saying, who hurries in to help with a "code," even if they are people never before seen by the patient, as well as events going on miles away, back home.

Thus, Morse's conclusion (and Penfield's) is that NDEs are not hallucinations produced by stimulating the temporal lobe. If the temporal lobe is the "seat of the Mind," or the point of attachment, events in the temporal lobe can trigger an NDE. This explains why people sometimes have an NDE when they merely think they are going to die, as in Albert Heim's study. Albert Heim was a 19th Century Swiss alpinist who had experienced what we now call an NDE while falling. The experience intrigued him, so he asked other climbers if they had ever experienced such a thing. Many of them had, though in fact they were not dying, merely falling (Sutherland, 1992, p. 2). If believing one is about to die can trigger an NDE, it may do so via the temporal lobe.

Reincarnation investigators have done some of the best work in Psychical Research. Investigators either study young children who spontaneously recall a former lifetime, or they hypnotically regress adults to former lifetimes It has been thirty years since Professor Ian Stevenson published his epochal *Twenty Cases Suggestive of Reincarnation*. This was the first lengthy, hands-on investigation of young children who spontaneously recall a former lifetime. There had been a few prior scattered reports in PR literature of the same phenomenon, referenced in Stevenson's book. He selected twenty examples which rule out alternate interpretations of the phenomena, such as ESP-Personation.

Normal channels of communication are best ruled out by the study of Imad Elawar, since Stevenson found out about him before the family had tried to make any verifications, and before his past life memories had begun to fade. Imad was five in 1964, when Stevenson made his investigation, and Imad had been talking about his past life since age two. Stevenson made copious notes before he and the family visited Imad's former family, where

Imad made spontaneous recognitions of people and pictures, also recorded by Stevenson. Imad Elawar's family were Druse, a sect of Islam which believe in reincarnation. Imad Elawar, a five year old child, could remember more than seventy details about a quite obscure man, living in another mountain village with little direct traffic to Imad's village, a man who had died nine years before Imad's birth. Both Imad's village and Ibrahim's village have good direct connections to Beirut, but are connected to one another only by a narrow, winding forty mile mountain road.

It is impossible for a two year old child to find out anything on his own about an obscure individual in a distant village who died nine years before his own birth. Could he be coached? Not by Imad's family. The Druse believe that one incarnation follows immediately after another, without time in between, and Imad's family were also under the mistaken belief that he was claiming to be Said Bouhamzy.

I have never read about a spontaneous past-life recall in which the former personality was well-known, much less famous, contrary to the lies of the Psi-cops. Certainly there was nothing about Ibrahim's life or death on the radio or in the newspapers. If there had been any news, it was "news" nine years before Imad's birth.

The only contact Imad had with a person from Ibrahim's village turns out to be a strong point of confirmation. When Imad was about two, he was out on the street with his grandmother when Salim el Aschkar of Ibrahim's village came along. Imad ran up to him and threw his arms around Salim. "Do you know me?" asked Salim. "Yes, you were my neighbor." Salim had lived close to Ibrahim Bouhamzy's place, but had since moved away.

Imad had never mentioned the first name of the previous personality (Ibrahim), only the last name (Bouhamzy) as well as a member of the family named Said. So, Imad's family mistakenly thought he was claiming to be Said Bouhamzy. If they were coaching, they were coaching for the wrong person.

As a general comment about all twenty investigations,

coaching does not explain the identity of personality and character traits, much less the persistence of physical traits from one life to the next.

Past life memories of the present personality often cause problems in the village, or were unsavory and nothing to brag about. Wijeratne recalled being an executed murderer in the same village, named Ratran Hami. Jasbir refused to eat the cooking of his mother because she was not of the Brahmin caste, and may have starved if a neighbor Brahmin woman had not cooked for him. Ravi Shankar had been murdered in his former lifetime as Munna, (by having his throat slit) and named his murderers, who still lived in the village. There was even a trial, but the court decided past life memories were not legally admissible evidence.

So past life memories bring nothing but trouble. The children were told to keep quiet about their past life memories, and even beaten, though all of Stevenson's twenty children come from cultures where belief in reincarnation is universal. When reincarnation was back into the same family, or into the same small village, the identity of personality was always noticed by family and neighbors. Even if one had a book listing every fact about the former person, there is no way personality could be the same. Complex interactive skills rule out cryptomnesia, itself an obscure and rare phenomenon. Stevenson has studied cryptomnesia, a favorite theory of the debunkers, and knows it is like a recording of a forgotten incident. It always plays back the same.

Only the combination of ESP plus personation has some hope of providing an alternative to reincarnation. ESP plus personation can be produced by mediums, at least in trance states. These children are not in a trance state. Nothing but reincarnation can account for the physical marks related to the previous lifetime, which I call "karma marks." William George, Jr. had several. William George, Sr. had injured his right ankle severely as a youth, and walked with a slight limp. So did William George, Jr. The dying William George, Sr. had told his daughter-in-law that he would be reborn to her, and she would recognize him by two prominent moles. William George, Jr. had the moles, in the same locations, about half size.

Charles Porter had been killed in a spear fight in his former lifetime, and had a birthmark in the shape of a spear wound on his right flank. Stevenson observed the birthmarks of both Charles Porter and William George.

Karma marks not only rule out all alternatives to reincarnation for these cases; they also imply that the Mind forms the body, rather than vice versa. Young children who spontaneously recall former lifetimes may be rare, although I have encountered two myself. What is rare is for Psi investigators to hear about such children, especially when the child is still young and still able to recall the past life. These memories usually fade between ages seven and twelve.

Hypnotic regression is the other route to reincarnation evidence. One of the most famous books about past life regression is *The Search for Bridey Murphy*, by Morey Bernstein, published in 1957. This book became an international best seller. Debunkers attributed it all to cryptomnesia, on the grounds that a Bridget Kathleen Murphy lived on the same block when the present personality was a small child. The families were not acquainted, and there is no evidence they ever met.

Cryptomnesia cannot account for the veridical details (names of merchants, streets, buildings) that Bridey knew about mid 19th century Cork because these had never been published and were unknown even to scholars until after the publication of The Search for Bridey Murphy. After that book became an international bestseller, old diaries and letters were turned up to verify those details. So be sure to look up the second or later edition of this book.

Nor can cryptomnesia account for the interactive abilities of Bridey Murphy. Bridey could dance Irish Jigs and speak in the lilt and slang of mid-19th Century Irish county Cork, and much of this slang and many of these jigs had never been published and had been forgotten, like much of the ephemeral popular culture of any age.

Stevenson has published many studies of "responsive xenoglossy," which refers to the ability of a hypnotically regressed individual to carry on a conversation in a language unknown to the present personality. My friend and mentor, Bill Coates, collaborated with Stevenson in the investigation of a woman who spoke Old Norse under hypnosis. Bill (now deceased) was one of the few linguists who specialized in dead European languages.

So it appears that all we need are more reincarnation studies of the same kind, to guarantee reproducibility, and we need to allow time to see if any new alternative explanations are proposed. Over the past thirty years, these two conditions have been met for reincarnation studies.

By all the rules of scientific method, reincarnation is a well-established scientific fact. If you don't believe it, go do your own studies of the phenomenon. That is what scientific method requires of skeptics.

We will now take a closer look at HSP, which allows the OOB Mind to see physical reality and much more besides, without eyes, 360 degrees.

The pioneer of these studies was Shafica Karagulla, whose poorly titled book, *Breakthrough to Creativity* is one of the great classics of Psychical Research. An unknown classic! Although her work was definitely Psychical Research by my definition, she published in medical journals, not in PR journals, and the editors of PR and Parapsychology journals usually know nothing of her work (Karagulla, 1967). Shafica Karagulla was a noted neuroscientist about thirty years ago, and a practicing MD.

Karagulla often worked with "Diane," who was a successful businesswoman, who kept her powers a secret. First Diane examined a patient by her methods, then Karagulla did the standard analysis of an MD, and they compared notes. Karagulla found Diane to be at least her equal at medical diagnosis. Diane once spotted an obstructed bowel, which Karagulla's own examination had missed. The patient was hastily called back, X-rayed, and operated on, saving his life. HSP is a mode of perception, like ordinary vision. Those who can do it, can always do it. It is not an unpredictable, once-in-a-lifetime phenomenon like experiencing apparitions or poltergeists.

The "Mind" is "the non-physical component of a living creature, as seen by HSP." Diane describes the human Mind as a glowing structure with nine major vortices and numerous smaller ones, each having a characteristic number of sub-cones, and a characteristic place in the body.

Five vortices are on the spine, one at the tailbone, one at L5 on the lumbar, one each at the levels of navel, heart and throat. The sixth chakra is at the eyebrows, the seventh at the crown of the head, and the eighth at the back of the head. A smaller ninth chakra is at the pancreas.

It was the Yogis who labeled these things "chakras," meaning "wheels," revealing an ancient science. The chakras are connected by a web of light beams, or at least that is how they appear to HSP. The Yogis call these lines "nadi," while they are known as "meridians" in Chinese acupuncture. There is considerable evidence that these meridians really exist. It has long been known that analgesic acupuncture increases the endorphins in the brain. Now it has been learned that acupuncture on a meridian connected to a particular organ will "light up" that part of the brain responsible for that organ. For instance, the meridian for the eyes surfaces alongside the outside of the foot. Stimulating these "eye" points will "light up" the same parts of the brain used for seeing, on an fMRI scan. (*Discover Magazine*., September 1998, p. 61). Outside the boundaries of the body, there is the multi-hued aura. This structure of chakras, nadi and aura is what I call "Mind." Since the Mind is a stable object, always visible when looked at by people with HSP, it must be made of some kind of "stuff." I call it "Mindstuff." With HSP, Diane can see internal organs, as we saw in the obstructed bowel case. But she usually found it more informative to observe the internal workings of the chakras. Serious pathology is associated with breaks in these structures. Minor pathology produces a jerky rhythm in the chakras.

I suspect that chiropractors fine-tune the rhythm of the five chakras on the spine, and the manipulation of the vertebrae so they move freely serves to focus the aura on each chakra in turn. The real healing is done unconsciously by the aura of the chiropractor's hands. I have found that headaches can be healed by putting one palm on the bridge of the nose, covering the forehead, and with the other hand at the base of the head, gently applying pressure and massage. These are both locations of chakras.

Where the nadi enter or leave the surface of the physical body, there we find the acupuncture points. The physical needles focus the aura to restore the flow of energy in that nadi to its normal flow and rhythm. Thus, it requires "healing hands" to be a chiropractor or acupuncturist. Merely knowing the physical part is insufficient.

People who can do HSP in-the-body are rare. Everyone automatically has HSP Out-Of-Body. Fortunately, "Diane" is not unique, because scientific method requires reproducibility.

In Barbara Ann Brennan (see bibliography), we have a contemporary with HSP (she doesn't call it that), who even teaches others how to activate their own HSP, at her East Hampton, Long Island School for Healing. Indeed, Brennan has gone one step further than "Diane." Not content merely to observe pathological energy patterns, Brennan is willing to use her aura to change those energy patterns back to a healthy pattern and thus heal the patient.

Like "Diane," Brennan is unwilling to be a guinea pig in some scientist's experiments. One can easily see why. In the 19th Century, D.D. Home demonstrated levitation, not only before the crowned heads of Europe, but also before the scientists of the time. Uri Geller has demonstrated an ability to change the physical properties of objects before the scientists of the 1960s. Neither

Home nor Geller changed the minds of any of the scientists, and only earned the ridicule of the Extreme Skeptic. No one is so blind, as those who do not wish to see. A psychic is foolish to submit to people claiming to be scientists, who are unable or unwilling to learn anything from such study, which means they are not really scientists, just phuds (Ph.D.s).

That the "Mind is a natural object" is a matter of fact, by HSP observation. A natural object is part of nature, like a tree or a galaxy. The Mind is not made of the ordinary matter known to physicists. Because of the pioneering work of Vera Rubin, astronomers now know that most of the mass of the universe is also some kind of transparent non-ordinary matter (Morris, 1993, p. 2).

Our next subject is "blue sense," often called psychometry. People with this skill are rare. Those who can do it, can always do it. It is a mode of perception, not a once-in-a-lifetime event. Blue sense is an instance of conscious apparitional perception. It is called "blue sense" because of the use of such sensitives by "the men in blue," i.e., policemen.

When a "blue sense" sensitive holds objects found at a murder scene belonging to the victim, she receives apparitional visions of the victim's experience, not only the murder, but events leading up to it, as well as the victim's own body-image.

Of course, the owner of an object doesn't have to be dead. In the 1960s I saw a contest (broadcast over local TV in Los Angeles), run by Dr. Thelma Moss of the UCLA Neuropsychiatric Institute, which pitted a "blue sense" sensitive against a psychologist. Before the contestants came out to the stage, various items were contributed by a few strikingly different audience members. This was in the mid 60s, when men sometimes wore necklaces and other jewelry. I especially recall the readings given for a necklace of gaudy plastic beads. The psychologist said it belonged to a lower class woman with little education (wrong as usual) while the sensitive said it belonged to a man, a highly educated lawyer, which the sensitive proceeded to describe (right as usual).

"Poltergeist" is German for "prankster spirit," and one of the most noted poltergeist investigators, Hans Bender, also happens to be German. Apparitions are not ghosts. Neither are poltergeists.

Poltergeists are much less common than apparitions, children who recall former lifetimes, or people who have had OOBEs. Poltergeists are so dramatic, however, that the world is much more likely to hear about it. Some member of the household unconsciously produces poltergeists, since they follow the household from place to place. German investigators believe adolescents are unconsciously responsible, since families "grow out of" poltergeists.

What do poltergeists do? Two things, and they are associated, i.e., found in the same case. One is levitation and movement of small objects such as cups and saucers (psycho-kinesis), which sail across the room and smash, and the other is teleportation, the disappearance of an object from one point in space-time and its reappearance at another point in space-time. Hans Bender has witnessed both. Dr. Bender notes that an apported object that has just appeared, i.e. come out of teleportation, floats to the ground with a falling leaf motion, as if nearly weightless. UFOs exhibit the same behavior.

If apparitions are not ghosts, and poltergeists are not ghosts, what is a ghost? And are there such things? Yes, there are, but they are fortunately rare, since a ghost is a Mind trapped between two worlds, not really part of this world or part of the next. Ghosts sometimes learn to absorb energy from the heat energy in the environment, producing a physically measurable cold spot, which moves around as the ghost moves around. This energy may be used for Psycho-Kinesis (PK).

Most "haunts" are probably just apparitions triggered by the traces left behind by former inhabitants (who may or may not be dead). However, if there are also PK effects and measurable cold spots, then it is a true ghost.

In addition to these seven paranormal phenomena well-established by Western investigators, there is the work of the

East Europeans, done during the Cold War, between 1930 and 1970. The Eastern investigators took a completely different tack, and discovered things of great importance for my theory.

One of these discoveries is dermo-optic vision. This is the ability of people to "see" colors or read print with their fingertips (Ostrander & Schroeder, 1970, p. 158 ff.). Some of the subjects were physically blind, and the others had to read by putting their arms through a blind which prevented visual observation of the target. This phenomenon became something of a fad in Russia in the 1960s.

A man named Kirlian developed a kind of photography which shows auras. Kirlian photography involves a strong static electric field in the "box" where the hands or leaves are placed, together with an Electro-Magnetic oscillation of 75,000 to 200,000 cycles per second (Ostrander & Schroeder, 1970, p. 189). What the photograph shows is almost certainly coronal arcing, the kind of thing one sees around high tension lines during a fog. But what is interesting is the pattern of coronal arcing. For instance, if a freshly plucked leaf is cut in two and placed in the "box," the outlines of the entire leaf can be seen, or at least these are the results claimed by the Kirlians and demonstrated in photographs. To duplicate these results, one must control humidity, as well as duplicating a high voltage, low amperage box (so no one is electrocuted!). The Kirlians hold several patents on this device.

For theoretical reasons, I am going to lump these Eastern discoveries together with HSP into the general category of de Broglie phenomena, which include an indefinite variety of different effects. So we still have just seven facts: reincarnation, apparitions, poltergeists, OOBEs, NDEs, blue sense, and de Broglie phenomena.

All seven studies are reproducible, and follow the rules of scientific method. Don't be fooled by the Psi-cop's impossible demands that a genuine Psi phenomenon must be one that cannot be duplicated by an illusionist. An illusionist can duplicate any discovery of physics, too. The Psi-cops are following Hume's rule, not scientific method. Those genuinely skeptical about any of the seven facts presented in this chapter have a duty to reproduce that study. Those unwilling to do so have no right to pass judgment.

If these seven facts have been well-established, why haven't they been well-accepted? Because these discoveries break the reductionist worldview and because Psychical Researchers had provided no explanation of them, as I shall later.

If my theory is right, physicists will be able to produce Psi phenomena on demand in the laboratory. If this happens, the walls of reduction will come tumbling down, the psi-cops will be discredited, and a major change in worldview will occur. But this is only the beginning of our Long Journey.

A Testable Theory of the Mind

The first law of Mind is that it is composed of Dark Matter, not unlike the Dark Matter found by astronomers. We know this because the Mind is invisible to physical eyes and cannot be photographed. When we open up the head in a living subject to perform a brain operation, there is no sign of the Mind. The Mind is only visible to the HSP sense, which we all have, but which normally only comes into operation when we go OOB (Out-Of-Body), which can happen in a variety of ways, and is a fairly common experience. The Mind is a normal part of nature, in that it has size, shape, internal structure, mass, conservation of energy and interactions with other Minds and with matter. This basic idea could be tested by weighing a dying person who volunteered to be inside a completely enclosed and self-sufficient capsule.

The second law of Mind is that it has absolutely no interaction with the Electro-Magnetic force. That is why it is invisible and intangible. A person in an OOBEs can freely move through solid objects, such as in-the-body people or doors, walls, ceilings, floors, whatever. We know that the tangibility and visibility of objects is entirely due to the interaction of their component atoms via the Electro-Magnetic force.

The third law of Mind is that it interacts with the brain and the rest of the body via de Broglie vibrations. These are the same de Broglie vibrations we encountered in physics, the ones that determine what is possible, and the probabilities of each thing that is possible at any given moment. In this way, some unconscious and low level structure of the Mind gets input from the brain, reading the de Broglie vibrations output by every part of the brain. Similarly, the same low level unconscious part of the Mind can radiate de Broglie vibrations, which is like writing or changing some part of the brain. This is how we control the body. We have far greater potential control of the body than you can imagine, since we can potentially affect every atom and molecule.

The fourth law of Mind is that it can effortlessly affect the geodesics not just of space-time, but also of the multi-dimensional manifold in which space-time is embedded. This happens every time we sleep. How can we tell that someone is really asleep, and not just lying quietly with their eyes closed? By their deep, slow, and labored breathing. This is the physical side of the Prana-pump, also known as the body-mind generator. The only force which the Mind can produce which affects physical matter is the Einsteinian force, changing the geodesics of space-time, producing levitation and apports. Not every day, not at our present stage of development. But we do operate the Prana-pump every day, or every night, if at all possible. By generating a cyclic force which opposes the movement of breathing, energy is converted from the physical world to the mental world. Without mental energy, we first go crazy, and then we die. The basic formula for all types of generators is that energy equals the resistant force times distance, or $E = F*D$.

The fifth law of Mind is that it has two intrinsic powers which come into operation automatically when the mind leaves the body, either temporarily in an NDE or OOBE, or permanently, when we die. The mind, of course, does not die. These two intrinsic powers are the apparitional power and HSP. Both powers are creative as well as reactive. When OOB, we can create apparitional realities, or we can observe apparitional realities created by others.

Generally, apparitional realities are created on an unconscious level in a cooperative way by the expectations and sensory or extra-sensory inputs to all the sentient beings physically present. Such apparitional creations can mimic all the physical sensations, such as sight, sound, smell, taste, and touch. HSP and the apparitional power can be used simultaneously. In an NDE, we see physical reality with HSP, but we hear what people are saying by the apparitional power, by telepathy if you will.

The sixth law of Mind is that it can enter higher dimensions, which physical matter cannot. One of these higher dimensions is usually referred to as the astral dimension. This is where we find heavens and hells. The astral dimension has both space and time, and we can travel to anyplace in the astral past or the astral future, but these do not necessarily reflect physical past and future. Seers see the astral future, a probable future. Precognition is a minor and common type of seership, seeing something in the nearest and most probable astral future.

There are conscious powers and unconscious powers. Most of the Mind consists in unconscious powers, such as the Prana-pump and the low-level details of interaction with the brain and perhaps other parts of the body via the HSP (de Broglie) power. There are powers which can be learned by simple practice, and those which cannot. For instance, I would say any de Broglie power (also called HSP power) can be learned by diligent practice.

Any physical macro-state which depends on quantum micro-states in a near state of equilibrium can be affected by HSP. You can learn to push the probabilities one way or another. Examples of such macro-states are cumulus clouds, which are constantly dissolving and condensing. If you live someplace where you have daily cumulus clouds, you could learn how to dissolve them completely, or make them build up into thunderheads, but only by diligent practice. Some Toltec Brujos can make an engine stop. They do this by pushing the probabilities of the sparking mechanism. It is naturally set close to equilibrium, thus one can push the probabilities to not sparking. In a similar fashion, one can make old fashioned watches or clocks stop, or make watches run that haven't worked for years. Stick-and-slip friction is subject to de Broglie probabilities.

Powers that cannot be learned by simple practice are levitation and apports. The Prana pump is somewhere deep down in the unconscious mind. However, Yogis learn to affect such normally unconscious parts of the Mind, and therefore Yoga might provide a path to control over such powers. But I haven't seen a Yogi do it yet! Why not? The low state of civilization in India might be the reason. As long as there are people who are hungry, or overpopulating the Earth, or committing acts of war, the level of spiritual evolution is not high enough to allow advanced Psi powers.

Interstellar enthusiasts have been looking for a warp engine somewhere in the bowels of theoretical physics. But they won't find it there. They will find it in the everyday act of sleep. This is the only phenomenon which appears likely to involve an effortless bending of the space-time geodesics, in order to produce the resisting force necessary for a dynamo.

It should be possible to test this idea. Pass a laser beam over a sleeping person and see if we can detect a rhythmic bending of the beam. The amount of the bending is likely to be very small, only detectable miles away, and only when the beam is focused to a point, and then magnified, so that the most minute movement can be detected. Only physicists or geologists have the equipment to make that test. Philosophers don't have the equipment, or the temperament. It might also be possible to detect rhythmic changes in the gravity field by mounting a gravity meter over a sleeping person. Gravity meters are very sensitive. So perhaps that is the most promising experiment.

If the results of this test are positive, there will be an overnight revolution in our intellectual history. Finally, the hold of reduction will be broken. The reason is that physicists will have the first reproducible produce-on-demand Psi phenomenon, one that will work with anyone, since we all require sleep. Physicists will go nuts. Our intellectual world will change in a flash, and all the other discoveries of Psychonics will become believable, and the leading edge of science.

We don't know much about dark matter. It may be a property of the vacuum, i.e., a property of space-time itself, which would explain why the Mind can effortlessly bend the geodesics of space-time to produce levitation and apportation. Perhaps there are different levels of energy of the vacuum, or perhaps the vacuum can organize itself into different levels of complexity. I don't know. That is just speculation, and is not part of my theory. What my theory does accomplish is to make the Mind a thing, an object in nature, something with mass, size, shape, internal structure, conservation of energy, and interactions with physical matter. Thus, the Mind ceases to be the "ghost in the machine." It becomes part of nature, and can be weighed and measured just like other parts of nature.

A larger question is whether the Mind is that non-physical part of a person which can be seen by HSP, a structure of chakras, nadi, and auras. To state that more clearly, is the Mind known from Professor Stevenson's studies the same as the Mind known from Dr. Karagulla's studies? I believe we could settle this question by having a clairvoyant observe someone going OOB and returning. I shall define a clairvoyant as someone like Joan Grant (see Kelsey and Grant, *Many Lifetimes*) or "Diane" (see Karagulla, *Breakthrough to Creativity*). A real clairvoyant must have all the natural powers of the mind, which come into operation automatically when going Out-Of-Body. Yet, the clairvoyant must still maintain conscious contact with the ordinary physical world. Joan Grant did something she called a "level shift" when she wanted clairvoyant powers. I suspect this is partly in the body, and partly out of body.

If the structure of chakras and nadi remains in place in the body during an OOBE, then the mind is not this chakras and nadi structure, which is traditionally known as the "astral body." I suspect that is, indeed, the case, for without that structure, the body dies. So the second question is whether the clairvoyant can see anything leaving during an OOBE and returning at the end of it? Whatever that is, it is the seat of consciousness, although consciousness can be bi-located during an OOBE, aware of all physical inputs to the body, as well as having a traveling component, independent of the body! So things are complicated, and many questions arise. Where does the astral body come from? Does it dissipate and disappear after death? If so, where does a new one come from in a new human body? Only really good clairvoyants can answer such questions, and then only if they are given access to people dying and being born. My theoretical speculations apply to the combination of mind and astral body, which I shall call Mind with a capital "M."

Even if tests of this theory allow us to understand the Mind, we may still not fully understand consciousness. As we have seen, consciousness can be bilocated, and I don't know if this correlates with anything visible to clairvoyants.

Let's look at some of the consequences and details of this theory.

It is by de Broglie radiation that the Mind can see in the dark via HSP, and can focus on successive internal layers of both ordinary physical objects and the more exotic Mindstuff objects, with their chakras, nadi and auras. It is the reception of de Broglie waves from the brain that allows ordinary perception by the Mind. Mindstuff controls the brain by emitting de Broglie waves in a controlled way, to alter the probabilities of physical events. The low level details of this are unconscious.

Dermo-optic perception (seeing with the hands) is de Broglie wave reception, by the aura around the hands. Look in the bibliography for a 1970 book by Ostrander and Schroeder for the evidence pertaining to this paragraph. I make references in this way (Ostrander & Schroeder, 1970), which provide the minimal information needed to locate the work in the bibliography. Kirlian photography and the "thoughtography" of Ted Serios (Eisenbud, 1967) are instances of "probability pushing," where the probabilities of an unstable reaction are pushed one way or another, in a patterned fashion, by the emission of de Broglie waves from the aura. The colloidal suspension of silver in film is inherently unstable. Eastman Kodak has encountered many workers who unconsciously stimulate the photographic response in unexposed film. These workers cannot be allowed to come near film.

Since the HSP power can also radiate de Broglie waves, it can shift the probabilities of physical events. If the probabilities of two different physical states are nearly equal, the Mind can learn with practice to tip the balance using HSP, one way or the other, to produce the Mind-brain interaction, spoon-bending, rain-making, making cars stop running, thoughtography, spontaneous combustion, healing, and much more, without understanding the low level details.

On the other hand, some HSP powers rely on using the aura of the eyes or the aura of the hands to receive inputs, producing such things as dermo-optic vision. According to Ostrander and Schroeder, the Russian children could learn dermo-optic vision after about 6 months of daily practice. Sometimes, auras can directly affect other auras, probably explaining the staring-at-someone phenomenon (making them turn around and look). Auras may also be able to transfer energy to another aura. There is something called "healing touch" which actually does not involve physically touching another person's body. Instead, one moves ones hands above the body. This is another skill that can be learned with practice and sensitivity, since it requires detecting wrong energy patterns in a sick person, and correcting them with ones own mental energy. One must be careful not to overdo this. No more than one patient a day. It requires sleep, or the special breathing exercises used by Yogis to restore ones mental energies. If you let your mental energies run down, it will adversely affect your mental sharpness, your physical health, your emotional state, and of course, your ability to do "healing touch."

Except for a few rare individuals like D. D. Home (a famous psychic of the 19th Century, who once levitated himself out the window of one floor of a hotel and into the window on another floor), bending the geodesics is not under conscious control. And even Home could not explain how he did what he did (Macklin, 1965, p. 19). There have been a number of unconscious levitators, such as a priest who levitated when he conducted Mass.

Can psychonic matter or Mindstuff be created? Psychometry suggests that it can indeed, and that this matter behaves much like physical matter. Sensitives who can do psychometry are sometimes used by police in their blue uniforms, which is why it is sometimes called "blue sense."

In physics, sufficiently energetic signals can condense as exponentially decaying particles with a certain half-life. The relationship between the energy of the signal "E" and the mass "m" of the particle(s) formed is given by Einstein's famous (E=m*C**2) formula. This same rule may apply to psychonic matter.

Some normally unstable particles of physics are stable within a strong field. For instance, a neutron is stable inside a nucleus, but is unstable outside the nucleus, with a half-life of about fifteen minutes. A Kaon is stable inside a neutron star, but not otherwise. Apparitional signals condense on our possessions as Mindstuff and later decay as apparitional signals. Mindstuff is stable within the aura. Outside the aura it is unstable, with a half-life measured in months. This means we can leave a trace of ourselves behind in the physical objects we use everyday.

When we leave possessions behind (no longer in the aura), the Mindstuff begins to decay back into apparitional signals, which a "blue sense" psychic receives. This explains how blue sensitives help in murder investigations, if given objects always worn by the victim and found on the body, such as a ring.

But, how do those with "blue sense" find missing persons, especially dead ones? I guess the first question is whether any of them can actually do that. If so, only sometimes or all the time? Suppose the victim had a premonition of her fate? Then that message would also be imprinted on personal objects, which a "blue sense" sensitive could read. Of course, such premonitions are seldom accurate, or they might be right in some details, but not in others. So I would expect that psychometry would be more successful in describing the guilty party from clothing and jewelry found on the murdered victim, than in finding dead bodies from examining personal objects left behind at home. Or it could be that tuning into the "vibes" of a person may help locate that person wherever they are.

Two of the strangest phenomena in PR are precognition and teleportation. Precognition is learning about something before it happens, and teleportation is the disappearance of an object at one place and time, and its reappearance at another place, without traveling the intermediate space-time. Yet, both are easily explained if the universe is five dimensional. Mindstuff and apparitional signals can move in five dimensions. Physical phenomena are confined to a single 4-dimensional slice of this five dimensional manifold (if time is a dimension).

Imagining five dimensions is not easy, so consider this analogy. Suppose we reduce the physical world to a sheet of paper, with width representing space, and length representing time. Physics gives us the laws of this sheet of paper, and everything known to physics is confined to the sheet of paper. Thus, to get from one point in space-time to another, one must traverse all the points in between on the sheet of paper, and we cannot exceed the Einsteinian speed limit, which is the speed of light. But what if we bend the sheet of paper in 3-dimensional space (which represents 5-dimensional space) so that two points separated on the sheet of paper come in contact in 3-dimensions? At that contact point an object could be sent over by levitation, producing teleportation.

Unfortunately, this theory of apportation is untestable. It is also wrong. If there were only one humanoid in the universe doing apports at any given time, it might work. However, there are dozens of species of humanoids visiting us from distant stars, and they apport at will. Furthermore, in the Chinese studies

("Mind-Bending the Space-Time Geodesics"), there are several girls doing apports at roughly the same time, in the same place. With all of them bending space-time at once, there is no telling where anything would go. All we really know is that levitation and apports are associated. People who can do one can often do the other. Both are found in poltergeist phenomena but not associated with other Psi phenomena.

I do have a theory of apports, based on the latest theories of physics, which have to do with supersymmetry, imaginary time, and a fifth dimension. In his new book *The Universe in a Nutshell*, Stephen Hawking actually draws a picture of the history of the universe as a somewhat lumpy and wrinkled nutshell. P-branes and M-branes can be represented as a surface, and in Hawking's nutshell, the surface is a "brane" of space-time, while the interior of the nutshell represents a fifth spatial dimension. It is my theory that apports take a shortcut through this fifth dimension. In all of the "brane" theories, there are 10 or 11 dimensions, most of them curled up very tightly. In the latest theories, one of these extra dimensions is not curled up, and becomes our fifth dimension of space.

It is difficult to put the astral planes into Hawking's "Nutshell." On the astral planes, there is both space and time, and the mind can freely travel in all 4 dimensions, or even be aware of everything at once, as in the mystical state of Cosmic Consciousness.

Apports and precognition suggest the possibility of time-travel. Why not apport an object, even a person, to a different time as well as a different place? I have never heard of a physical object arriving from the future or the past. As Stephen Hawking says, if time-travel were possible, we would be overrun with tourists from the future.

What about those rare reports of people suddenly being transported into the past for a few moments? This is an apparitional experience. They have witnessed an apparition of the past. And what about the future seen by Seers or Prophets? This too is an apparitional experience. Prophets are witnessing an apparitional reality, which may be a kind of copy of the physical past. The apparitional future is the probable future, the expected future, given what has already happened. Some of what is seen may have a symbolic rather than a literal meaning, and the meaning may be personal rather than objective. Such visions may be warnings, or visions of possibilities, not inevitabilities. The future is never fixed, and is always subject to change, until it actually occurs in physical reality.

Why is time travel NOT possible? Because the physical past and future do not exist. There is only one physical universe, and time is the flow of energy in this universe. Time is motion and change. Despite Einstein's theory of relativity, we are not required to treat ordinary time as a space-like dimension. Physicists find imaginary time more useful in their theories. An imaginary number is a number multiplied by the square root of minus one. Imaginary time would be a dimension of imaginary numbers, and it does behave like a spatial dimension. It can be curved like space, and represented in physical models in a spatial way. The nutshell used by Hawking as a model of one history of the universe uses imaginary time as one of its dimensions.

Doesn't special relativity imply the real existence of time as a dimension? Only if we accept Einstein's operational definition of simultaneity. Operational definitions are one of the unfortunate leftovers of logical positivism, which was a very popular philosophy about the time relativity and quantum mechanics developed. But operational definitions never really work.

Suppose we wish to maintain simultaneity between the earth and a spaceship traveling at speeds approaching C. We know that our perception of things is going to be different from that of people on the space-ship. For instance, from their point of view, the universe seems to be shrinking and speeding up. Soon they will be able to go from one star to another in just a few minutes. Simultaneously, the rotation of the galaxy will speed up, and they can actually see it rotate. Meanwhile, on Earth, we see clocks on their space-ship slowing down, along with aging. So eon after eon arises and passes away on earth as the space-ship slowly creeps across the sky. Yet the astronauts do not age. Radioactive elements on their ship do not decay. Their clocks run slower and slower. It is nevertheless possible to maintain simultaneity. All we have to do is occasionally apport to the spaceship and give them the universal standard galactic time.

Of course, universal simultaneity does not by itself deny that time is a dimension. I merely demonstrate that special relativity does not by itself imply that time IS a dimension. I should also point out that time is an imaginary number in relativity, related to real time, but not identical to it.

If this theory, or some other, should pass its tests and become well-established as an explanation of psychical phenomena, it would instantly make psychical phenomena intellectually respectable. A theory like this heals the rift between the physical world and the psychical world, since both are parts of nature, subject to the laws of nature. There is nothing supernatural or philosophical about this theory.

Fermi's Paradox

To recapitulate this section of the book: How do we know that an advanced state of spiritual evolution is required for interstellar travel? Because of Fermi's paradox. Enrico Fermi, the great Italian physicist, said "If extra-terrestrial civilization is common, why isn't it here?" This is a paradox only if we assume that ET would behave like humankind in our present state of spiritual evolution. If WE found a planet like Earth, as it has been for 1.5 billion years, with plenty of oxygen, and plenty of water, we would certainly colonize it. But obviously that has not happened. Indeed, except for the occasional asteroid or comet, Earth has evolved to its present state without any outside interference.

Yet, we know that ET is here, and probably has been here many times in the history of the planet. Only a spiritually advanced culture would behave like anthropologists and not like conquistadors, and allow the planet to evolve in its own way. That is why I am sure that our own higher Selves would not allow us to develop the power to levitate large space-ships, must less to apport them hundreds of light-years in an instant. Not now. Not until we have outgrown our childish greed, and learn to see things with a god's eye view of time and space.

Those who follow mystical paths sometimes do gain conscious control over psi powers. I suggest we do the same. We must lift our entire civilization, our entire species to a new level, if we wish to go to the stars.

Now we enter the Royal Maze, with no fixed gates or pathways. We each must find our own way towards spiritual evolution. Forget the books, forget the ancient Oriental traditions. The books about them are dusty relics, mistranslated, misunderstood, just like the teachings of Jesus. Rely on your own experience. Or rely on my experience. I have experienced the Illumination of Fire, in which the divine purpose that runs through all things is made evident.

Spiritual evolution is not something I can easily define. But I know it when I see it. Lord Kenneth Clark made a similar remark about Civilisation. A society which takes care of its homeless and jobless is more evolved than one which does not. Knowledge is more evolved than ignorance, especially knowledge about things that matter, such as psychonics, metaphysics and utopian analysis. A cultural peak with many geniuses is more evolved than a dark age, no matter how necessary an occasional dark age might be. Arts which uplift are more evolved than those which incite to murder and riot. All forms of prejudice and discrimination over trivial matters is primitive. Our persecution of people just because they enjoy different recreational drugs is primitive. On the other hand, the grand ideals of the Enlightenment are very evolved, if only we could learn to follow them, and recognize instances of tyranny. The life of the Seeker is more evolved than a life of greed and brutality. Not that everyone must cease productive work. One can still meditate, one can still seek to erase hatred and greed in oneself, even with a job and a family. Still, the highest state of spiritual evolution may develop in those Seekers who do withdraw from the world to devote full time to spiritual evolution.

Western Civilization is at a cultural peak in science and technology, but not in the arts or architecture, nor in the spiritual life. Nor can it ever produce a high civilization as long as the prevailing dogma is reduction, which says that nothing is real unless we can photograph it. Or, nothing is real unless we can explain it in terms of Atoms and the Void. Such a narrow view leaves out everything interesting and important. There is excellent evidence from Ian Stevenson's reincarnation studies that the mind is real, is the seat of Self and consciousness, and survives death, eventually to reincarnate with new memories and personality, with a continuity of Self and consciousness. Clearly, the mind has no interaction with the electro-magnetic force. So it cannot be photographed. We do not see it when we look inside the living brain. Nor can it be composed of Atoms. Scientists must either accept this result, and enlarge their definition of science, or science becomes just another religion, a particularly unpleasant one, since it denies us life after death, immortality, or a meaning to life. Therefore, as a religion, it must eventually disappear.

Let us be optimistic, and assume that the scope of science will be enlarged to include everything which satisfies the essence of scientific method. Then, we shall have A New Science of Civilization. This is my invention, building on the "moral sciences" of Thomas Hobbes and John Locke. My professors and colleagues said it couldn't be done, but I did it. The solution of major social problems such as war, poverty, ignorance and despair is a necessary step in our spiritual evolution. It doesn't solve the problem if only a few Seekers go off into the desert or mountains or forests, and become highly evolved. Only the spiritual evolution of the species will open up to us the possibility of interstellar travel. For one thing, it is impossible for even a few to evolve in the midst of war and revolution. War, both conventional and unconventional, are the products of poverty, denial of basic human rights, and ignorance. In this new millennium, the greatest threat comes from religious fanaticism, such as the feudal mindset of the terrorists who brought down the World Trade Center Towers on 11 September 2001.

Religion is no longer needed, if we expand our sciences to include Psychical Research and Empirical Metaphysics. It is not so hard to see why religious extremists of all stripes would reject the secular reductionism and naked materialism represented by the World Trade Towers. I reject it myself, and always thought the World Trade Towers to be a particularly hideous example of 20th Century Heroic Materialism. I also reject religion, whether extreme or mainstream. The alternatives are not restricted to religious faith or secular humanism. A new spirituality is springing up everywhere, one which is based on experience and rejects all dogma and rules.

I have one more hypothesis about spiritual evolution. The more clearly a person understands and applies the divine purpose which reveals itself in the illumination of fire the more spiritually evolved they will be, and thus the more ready to undertake whatever spiritual exercises may be required to gain conscious control over levitation and apports. What those spiritual exercises are exactly, I do not know, but I believe the proper functioning of the chakras is shown to us in the Book of the Citadel in the New Tarot. It is not that I practice fortune-telling. That would be a strange occupation for a physicist and philosopher. No, what I find infinitely fascinating is the symbolic message in the New Tarot, and I have spent quite a bit of time deciphering it. I do believe in a divine purpose, and thus in divinity, because of my own experience of Cosmic Consciousness at age 31, exactly 31 years ago. This is the impersonal ONE, the divinity of the mystics, not the personal god of religions. I reject all named gods, all religions and all gurus, while I encourage Seekers to find mystical and transpersonal experience for themselves.

No doubt this seems an unorthodox way to the stars. To that I reply "Sic Itur Ad Astra"—a way to the stars and to immortality. I can also add that there is no *orthodox* way to the stars. So any way to the stars that works will be unorthodox.

We do not have to choose between the nihilism of science and the dogmas of religion. Separate out the good from the bad. That is my job. Apply the essence of scientific method to every philosophical question. For every question, there is a realm of reproducible experience which can provide answers. UFOs are real, the Mind is independent of the body and there is a Divine meaning to life, though not a divine plan. We do not have souls, we are Souls, a piece of the divine and immortal Atman. This is all well-known and easily established. It just isn't in the textbooks or taught in the universities. My contribution is to discover, uncover and recover new sciences.

A Science of Civilization

The function of philosophy is the creation of sciences. Or at least, that is its only achievement. This section of the book presents a science of civilization, called "utopian analysis," which supersedes the philosophy of ethics and aesthetics. It builds on the moral science of Hobbes and Locke, and does not commit the naturalistic fallacy. In it ideals take the place of theories, and political experiments test the truth or falsity of ideals.

Utopia is not a place. The word "utopia" is Latin for "nowhere." Utopia is not perfection, and it is not one particular form of society. There are countless ways of realizing the seven well-established ideals, which are (1)life, liberty and the pursuit of happiness; (2)reciprocity, (3)democracy, (4)hierarchies of community, (5)equal opportunity, (6)justice, and (7)the beautiful city. It is by building a higher community that includes both sides that we prevent war. Reciprocity is a fancy name for the golden rule. The science of utopia is all about establishing or refuting ideals. But most of this book is devoted to a utopian dream. This is my dream, not the only possible dream, and if I lived in the year 3000 CE, I might dream a different dream. And there is no reason why all utopias based on the same ideals couldn't simultaneously exist, in different cities, or counties, or states, or countries, and cooperate perfectly. Such a unity in diversity is actually much better than bland uniformity.

On the web, we see countless other utopias, which seem self-evident to their authors. And to each of them I say where is your evidence? Where is the analysis that shows the ideals on which the utopia is based? Where are the political experiments that refute alternatives and establish this one? In other words, how do they know? What seems self-evident to one author may seem a recipe for anarchy or tyranny to another. That is why we need a science of utopia.

Reading Plato's *Republic* at age 15 turned me into a life-long utopian dreamer. There is no greater pleasure for me. However, I was never attracted to his utopia. It is authoritarian, and I have always been libertarian. Liberty is the right to do whatever you like in private, so long as it places no one at involuntary risk. So in my utopia, there would be no DEA, no one in jail on drug charges, and everyone could smoke pot and ingest entheogens, at least at home. The War-On-Drugs is like the War on Vietnam. It should never have been fought in the first place, and creates a great evil in the form of gangs, drive-by shootings, and corruption of officials. Did we learn nothing from Prohibition? Does no one understand the First Amendment? Apparently not.

"We hold these truths to be self-evident, that all people are endowed by their creator with certain unalienable rights, and that among these are life, liberty and the pursuit of happiness." These are stirring and beautiful words, written by Thomas Jefferson in the Declaration of Independence of 1776, which set off our first revolution, and created the First Republic. There was a second, peaceful revolution in 1789, which created the Federal government, which is the Second Republic. I made one change to Jefferson's words. I changed "men" to "people," which is what he meant, anyway. Stirring words, but wrong in 2 places. Apparently these truths are not self-evident or we would not have outlawed drugs, gambling and prostitution about 1919, first fruit of the enfranchisement of women, oddly enough. Either people do not understand what the ideal of liberty means, or, more likely, it is not self-evident that it is the best rule. Most people seem to prefer dictatorship, so long as they get to do the dictating. Jefferson's second mistake was in saying these rights are unalienable. Murderers and traitors forfeit those rights by their own actions.

Liberty is not the same thing as anarchy. Indeed, the two are opposites, because anarchy always leads to authoritarian regimes, and the end of liberty. That's what happened in the French Revolution. Liberty applies to private actions, but if everyone does whatever they want in public, chaos ensues. Imagine some people driving on the right side of the road and some driving on the left. Liberty is not license. Serial killers want to kill, and the fact that they usually do it in private does not make it a liberty. Terrorists want to destroy buildings, poison the water supply, blow up planes, and kill thousands of people. But just because they want to does not mean they have a right to. Out in the country, everyone has their own car and they drive wherever and whenever they want. In a congested metropolis, this same rule leads to gridlock and smog.

There can be no liberty without justice or a defense against murderers and terrorists. Indeed, Thomas Jefferson put them together, because that is the full meaning of "life, liberty, and the pursuit of happiness." It is in the name of preserving our life that we protect ourselves from terrorists and serial killers. That is why I propose identity cards, which are used to transfer funds, get on or off public transport, enter or leave a city or a neighborhood or a business or a mall, with every transaction recorded on a location database. These and other related measures are the only way to catch terrorists or serial murderers or find people who have gone missing before they are killed. Anarchists would disapprove of identity cards. But remember, anarchists and libertarians are opposites, not close relatives.

Some people accuse me of being a neo-fascist, because, (they say) I want government interfering in everyone's life. Not true. I do not believe in city planning, or economic planning. A more libertarian society has never been proposed. I do ban cars, trucks and buses from the metroplex in the name of "the beautiful city," where people don't need cars, because of the excellent public transportation system. Every metroplex has to choose. You can't have both. Either cars and gridlock, or a smooth flow of traffic on subways and freeway trains. Likewise with the identity cards. Without them, it is impossible to catch all the terrorists and serial killers or track missing people. So choose. Which would you rather have, the slight inconvenience of using your card all day, or terrorists and serial killers? If you think Anarchy is a feasible political theory, study that phase of the French Revolution called "The Reign of Terror."

Do not imagine that your movements will be restricted in any way by the identity cards, nor should you imagine that anyone is watching you. The location databases spring into action only when there has been an abduction, a murder, a rape, or a terrorist act, and all that the location software does is produce a list of possible suspects certain to contain the culprit(s), because it is a list of everyone who could have been at the right place at the right time. So everyone on the list will get questioned, but most will be easily eliminated from the suspects list. The location database system would be designed so that it could not be used to invade personal privacy, could not be used by any private individual, could not be abused by political officials to follow the actions of anyone, and could be used only by the local magistrate, not by the police. Even the list of suspects would be kept secret and destroyed once the abducted person is found, or the culprit is caught and convicted. This is not a version of Orwell's *1984*.

Our form of democracy in the USA is tricameral, justice superior, with a constitution. The three branches are executive, legislative, and judicial. But there are really two more branches, the lobbyists and the bureaucracies. I have invented a form of democracy which gets rid of the lobbyists and the bureaucracies, reduces tricameral to unicameral, and eliminates the duplication of the same system in every state, county and city. I call it Aristarchy. It requires a vote by 3/4ths of the citizens in a given jurisdiction to make or change a law. The Aristarchy does not make laws. But it does make decisions, combining the executive and judicial branches into one, just like the Mandarins of Classical Chinese Civilization. That is also what bureaucracies do, make decisions. It takes the vast bureaucracy of Social Security two years to make a decision on disability. The local magistrate can make that same decision in two hours. Lobbyists would be powerless, because Aristarchs would be selected by essay exam and interview, and promoted by merit. They would not have to run for election, and they would not be allowed to accept gifts. If the Aristarchy seems too powerful, just remember, they cannot make or change the laws. Only the people can do that.

So what does all this have to do with interstellar travel? This is essentially why the Yogis of India never achieved interstellar travel. Going to the stars requires spiritual evolution, which clearly means more than just mental evolution. Social problems must also be solved. Liberty and justice for all. It is not enough to mindlessly pledge allegiance to this grand ideal. It is also necessary to understand it, and do it.

Seven True Ideals

Utopian analysis is the first science of civilization, the first normative science which does not commit the naturalistic fallacy (for those who have taken Philosophy 101). It builds upon the "moral sciences" of Hobbes and Locke, which in turn can trace their ancestry to Aristotle's *Ethics*.

A science must have the equivalent of a fact, a theory, and a test. We must be able to rule out the alternatives. An idea which is neither testable nor reproducible is useless. The analysis of a social controversy like abortion or capital punishment relates each side to an underlying ideal. A proposed solution nearly always requires a deliberate (i.e., "utopian") change to community institutions, laws, or traditions. "Utopian" does not mean "perfection," does not mean "hopelessly impractical," nor does it mean "planned." City planning never works. Planned economies never work. I am a libertarian, which means leaving most things unplanned, and allowing things to evolve naturally, like a forest preserve which just requires occasional pruning.

The equivalent of a theory in utopian analysis is an ideal, such as socialism. That particular ideal is "from each according to ability, to each according to need." The equivalent of a test is a political experiment. Socialism was made a political experiment by the Soviet Empire, by the British after WW II, and by the Cubans. The equivalent of a fact is the observed outcome of a test. The socialist experiments have all been failures. Apparently, socialism provides no motivation to produce according to ones ability. The failure of socialism is a normative particular, something we had to learn by experience, something that could not have been known without the trial. Indeed, there may still be some devout leftists here or there in humanities departments.

Political experiments show us that every deviation from reciprocity in economics, justice or marriage will fail. Utopian analysis is the science which supersedes ethics and aesthetics, without committing the naturalistic fallacy, since we never leave the normative realm or prove ideals. We rule out the alternatives. As in all sciences, a theory is well-established when we have ruled out the alternatives.

I have found seven ideals which are both fundamental and true. There is evidence that they work and that the alternatives do not.

[1] Life, Liberty and the Pursuit of Happiness: adult citizens can do whatever they like in private, whatever the risk, so long as no one is put at involuntary risk. Among the corollaries are the right to self-defense, freedom of expression and access, freedom of association, religion and privacy. This ideal does not require streetwalkers or crack dealers on every corner. Every community has a right to decide which of these things, if any, is allowed in public.

[2] Reciprocity: This is give and take, wages for labor, profits for risk successfully taken, the Golden Rule and the Mosaic Law. This is the foundation of every successful form of economics, justice or family that has so far been created.

[3] Democracy: Government by the consent of the governed. The people own the government, rather than vice versa, so no military draft. Separation of church and state, and separation of military and state. In other words, we don't want religious coups, or military coups. These always turn out badly.

[4] Union: The only permanent solution to the problem of war is to create a union of the warring communities in a hierarchy of communities. In the US, we fought a horrible Civil War to maintain the union, and the long range benefits are worth it. Alabama will never again fight Ohio, except on the football field.

[5] Equal opportunity and responsibility: equality under the law for every gender, class, race, tribe, religion, family, ethnicity, and age, both in prohibitions and in benefits. In the US, it has become difficult to get a movie made, become a college professor, or rise high in the financial or legal worlds unless one is a member of the overclass. Middle America has been disenfranchised.

[6] Justice: symbolized by Lady Justice, with her scales, blindfold, and sword. The scales imply that what the perpetrator did to his victims shall be done to him, if possible. The blindfold implies a blindness to irrelevant factors, such as intent or mental state. Only the act itself matters. Only the actions of the victim can lessen the responsibility of the perpetrator. The sword implies decisiveness. No bail, no appeal. Once the facts have been determined, judgment shall be made and punishment carried out immediately. In the 19th Century, the US had this kind of justice system. We lost it by successive decisions of the Supreme Court, which have fattened the purses of lawyers, by delaying justice indefinitely, and making the taxpayers pay for the lawyers. This has not improved the accuracy or fairness of the courts.

[7] Public Aesthetics: Aesthetic pleasure derives from intelligible novelty.

Nothing is more hideous or brutalizing than the endless boxes which passed for architecture in the 20th Century. No place is more dangerous than the high rise boxes put up in mid-century for public housing. We each have our own likes and dislikes in architecture and the arts, but there are a few urban environments universally admired, as places to visit, or to live, such as Amsterdam, Paris, Greenwich Village in NYC and Albuquerque Old Town. These successful urban environments permit the greatest population density, 100—200 households per acre. They mix, rather than segregate, work and play, business and residence. These are neighborhoods made for walking, and for outdoor cafes, and for street-life. They are improved by excellent mass transit, as in Paris, and by banning cars and dogs, as in Albuquerque Old Town. They have a mix of the old and the new.

Social problems require utopian analysis. We must resolve the dispute into its underlying ideals, and their consequences. If a solution can be found, it will be a "utopian" change to the laws, institutions, or traditions of that community. "Utopian" does not mean "impossible," or "unrealistic," or "planned;" it just means "deliberate." Utopians want to improve society with a deliberate and conscious change. A society is utopian if some parts of it have been consciously created according to true ideals, even if it sometimes fails to live up to its ideals. Thus, the Netherlands, the US, the UK and France are all utopian societies, as are all societies which succeed in emulating one or another of these utopias. The USSR was a dystopia, not a utopia, because it was based on the false ideals of socialism and authoritarianism, which in turn reflects the failure of Karl Marx to create a true science of civilization. Marx thought he had also found a science of history. He was wrong about that, and wrong about everything else as well. Considering the evil that Marx caused, it is really important to get the Science of Civilization right.

Those in favor of execution are applying the scales of Lady Justice. Nothing balances a life but a life. The problem is in the practical application. In the US, since the development of DNA technology, dozens of people on Death Row have been found innocent and released. We must call a moratorium on executions until our justice system has developed to the point where it does not make mistakes . . . if that is possible.

In the Middle East there are fanatic mullahs teaching the masses to reject and destroy the secular modern world. How can we create a global community that can encompass such wild eyed lunacy? We can't. We must make secular democracy more inviting by opening society to the new sciences and the new spirituality with its new aesthetics. Fanatic sectarianism cannot be defeated by reductionist materialism.

In the US, we pledge allegiance to "liberty and justice for all." We sing of "sweet land of liberty" with no sense of irony. Whenever we memorialize a fallen hero, we say "he gave his life to preserve our liberties." True enough. But the liberties we enjoyed in the US in the 19th Century were lost at the ballot box in the 20th Century. Neither the Supreme Court nor our political leaders recognized this.

Liberty may be defined as "full citizens doing whatever they like in private, whatever the risk, so long as no one else is put at involuntary risk." Prohibition was a violation of the ideal of liberty, as well as a disastrous political experiment, since it resulted in gangs, drive-by shootings, robbery-killings by desperate addicts, and the corruption of police and public officials. It should not be surprising that we have the same result from the War-On-Drugs. Utopian analysis should allow us to learn from our mistakes and be able to counter religious fanaticism (the root of all evil).

Like every act of tyranny, the War-On-Drugs is supposed to be for our own good. It isn't. Every person must make her own discoveries about what is good for her and worth the risk, the trouble, the expense and the time for her. It is not simply a matter of protecting people from things that are risky. If we did that, we would ban cars, not marijuana. In the US, 60,000 people are killed in or by cars every year, whereas no one has ever died from smoking pot. Everything has its risks, including doing nothing. The Blue Laws savagely persecute a minority over a difference in lifestyle and recreational drugs. The DEA takes their property and lets them rot in jail. The USA jails more of its population than any other industrialized country. Land of the Free? I don't think so.

Public education is a violation of the freedom of access for children. To put that in another way, adults have a right to go to school or not to go to school, and a right to pursue whatever subjects they find interesting, no matter how the majority may disapprove. Sadly, education is nothing like that. It is just indoctrination in whatever the powers that be decide every kid must learn. It never works. It only alienates students and kills their natural curiosity and creativity.

I am surprised that no one ever noticed that required education for children is a direct violation of our ideals of liberty. Are not children citizens? Do they have any civil rights? At what age do children become citizens? I argue that it is between 8 and 12, since historically children began their apprenticeships at that age, and went off to boarding school at that age. Eight year olds are capable of committing cold blooded murder. I was driving a tractor at age 8, and so do most kids raised on a farm. There should be a "coming of age" ceremony, like a Bar Mitzvah, at whatever age the community deems appropriate, where we welcome a child to the full rights and responsibilities of citizenship. After that, education cannot be compulsory. After that, a child may decide where to live, and with whom. This doesn't mean we allow them to drive cars, which is dangerous enough for 16 year olds. Driving carefully and responsibly requires a level of maturity not usually found in 8 year olds. It seems to me the right to drive, to drink, or to vote should be based on some objective test of maturity, and could be taken back for a few years if an adolescent behaves irresponsibly.

Evidence

[1]. Liberty: Let us examine in more detail the personal, religious, free speech, right to access, free press, right to privacy, 4th Amendment and 2nd Amendment liberties. These rights apply only to private affairs, not to public spaces, places, airwaves, etc. See "Public v. Private". For instance, we are under no obligation to allow pornography, prostitution, or drug taking in public or at work. Similarly, we are not required to allow street preachers to make a nuisance of themselves, nor are we required to allow religions to own radio or TV stations, or to make advertisements for their religion.

Personal liberty is the right to take whatever risks we wish in pursuit of our personal career or avocation or hobbies, spend whatever amount of money we wish at these things, and spend whatever amount of time we wish, in private, of course, and placing no one at involuntary risk. It follows that the Puritanical Blue laws against drugs, gambling and prostitution must be struck down, as unconsitutional (violating the first amendment) and just plain wrong. It is apparent that voters and Supreme Court alike are perfectly capable of giving lip service to an ideal, while failing to recognize a clear and obvious violation of that ideal.

As evidence, I should point out that liberty was the rule in the US during the "gay nineties," or "La Belle Époque," when immigration to the US was at its peak. Brothels and recreational drug use were all permitted. Justice was at its peak. Opportunities abounded. So it is difficult to pick out just one thread, since we have at least three ideals which reached their maximum during this period. The best we can say is the popularity of the US for emigrants during this period constitutes evidence for the truth of all three ideals.

Life was not easy for the immigrants, especially the first generation. They could not speak the language. They could only qualify for the worst and most dangerous jobs. Each new wave of immigrants moved into the slums, as the previous wave became middle class and moved out. Though life was hard, they wrote letters back to their home villages, persuading the rest of the family, and sometimes whole villages to emigrate as well.

The collapse of Communism and the failure of Prohibition are the latest examples of the failure of the only known alternative to Liberty and Democracy, namely the Ideal of "Big Brother Knows Best." While it has often seemed reasonable to intellectuals that an elite would know better than you what is best for you, this never works out in practice. Different people have different tastes, which they discover by experience. This is the root of liberty, the reason why everyone must make their own choices about how to spend their risks, their time, and their money.

Freedom of religion: Like all liberties, religious freedom only applies to private activities, and only those which place no one at involuntary risk. Thus, we must forbid the ritual mutilation of infants in the name of religion. If someone is going to be mutilated to mark their entrance into a religion, it must be voluntary. And someone must be "of age" to make a voluntary choice. I place that at a mental age of eight to twelve.

Freedom of religion is just a special case of freedom of private associations. In the Constitution of the Second Republic, it is called the Freedom to Peaceably Assemble. Understanding this liberty would help to clarify a lot of recent cases which have come before the Supreme Court. For instance, do the Boy Scouts have the right to reject homosexual scoutmasters? Of course! The Boy Scouts can do anything they like, so long as (1)they do it in private, and (2)no one is put at involuntary risk. You see that Utopian Analysis is often at odds with the Politically Correct opinion indoctrinated at our allegedly elite colleges and universities. This does not mean that fraternities can force pledges to chug a fifth of whiskey, since this puts the pledge at involuntary risk. Indeed, chugging a fifth of whiskey will kill anyone, unless they are forced to vomit immediately with a dose of Syrup of Ipecac. Furthermore, any fraternity which has such dangerous hazing rituals is, and should be, kicked off campus, and kicked out of the national organization.

Free speech and free access: This is the right of every individual to artistic, literary, musical, scientific or philosophical expression to the world and the right of every individual to private access to all such public expressions; and the right of every full citizen to decide for themselves what they want to learn. No more government propaganda. I define a "full citizen" as someone who has come of age, who is not a convicted felon, and has not been declared incompetent to manage their own affairs.

One immediate consequence of this ideal is repeal of compulsory education for those who have come of age. Maybe we can force the little ones to acquire the basic skills of reading, writing and arithmetic, but once a child has come of age, they may be allowed to become an apprentice and get a job, leave the public schools and use their vouchers in other ways. I would give everyone vouchers, and let them be collectable over years, tradable, salable, and usable by other members of the family. The whole family might go together to send someone to Harvard or to pay for Enlightened Hospice for Gramma. Enlightened Hospice would have lectures by people who have experienced NDE, and would allow Gramma to try any recreational drug or alternative therapy. Dying made easy. It can be done.

Evidence for the truth of this ideal of freedom of expression and access comes from the effect of the Catholic Index of prohibited books and ideas. Because of the Index, southern Europe played no role in the Enlightenment, or the social revolutions of the 18th Century, or the industrial revolution of the 19th and 20th Centuries, even though Italy and Spain had been the leaders of Western Civilization in the Renaissance. Tiny England and Holland grew mighty because they respected liberty. We have not yet applied this ideal to our schools.

Web publishing now gives everyone the right of World Wide self-expression in any medium, or soon will, at the cost of learning HTML.

The boundary of every liberty is involuntary risk to others. In the case of freedom of information, this comes either in libel or invasion of privacy. In another piece of judicial legislation, the Supreme Court has apparently ruled that—public figures, members of the government, and celebrities—have no right to privacy, and anything can be said or printed about them, so long as it is not libelous.

I can see no justification for denying anyone the right to privacy just because they are famous. Some situations may be defined as "public," for instance, the red carpet at the Emmys and Oscars. Even now, celebrities who do not wish to be photographed or interviewed are allowed secret entry in the back of the building. A person who walks the red carpet is giving implicit permission for interviewers and photographers to use their images and words. In other situations, in private life, no one's image or words or even well-known facts about them may be published or broadcast without their explicit consent. This rule used to be followed. For instance, during their careers, many famous movie stars in the Golden Age of Hollywood were openly homosexual, but this was never published, and unknown to the general public. Such public knowledge would have destroyed their careers.

Fourth Amendment rights and privacy rights go together. No one should be able to search my house, my office, my bag, purse, wallet, car or clothing unless they have reason to think I have committed a crime (for instance, seen fleeing from the scene of a crime), or unless they have a search warrant or an arrest warrant signed by the local magistrate. A person may have to voluntarily give up these rights in order to enter high security areas, such as commercial airports. Let us hope there will always be other means of travel.

Second Amendment rights: The Second Amendment to the Constitution of the Second Republic actually refers to military weapons, and the right to form local militias, what we today call the National Guard. But let us say people have a right to arm themselves for their personal protection. Modern firearms are definitely overkill. I suggest that arms concealed in a pocket or a purse must pass the metal detectors, and cannot be used frontally without giving the target ample time to duck. This might include ceramic (Ginzu) switchblade knives and throwing knives. Such weapons would be sufficient to allow a woman to defend herself against a mugger or rapist. Non-concealable weapons, suitable for home defense might include the modern compound bow (but not crossbows) and black powder smooth bore flintlock muskets or blunderbusses. Either type of gun would be sufficient for home defense and yet useless for assassination, armed robbery, armed insurrection or suicide.

Evidence for this elimination of modern firearms lies in the large number of crimes, suicides and fatal accidents involving them. It is still possible to commit armed robbery, suicide or have a fatal accident in other ways, but it is not made so easy. The target has a chance to duck. Black powder muskets are inaccurate at any great distance, and the large cloud of black smoke marks the location of the shooter.

[2]. The Ideal of Reciprocity: The only known alternative to reciprocity is the ideal of socialism, refuted by the collapse of Communism in 1989, and by the failure of socialism wherever it has been tried, e.g., in Post-War Britain, present day Cuba, and in the Soviet Empire. Reciprocity is the basis of my analysis of social welfare, morality, family and free enterprise. Figuring out how any institution works means

figuring out the pattern of motivations. This is always easy to do if the institution is based on reciprocity. Many of the proposals of Utopians seem to work only by idealism, not self-interest. In the long run, these always fail.

In the economic sphere, we now know that people will not produce according to their ability, unless there is some incentive to do so. The socialist economy is something like the slave economy, where everyone tries to do as little as possible, as little as they can get away with. In a free market, some will prosper more than others. This bothers some Utopians. But there is no known workable economic system that is based on the principle of equal income for all.

Envy can become a socially divisive problem if it becomes impossible for the poorest to rise to become the richest. Clearly Bill Gates in the US and the founder of Virgin Atlantic in the UK show that both nations have freedom of mobility. Envy is lessened by the philanthropic activities of the very rich. Indeed, the long term stability of free enterprise may depend on such wise philanthropy. Charity balls are one of the chief social activities of the very rich, so I expect philanthropy to continue, and to be a natural part of the lifestyle of the very rich. But I certainly don't believe in giving rich people more power in government. Each rich person has one vote only, just like the poor.

[3]. The Ideal of Democracy: The people own the government, rather than vice versa. All the people, not just some of them. Thus, the government must treat each and every person as if they have an inherent right to life, liberty and the pursuit of happiness, unless by their own actions, a citizen forfeits that right.

It follows that a military draft is undemocratic, since it turns draftees into war material, objects which may be used up in the name of "national interest." Not only must military personnel be volunteers, they must volunteer for every mission, and have a right to voice objections to the detailed plans of the mission, if they think their lives will be put at more risk than is necessary.

Democracy is government by the consent of the governed. A stronger requirement is that it be "government of the people, by the people, and for the people," not government by bureaucracy, choked by endless red tape and stymied by idiotic bureaucratic or judicial rulings.

There are many different possible forms of democracy, including the tricameral, multi-level, judicial superior form we have, and the Parliamentary, Commons superior form found in the UK. "Judicial superior" means that the Supreme Court may overturn the decisions of any other part of government. Furthermore, there is no mechanism for overturning their decisions or ousting members. "Commons superior" means that all other decisions may be overturned by Commons in the UK, including the decisions of Barristers, Church of England Primates, House of Lords decisions, and the decisions of the monarchy. I will call the UK system "parliamentary government" and the US system "tricameral government."

Parliamentary government works better than tricameral government. How can we tell? One clue is voter turnout, which is high in the UK and other countries with a commons-superior Parliament, low in the US. Another clue is citizen apathy. There is no apathy under Parliament, because it is possible to create new parties, which may even come to power. In the US, we are stuck with the same two tired old parties we had in the Civil War. And because of the "winner takes all" rule on the state level, it has so far proven impossible to create a viable new party. A third clue is the degree of allegiance by elected officials to special interest groups which pay for elections. Countless polls show the majority of people in the US want gun control, but the NRA is so strong that they can easily defeat any congressman who votes against them. This undemocratic allegiance to the financiers is high in the US, almost non-existent in the UK. A fourth clue is efficiency. In the US, efficiency is low, and overhead is high. There are as many people working for government on all levels as there are tax-payers. The American government has become the butt of jokes by Late Night comedians, for it seems government against the people, by faceless bureaucracy, for special interest groups (PACs).

Sometimes a government will do something which is fundamentally undemocratic. An example in US history is the draft of soldiers for WW II and Vietnam. These men were used up like other expendable supplies of war, so they named themselves "GIs," which means "Government Issue," no different from all the other olive drab munitions used up to take some meaningless hill or hamlet, which benefited the GI not at all. The GIs were given no choice at all, about anything. They could not even refuse suicide missions. I grieve for these GIs, and cannot stand to watch war movies. If allowed to volunteer, many would have, and perhaps the generals would then have been more careful with their lives, as they have been in more recent wars, such as Desert Storm.

I advocate a third form of democracy, which I call Aristarchy, based in part on the classical Chinese mandarin system of the T'ang, Sung, and Ming dynasties. It replaces bureaucracies with individuals, highly qualified individuals. This is the only way we will ever get rid of the bureaucracies, although we could get rid of the lobbyists by adopting the Parliamentary system. Local magistrates would combine powers of chief of police, mayor and judge. Above them would be metropoles in charge of a metroplex and surrounding countryside, governors in charge of regions of the country, and archons in charge of national government. It would be a single unified system, unicameral, without the duplication of legislative, executive and judicial functions at each level of community that we now have.

Do not imagine that this would be government by college professors, who are notoriously specialized, and ignorant and irrational outside their own narrow field of interest. Broad knowledge and good people skills are required. And wisdom. Do we ever find that in academia? I don't think so.

Laws would be made or changed by a vote of three-fourths of the citizens in the jurisdiction in question. The Aristarchy would have broad powers of interpretation of the spirit of the law, rather than the letter of the law. The basic idea, both in the Chinese mandarin system, and in Aristarchy, is to find the wisest and best informed person, and make him or her personally responsible for government. Then we would know who would listen to our complaints against a neighbor or a business, who to blame for bad government, and who to praise for good government.

The evidence for this system is the millennia of high success of the Mandarin system in China. During the T'ang, Sung, and Ming dynasties, the people enjoyed a peaceful anarchy, seldom troubled by the government. The Chinese avoided a disruptive hereditary aristocracy, while members of all classes could and did become Mandarins. All they had to do was study the Neo-Confucian classics and pass the essay exams. I propose something similar. The Chinese experienced repeated foreign conquests and natural disasters during this period, but the Mandarin system was restored in each new dynasty, after stability had returned.

[4]. The Ideal of Higher Community: The only permanent solution to the problem of war is to combine the warring communities into a higher community. In medieval times, cities fought cities and duchies fought one another (as in the War of the Roses, the Hundred Years war, and even the 17th Century Thirty Years war) until the rise of modern states, such as England, France, Italy and Germany. Then there was a period of fratricidal war between states until the emergence of the strong Nation of States, such as the USA. Europe is becoming a nation under the EEC and NATO. France and Germany will never again battle each other, and neither will Alabama and Ohio, except in the realms of sport, business, or culture.

This ideal naturally leads us to world community, something which we have been unconsciously creating for more than a Century, with the Olympic Movement, the jet plane, satellite TV, international science and business. The UN would suffice as a world government, but first the process of creating the global community must be completed. We must all think of ourselves as Citizens of Earth, first and foremost.

Note that a hierarchy of communities does not require all sub-communities to be the same or have the same laws and customs. But it does require giving up ancient hatreds, something which the ethnic groups in Yugoslavia did not do during the 50 years or so they had a single government. Community and government are two different things. Before the US Civil War, there was one Federal government, but unfortunately, two quite different communities, one slave-holding, the other industrial. We used to hear about "the melting pot," something undergone by all groups emigrating to the US. This is still a valid idea. It does not mean miscegenation, nor does it mean giving up distinctive music or cuisine. It just means melting down all those ancient hatreds, those tribal attitudes nurtured in the old country, and we must view with suspicion any group or tribe which refuses to undergo the melting pot.

Incidentally, allegiance to a higher community can make it easier to loosen the bonds to lower level community. Self-Determination or nationalism is a widely held ideal, although insofar as it is correct, it must be folded into the ideal of higher community. So, it would be all right for Yugoslavia to burst apart into Serbia, Bosnia, Macedonia and so forth, so long as these new states join the EEC and NATO, so they can be part of Europe and yet maintain their local customs and religions. Similarly with the UK. If Scotland and Wales wanted to separate from the UK, this would be all right if they were once again members of the new Nation of Europe, which of course means the EEC and NATO. Perhaps that is the only solution for the Basques as well. They might carve out their own state from Spain and France and join the new United States of Europe, when that comes into official existence.

[5]. The Ideal of Equal opportunity / responsibility: Everyone should have the chance to go as far as their talents and ambition will take them, regardless of race, religion, sex, tribe, age or family, but must also take up the responsibilities of a good citizen, such as paying taxes, voting, obeying the laws, giving ones children a conscience and a sense of civic duty. If everyone did feel that they had equal opportunity, they would probably also be more willing to take up equal responsibility. Every criminal or tax cheat represents a failure on one side or the other of this ledger. Crime grows out of a sense of hopelessness quite as much as a lack of discipline.

This ideal forbids discrimination for or against people on the basis of irrelevant factors. Usually tribe, age, gender, race, family or religion are such. I include in "gender" sexual preference. However, any of these things can become relevant factors. If we were casting the part of Abraham Lincoln, we could not be accused of arbitrary discrimination if we restricted our casting to tall, thin, white males. Similarly, in the army, where fighting unit cohesion is all important in combat, the highest level officer who leads them into combat could decide that she didn't want this or that. If she thinks it's relevant for cohesion, then it is. Similarly, scout leaders, who are alone with young boys or girls in campouts, can be required to be married and heterosexual, since pedophilia is usually found only among homosexuals. There is evidence that girls do better in math classes if there are no boys present. In other words, gender becomes relevant, and we could allow voluntary segregation of the sexes in classes and even in colleges.

More harm is done by discriminating for ones own family, tribe, gender, race, etc., than by discriminating against. Tribalism is especially problematic. Tribes like the Basques, Croats, Serbs, Bosnians, and Jews insist on having their own sovereign country and are quite willing to commit ethnic cleansing to eliminate other tribes or to scare them out. I suppose they could invoke a contrary ideal of Nationalism, or Self-Determination. But I think this is a false ideal. Great nations are open to all types.

On an individual basis, if a particular tribe or family always discriminates for their own kind in hiring and firing or giving out contracts, soon an entire industry or profession can be so dominated by members of that tribe or family that none other need apply. This should be illegal, and should be punished by deportation, as well as the firing of all those hired by the discriminator.

It isn't just tribalism we have to worry about. There is also class discrimination.

In the revolution of 1776, we thought we had rid ourselves of the oppressive class structure of England, because we had gotten rid of titled Lords and the hereditary ruling class. But in the 20th Century, a new Overclass appeared, which dominates academia and media in the US. The creation of Aristarchy would overthrow this Overclass. Only non-tribal members of middle America (not the underclass nor the overclass) may enter the Aristarchy; otherwise it could become dominated by a tribe or a minority class.

The ideal of higher community is contrary to the false ideal of Nationalism or Self-Determination. Why did we fight the Civil War here in the US? To avoid Balkanization. The US would not be a great nation if it were broken up into smaller States or confederations of States. The Confederate States of the Old South would not be a great nation, would never be a factor on the world stage. Neither would the sovereign state of Texas, or of California. This was a war fought over the Ideal of Union, not over slavery. And tragic as that experience was, citizens of the present United States are glad of the outcome, whether they live in Atlanta, Miami, New York City, Austin, or Los Angeles.

[6]. The Ideal of Justice: This is defined by Lady Justice, with her scales, blindfold, and sword. The scales make punishment

equal to the crime in order to restore peace in the community. The sword of decision suggests that we restore the ancient power of the jury to decide guilt or innocence, by eliminating appeal, with immediate execution of sentence. The blindfold means Lady Justice does not take sides; her only interest is in finding the truth.

The test of an ideal of Justice is the amount of suppressed rage in a society, and the resulting number of berserk mass killers. Simply comparing crime rates is irrelevant, because crime rate depends on many things, such as morality, community solidarity, and respect for authority.

It is my hypothesis that the primary function of Justice is to restore emotional harmony in the community by releasing pent-up rage and sorrow, rather than "correction" of criminal character or warehousing of violent people. The function of justice is revenge. This is a natural desire, a natural reaction to evil, which must be given an outlet, or it will build up like a festering boil, and burst out in mass killings. Compare the unrequited rage in the USA in the 1890s, when justice was swift, to the 1990s, when it takes forever, if it is attainable at all.

Lady Justice implies execution of murderers, if we can establish the truth. Executions should not be public, nor should reporters or family members be given any access to condemned criminals. Execution of sentence should be immediate. No details of executions should be made public. That merely panders to the public's love of violence as a form of entertainment. I have shown in the "Abortion" chapter that the execution of murderers is not itself murder, because the murderer has broken the social contract. In the chapter on "Justice" I have shown how we can find out the truth, because we must be very sure of the truth before handing down a death sentence.

[7]. The Ideal of Public Aesthetics: Aesthetic pleasure derives from intelligible novelty. Building our cities according to

intelligible novelty gives us beautiful cities. This can only be seen by example. Compare the anonymous boxes of the 20th Century, with their endless rows of identical rectangular windows, to the Taj Mahal, for instance, or a Gothic cathedral.

Aesthetics is not just beauty. It is everything we do to keep from being bored. Some people play the ponies. Some people play chess. Let everyone make their own choices. How then, can there be any universal truths about aesthetics? The universal truths of aesthetics all apply to community action, and all somewhat resemble zoning laws. We may not be able to guarantee beauty or other kinds of aesthetic pleasure (friendship, love, adventure, competition), but we can sometimes identify rules of boredom and exclude them. For instance, I would suggest that no new building shall be rectangular, with rectangular and repetitious window treatments. This describes the vast majority of 20th Century skyscrapers. Of course, there are attractive and unattractive skyscrapers, and a place like Manhattan is so crowded that skyscrapers may be a necessity.

The Public Vs. Private Rule: A corollary of the ideal of liberty is the Public Vs Private rule. Public is some or all of the following things: what is done at work, or on public transport, or in the street, or on the sidewalk, what is allowed to be broadcast, or put up on billboards, or sold in public stores.

A community may forbid religious activities in public places (streetcorner preachers), advertisement of religion, or public broadcasts of a religious nature. Why would they want to? Later on, I show that religion is faith, a euphemism for dogma and superstition, and quite unnecessary in this age of psychical and mystical knowledge. Religion is the chief obstacle to rational thought and rational action, such as population control. It remains powerful enough to get the teaching of evolution and the Big Bang banned in Kansas, of all places. In Tulsa, most of the channels on cable are religious channels, taken up by shouting evangelists, spouting a hateful stream of lies and greed. I would much rather see these channels replaced by the Discovery channels, A&E, Bravo, and BBC.

It would ease the repeal of the blue laws against drugs, gambling and prostitution if we at the same time made these things illegal in public. To be more specific, we could have "Sporting Houses" for licensed and inspected courtesans and gamblers, while prohibiting street-walkers. As for drugs, I see no reason why we could not allow marijuana, coca leaves, opium gum, magic mushrooms, tobacco leaves and the dried and fermented forms of these plant materials to be sold in public stores, perhaps only in a special store called the herb shop, which would also have spices, aromatic and medicinal herbs, as well as alcoholic products from the farms that grow the raw materials. Camels, Cocaine, Heroin, and Jack Daniels would only be available from the local drug dealer (a perfectly legal business) who would deliver it to your home.

The Ideal of Equal Opportunity trumps the Public Vs Private rule. This can happen if membership in a club is a prerequisite for financial or political advancement. If that is true, the club cannot be allowed a restrictive membership. Qualification for membership cannot depend on gender, race or tribe, although it could still depend on income or intelligence or other relevant factors.

Liberty and the War-On-Drugs

We always memorialize the fallen heroes of our wars by saying "They fought to preserve our liberties." True enough. However, no Fascist or Communist has ever taken away any of our liberties. The liberties we lost in the 20th Century were taken away by people who regarded themselves as fine, upstanding citizens. Tyranny was voted by Congress, signed by a President, and upheld by the Supreme Court, despite the First Amendment. It does no good to pledge allegiance to "liberty and justice for all" if we are unable to recognize transgressions, or if we are unwilling to allow people to do things which are disapproved by the majority. I refer, of course, to the War-On-Drugs.

The failure of Prohibition should have told us exactly what the outcomes would be of the War-On-Drugs. They are the same as the outcomes of Prohibition: gangs, drive-by shootings, corruption of the police and other officials and a general decline in law-and-order. It is like the war in Vietnam. It was a war we could not win, a war that should never have been fought in the first place.

The whole point of the science of civilization is to learn from experience. Perhaps as a society we failed to learn anything from the failure of Prohibition because the science of civilization did not exist, so there were no scholars to point out that the War-On-

Drugs is a direct violation of the Ideal of Liberty. Social ideals are the hypotheses of this new science, a science which I have invented, and set forth here for the first time. The Ideal of Liberty says that all citizens may do whatever they like in private, no matter how risky, so long as it puts no one at involuntary risk. I can show by many examples that this is the Ideal of Liberty and that the War-On-Drugs violates it.

Some of the illegal drugs are very risky, but fewer people die of them than die directly or indirectly as a result of tobacco and alcohol. Besides, everything is risky. Voluntary risk is irrelevant. We allow people to drive in cars, even though forty thousand people a year die in them. At least another hundred thousand become paralyzed or severely brain damaged. Another twenty thousand pedestrians and bicyclists are killed by cars every year. We allow people to climb eight thousand meter mountains, even though a third of the participants in this sport die of it. For every four people who climb Mount Everest, one will die. The glaciers around Mount Everest are graveyards, containing hundreds of bodies. Voluntary risk is apparently irrelevant, as it should be.

It is not just the War-On-Drugs that is wrong. It is all the blue laws that were voted in when women got the vote in 1919. This includes the outlawing of drinking, gambling and prostitution. It is not that I advocate or wish to practice these things. Liberty means allowing other people to do things you disapprove of, if they will give you the same right. We all have different lifestyles, different tastes. It doesn't matter if something is a sin according to the preachers. I could say preaching is a sin, since it is a revival of the Puritanism which burned heretics and witches in our early history.

I have a lot of Web friends who enjoy marijuana and magic mushrooms. And they are very nice, kind, loving, spiritual people, the best people I know. Yet, they run a terrible risk of persecution at the hands of the jack-booted Nazi thugs of the DEA!! ARGHHH! We should rise up in righteous indignation and overthrow the government that imposes such tyranny upon us.

After all, that is why America was founded in the first place. "We hold these truths to be self-evident, that all men are created equal, endowed by their creator with certain unalienable rights, and that among these are life, liberty, and the pursuit of happiness." These stirring words in the Declaration of Independence, written by Thomas Jefferson 225 years ago, set off a rebellion and a revolution. It must have seemed to the Founding Fathers, scions of the Enlightenment, that Puritanism had been put down and rejected forever as a mere superstition of the dark ages. But apparently Puritanism was only lying low, gathering up its energies, to return with a vengeance in the 20th Century. A Puritan can be defined as anyone who is afraid that somewhere, somehow, someone may be having fun. And the hippies of the 1960s did seem to be having lots of fun, with pot and psychedelic drugs, free love, rock and roll, and freedom of expression in art, face-painting, spiritual and metaphysical pursuits. All of this was to be crushed out of existence in the following decades.

Which is the stronger allegiance? Our pledge of allegiance to "liberty and justice for all," or our actual allegiance to stamping out the production, sale and use of illegal drugs, no matter what the cost in money, the corruption of law and order in nations like Columbia, and the cost in blood on the streets here at home, as rival gangs shoot it out in the night? Whole neighborhoods of our big cities are blighted by gangs. Whole generations are swallowed up in the gangster life, with its blood rituals of initiation. These are the fruits of tyranny. There would be no economic basis for gangs if drugs, gambling and prostitution were made legal. And who are these tyrants? They might be your neighbors. They might be your grandmothers. Normal, law-abiding people, who sing the National Anthem without a shred of irony. We have met the enemy and it is us.

I grew up in Oklahoma, which remained a dry state long after Prohibition was repealed in every other state. There was a curious alliance between my grandmother's Women's Christian Temperance Union and the bootleggers. Neither wanted

Prohibition to be repealed. As the saying went, "The drys have their law, and the wets have their liquor." The WCTU seemed satisfied that the wicked were punished, while bootleggers and moonshiners made a good living, since liquor was made expensive by its illegality. And the same is true today of the Coca leaf, marijuana plants, opium gum and the various natural psychedelics. Prohibition creates another problem. Addicts have to come up with a lot of money to support their heroin or cocaine habit. So they turn to armed robbery of gas stations and convenience stores, which in turn, often leads to the murder of the clerks. Their blood is on your hands, you fine upstanding citizens, if you are one of the tyrants who support the war on drugs!

The violence of American society began with Prohibition, and continues because of the War-On-Drugs. We not only incarcerate more of our population than any other nation, we also have the highest murder rates among First World Industrialized nations.

As one piece of evidence for that claim, I refer you to a New York Times article of June 27, 1990, p. A10, which offers a comparison among industrialized countries of the number of murders per year per 100,000 young men between ages fifteen and twenty-four. The years of the study were 1986-1987. Austria was the safest place, with 0.3 murders per 100,000, followed by Japan with 0.6 per 100,000, followed by West Germany, Denmark, Portugal and England. England had 1.2 murders per 100,000. Over the entire nation, we had twenty-one murders per 100,000, but some regions were much worse. Michigan had a murder rate of 232 young men murdered per 100,000. Detroit's rate was higher still, well over 300, a thousand times worse than the murder rate in Austria. Murder has become the number one occupational hazard for women, in part because of the number of convenience store clerks murdered by utterly sociopathic robbers, and in part due to berserk mass killers. "Going Postal" is what we call it in the US. And this doesn't even count the thousands of young women who just "go missing" every year, and are never found, obviously the victims of dozens of serial killers like Ted Bundy, smart enough to hide the bodies where they will never be found.

Is the satisfaction the Puritans get from "punishing the wicked" sufficient to reconcile us to a murder rate 1000 times worse than other First World Nations? That is comparable to Third World countries like Liberia! Can we justify the murder of hundreds of convenience store clerks by desperate crazed junkies? Perhaps the Puritans think that legalization would produce more desperate crazed junkies. It wouldn't if we treated addiction as an illness rather than a crime. How do I know? Look at the example of the Netherlands.

Marijuana has never been illegal in Holland for citizens, and they treat addiction to harder drugs as medical conditions, rather than a crime. Addicts from other countries are deported. Treatment usually consists in free maintenance doses of the drug of addiction. And they have seen no increase in addicts nor any rise in other sorts of crime. The rest of Europe is now following their lead, and has begun to introduce a little bit of liberty and common sense into their drug policies. See *Newsweek*, "Europeans Just Say 'Maybe'," 11/1/99, p. 53.

The Puritan Overclass in the US may be afraid that legalization would result in chaos—streetwalkers on every corner and crack dealers in every schoolyard. But notice that the definition of liberty only applies to private behavior. It does not follow that it must be permitted in public. Every community should have the right to determine its own composition and to set standards for what is done in public, within that community. This is another ideal, that of Public Vs Private behavior. This ideal, one of several which I regard as true and well-established, says that every community has the right to set its own standards for what is allowed in public, what is permitted at work, or in stores, or on public media, or public transportation. See the chapter "True Ideals."

The Ideal of Liberty says we must allow prostitution, but we do not have to allow streetwalkers. We can instead have private "sporting houses," which was, in fact, the pattern in the US in the 19th Century, before the 20th Century wave of Puritanism. I suggest drawing a distinction between the public Herb shops and the private dealers, who must deliver to your home.

In the public Herb shops, we would find natural leaf tobacco, opium gum, local bottled wines and beers, marijuana, magic mushrooms, peyote buds, fresh or dried coca leaves, ayahuasca vines, and herbs and aromatic plants of all kinds. Cocaine, Camels and Jack Daniels would be purchased from a private dealer. Thus, you see that I advocate putting some things in the Private category that are presently in the Public category. Cigarettes and distilled spirits, for instance.

The boundary of all liberties, including religious freedom, freedom of the press, personal liberty, and free speech, is placing others at involuntary risk. Some say that drugs, gambling and prostitution do have involuntary victims, because legalization increases public health problems, such as addiction. While this factual claim is untrue, let us ask if drugs, gambling and prostitution in private would put anyone at involuntary risk. I freely admit that doing it in public would place people at involuntary risk, which is why it should be kept in the private category. Drinking and driving is not allowed in public, either.

Any activity can be said to have unwilling victims, in the grievous loss suffered by friends and relatives of the diver who is now a quadriplegic, or the parents of the toddler drowned in the backyard pool. These are accidental victims, not covered by the rule on involuntary risk. Note that "victimless crime" is an oxymoron. How would you punish it? Do to the pot smoker what he did to the "victim" (himself)?

It is possible to do something about the public health problems associated with drug use. Communities with long exposure to a particular drug have developed customs which protect them from addiction and disease. Pre-Columbian Native Americans did not have lung cancer or emphysema, because they didn't smoke all day or every day. Smoking was part of a social ritual, when entertaining visitors, or conducting pow-wows. Italian peasants don't become alcoholics because they use wine as a food. It is only consumed at meals, with grandma and the children present (who get watered wine). It is shameful to become inebriated at the family table. Distilled spirits are avoided. Andean peasants don't have a cocaine addiction, because they chew the raw coca leaves, with lime, and they do so to give them strength and endurance in the rarefied atmosphere of the Andes. Turkish peasants don't have heroin addictions because they use the raw opium gum only to treat toothache and other pain. It is apparent that we should all try to emulate these folk customs. Just to take opium as one example, the experience of physicians is that one never becomes addicted to opium if it is only used to alleviate pain, no matter how much opium it takes to accomplish that.

But how do we treat addicts? I would suggest two routes. Those who wish to get rid of their addiction can be admitted for a free 6 month stay in the locked grounds of a rehabilitation center. Those who do not should be given a free maintenance injection every day at the local Free Clinic. As for the rehab center, once a person voluntarily signs himself in, she has to stay for 6 months. There would be doctors and medicines to help with the initial detoxification. Everyone who has passed that phase would be put on a low dose of Prozac to increase the Serotonin level in their brains. Serotonin induces neurogenesis. It takes 3-4 weeks for a neuron to become mature, and several more weeks or months for it to be put to use. That is why a person must stay for 6 months. That is long enough for the brain to heal and relearn how to live a sober, unintoxicated life.

Wouldn't we have more junkies if we legalized drugs? The Puritans were sure there would be more alcoholics as a result of repealing Prohibition. But that did not happen. So the question now is whether or not the ideal of liberty (now that you understand its implications) is true or not?

How do we apply scientific method to social ideals? What we need is the equivalent of a theory, a test, and the results. Then, as the Great Detective Sherlock Holmes said, "When you have eliminated the alternatives, my Dear Watson, whatever remains, no matter how unpalatable, must be the truth." I have taken a few liberties with this famous passage from "The Sign of Four." The alternative that survives all testing is the well-established conclusion. Maybe at some future time, a better theory will be thought up, or continued pushing on the envelope of testing may eventually refute even a well-established theory. But for the time being, it is the best we can do. It is the only known solution. See the chapter "Scientific Method" for more details.

In the Science of Civilization, which I sometimes call "Utopian Analysis," for reasons to be explained later, the equivalent of a test is a political experiment, such as the 75 years of the Socialist experiment in the Union of Soviet Socialist Republics, or the afore-mentioned experiment in Prohibition. The result of such a test is what I call a "normative particular." I suppose you could call it a "value fact," so long as it is understood that values are not facts, nor facts values, nor can one be inferred from the other, which would commit the Naturalistic Fallacy. What we observe is the failure of socialism, whenever and wherever it has been tried. We also observe the failure of prohibition. The collapse of the Soviet Union is an historical fact, but the failure of the Soviet Union or of Prohibition is an observed normative particular. We did not infer it. We could not have predicted it without making the test. It is an object lesson from history. And we shall see in the course of this book that every social controversy is a consequence of two conflicting social ideals. This is the "analysis" part of Utopian Analysis, digging out the relevant ideals. And we shall also see that every major ideal and its alternatives has been tried, somewhere, at some time. So history provides us with all the political experiments we need to study. I do not regard communes (intentional communities which have withdrawn from the larger societies) as adequate political experiments. A commune can live on idealism or the charisma of its leaders. Real world political experiments cannot.

An ideal is something to be pursued, but rarely perfectly attained. "Utopia" is often taken to mean "perfection," where every true ideal is fully realized. I do not use the term that way. In my usage, any attempt to improve society is utopian, and ideas about improving society should be practical. "Utopia" does not mean "the impossible." In looking for evidence for liberty, we must compare societies which are relatively authoritarian with those which are relatively libertarian. So it is Sparta versus Athens, Rome versus Classical Greece, France of the Sun King versus England of the Glorious Revolution, which made Commons superior to monarchy, Lords or Barrister. More recently, it is 19th Century America versus the monarchies, Czars and Emperors of 19th Century Europe, and during the Cold War, it was the democratic West versus the autocratic East.

The Hellenic world imitated Athens, not Sparta. Two thousand years of scholars have preferred Classical Greek culture over the brutal world of the Roman Empire, at least in most respects. During the Cold War, the Soviets had to put up walls to keep their population in, since it was rapidly evaporating to the West. And 19th Century America was the light of the world. That is why immigrants poured into this country from all over the world, and still do. The people of France gave us the Statue of Liberty because they admired our society above all others. "Send us your tired, your poor, your huddled masses, yearning to breathe free," wrote Emma Lazarus in the famous poem now found on a plaque at the foot of Lady Liberty. "I lift my lamp above the Golden Door," says Lady Liberty, and so she does. Our ideals of liberty are the light of the world, and have spread the ideals from the Book of the Law she holds in her left hand around the world. Now if only she would shine a little light on the darkness we have built right here at home!

Lady Justice

In California, a man raped a young girl, cut off her arms and left her to die. The community was outraged and wanted this monster to die. The rapist's punishment was to receive free room and board, free legal and medical services with no responsibilities for several years at vast expense to the public. This is known as prison. When he was released to his home community, lynch mobs formed. Instead of helping the community take revenge on this man, the justice system mobilized considerable resources to protect the criminal. They moved him to a different community, where lynch mobs again formed. Eventually the police moved him to a penal community, the only place where they could protect him.

In Tulsa, a drunk slammed into a legally parked police car. The police car was clearly visible, as it had all its lights flashing. Inside the police car was a popular young police woman, writing a traffic ticket. The collision jammed the doors and set the police car ablaze. The woman inside burned to death, desperately struggling to break out, while onlookers also tried to break into the car. Television crews appeared on the scene and filmed the drunk being led away. He was laughing.

The community wanted to crucify this man. And why shouldn't it? Anger at evil is a legitimate and natural human emotion. Is not the function of the justice system to take revenge on evildoers? Is not this the very meaning of the phrase "justice was done?" The principle function of the justice system has always been to punish the wicked, not too harshly, nor too leniently, but as the scales of Lady Justice imply, in exact measure to the crime itself. And we also want to make sure the criminal can do no more mischief, at least not the same kind of mischief, at least not to the same victims.

The best evidence for Lady Justice comes from comparisons of La Belle Époque (1880-1920) in the USA to the periods which preceded it and followed it. La Belle Époque was a great time (though not perfect), a time when liberty and justice were most fully followed, at least for white males. The major change before the 1880-1920 period was the transition from the wild frontier to the settled civilization of the gaslight era, to a time of bicycles and ragtime. In earlier times, a boy could be hung for stealing a loaf of bread; today people are given free room and board for the most hideous serial killings. But in between these two extremes, there was a period in which the ideals of liberty and justice were followed in the United States. Trials were over in hours, or at most a few days, and if the murderer was found guilty by the jury, sentence was passed immediately and carried out the next day.

The best refutation of the alternatives to Lady Justice is the rise of suppressed anger since the 1920s, because so much evil goes unpunished, or not punished adequately. The symptom of suppressed anger is the berserk mass killer at the Post Office, or at McDonalds, or of an entire family, a phenomenon of our time. It may be possible to rehabilitate juvenile delinquents, but not hardened sociopaths. Permanent exile is impractical, since we have no equivalent of Siberia.

There has been a lot of irrelevant debate about capital punishment. An execution is not itself murder, according to the Law of Reciprocity, since anyone capable of cold blooded murder is not a party to the social contract that defines the scope of murder. Execution of a sociopath is more like extermination of a rabid dog.

Hobbes and Locke laid the foundations for modern notions of the social contract with a thought-experiment. They said "Let us imagine that everyone capable of committing murder agrees with one another not to, if given the reciprocal right to life." This is not history, but logic. It defines the scope of murder, since it is murder to kill someone or something only if they are a party to the social contract. Fetuses, infants, dogs, felons, people in a permanent vegetative state, or the mentally incompetent either cannot or will not agree to the social contract. That doesn't mean we can kill them without cause, but it also means that killing them is not murder. It may not be a virtue, and we may punish the perpetrators, but not with execution. We only execute murderers, where the victim is wholly innocent, and the murderer entirely responsible.

Why has this process gotten completely out of control? It is because of the Supreme Court. We have seen a steady expansion of "due process" until it has become "unending process," with the only winners being the lawyers, since taxpayers have to pay for the judge (a lawyer), the prosecutor (a lawyer) and the public defender (a lawyer). Trials have lengthened from hours in Judge Parker's court to years in Judge Ito's court. And is the quality of justice any better? Rulings by the Supreme Court in this century have a definite trend: they enrich lawyers by extending the length of due process, and increase the number of technical loopholes which allow appeals to set aside the original decision of a jury. That is why it costs a million dollars to execute a murderer. The million dollars goes in the pockets of lawyers, which is why lawyers are so unpopular, and are blamed for the decline in justice. In the days of Judge Parker, a century ago, the cost of an execution was a plain wooden coffin.

There is another reason why lawyers are unpopular. A trial is a contest between lawyers, not an objective search for the truth. It is more important for both the prosecutor and the defense lawyer to win rather than to find the truth. Winning advances ones career. Losing does not. As a result, prosecutors sometimes fail to hand over all the evidence to the defense lawyers. Perhaps the police had investigated a number of suspects, other than the one arrested.

Also, defense lawyers have never been known to convey all that they know to the prosecutors. The defendant may very well confess to his lawyers, but they are not required to reveal that information at trial. Lastly, too many trials depend on one bunch of criminals telling stories about another set of criminals. Why should such testimony be given any credence at all, given the motivations for the testimony? Many times a case doesn't even go to trial. A plea bargain is often forced on the defendant by his own lawyers, even if he is innocent, as the best alternative he can expect.

The whole system is rotten and needs to be replaced. I don't care how ancient it is, or how rooted it may be in English Common Law.

So, what sort of justice system should we have? One more like that of classical Chinese civilization, where the local aristarch/mandarin is the chief of police, the mayor, and the judge, all rolled into one. He or she will decide whether to call up a jury or not. The mandarins of China did not use juries, and given the notable incompetence of the juries on some famous recent cases in the US (the O.J. Simpson trial, for instance), the magistrate may decide to put the decision to a jury only when some matter of opinion is to be decided. The jury can then stand in for the entire community, and make a judgment which reflects public opinion. However, in most cases, swifter justice will be had with a trial that is public, where all the evidence is presented to both the public and the local magistrate, who makes the decision and gives the sentence, which is carried out immediately, within minutes. Critics rightly point out the number of convicted "killers" on death row, who have been saved by DNA testing. Quite right. But one cannot pull one item out of a utopia and examine it out of context. I would not be in favor of the death sentence either, in our present justice system, which does a poor job of finding the truth, and making the correct decision.

So, how can we find the truth, with such surety (which must be 99.999% accurate), that we can impose the death penalty and still sleep at night? Firstly, the walls, checkpoints, identity databases, and unforgable money/id/key cards is the first thing that must be put into place. We must always be able to say with certainty that we can produce a list of people which must contain the culprit.

Secondly, we must develop the interview into a science. Often the only person who knows the truth is the perpetrator. It is equally true that only the interview can save innocent people who would otherwise be convicted on circumstantial evidence. So a lot hinges on getting the truth out of the real perpetrator as well as people who look guilty on the basis of circumstantial evidence.

Doesn't reliance on the interview violate the Fifth Amendment? Yes it does, but I suspect that the real intent of the framers of the Constitution was to eliminate torture of suspects, and especially eliminate evidence extracted by torture. It is well known that anyone will confess to anything if subjected to enough torture. So I propose, not the elimination of the Fifth Amendment, but a revision of it which not only rules out the use of torture of suspects, but requires all interviews with suspects to be televised and available to the public if the suspect allows it. We must not allow any secret torture of suspects.

So, do we know of any way to tell for sure if someone is telling the truth or telling a lie? There are, of course, a variety of lie detector devices, but these can be defeated by a trained liar. Liars will be less able to defeat various brain scan devices, such as a PET scanner or a fMRI scanner. But that might be only a kind of last resort, to be used on people that we are 99% sure are the real perpetrators. I suspect that the best "lie detectors" are specially trained people, ones who have shown a talent for this. Liars give themselves away in small involuntary changes of expression and posture which interviewers can be trained to spot. These interviews should be conducted by the local magistrate, since they have no vested interest in convicting someone, and no prior history with the suspect. The trained "lie detector" person will be a silent participant, who can secretly signal the magistrate when she thinks a lie has been told.

Such a system of "proven interview" will save the innocent as well as convict the guilty. Without the interview, we must rely on circumstantial evidence, which can be misleading. Suppose our scientific criminologists find plenty of evidence of the presence of someone at the crime scene at about the time of the murder, evidence in the form of DNA typing of semen, sweat, and skin cells (which we are constantly shedding). A strong circumstantial case could be built up against this individual in a murder-rape case. However, it could have been the boyfriend, who left just before the perpetrator arrived on the scene. In that case, the scientific interview would clear the boyfriend. And if our system of scientific interview cannot free the innocent despite the circumstantial evidence, it is not a trust-worthy system of scientific interview.

The identity databases must contain indexed fingerprints, indexed DNA records, and other information on everyone who lives in this country or visits this country. Is this a police state or what? No, because this would simply be latent data, like the film in a security camera, which is never looked at unless a crime is committed, and is not publicly accessible. And we have the numerous location databases. One makes a record on one or another local database every time one buys anything, or passes through a checkpoint, even the passive checkpoints which do not require stopping and verifying that you are who your ID card says you are, with fingerprint, iris print, voice print, or signature, or all of the above in the most secure areas.

We add to this the most sophisticated criminalists, who know how to make microscopic examinations of crime scenes, who know all the ways of determining time of death, for instance, in a murder case. Then we query the location database system to see who could have been there at the time of the crime, and follow each individual back and forwards in time, to see if they are following their normal ritual, or doing something suspicious, like fleeing the area. The most likely suspects are subjected to the scientific interview, and this process continues until the culprit is caught. Criminalists will play a prominent role in the new police force.

In this new justice system, there will not be a "trial" with its echoes of trial by combat. There will be neither prosecutors nor defense lawyers involved. Once the magistrate believes the truth has been determined, there will simply be a public hearing, where all the evidence is laid out, and where anyone may object or enter additional information.

If the magistrate can think of alternative interpretations of the evidence, or if some member of the public can do so, then the case will be suspended until this point can be investigated and alternatives ruled out. It is better to convict no one than to convict an innocent person. Thus, a suspect always has the presumption of innocence on his side. But if we can really prove who did it, we should not hesitate to mete out the death penalty for murder. The only possible appeal might be to the magistrates immediate superior, who might stay execution for a time. But if the superior metropole has complete confidence in the local magistrate, then execution will be immediate. The next of kin should not have to wait years for justice, amid constant appeals, which could release the murderer at any time.

However, if the friends and next of kin of the victim ask for clemency for the convicted killer, then clemency they shall have.

Catching Terrorists and Serial Killers

Horrible images of the events of 9/11/2001 keep running through our minds, and we wonder how a free society can protect itself from that? It can be done, without losing any of our civil rights, such as our 4th Amendment right to privacy. And this same system provides absolutely the only way of catching serial killers and those who successfully hide the body where it is never found. It means converting our financial system to all electronic money. It means issuing an unforgable id to every citizen and every visitor, and tying it to an identification database. In the identification database, fingerprints are stored, and indexed. DNA is stored and indexed. Infrared photographs of the face are stored and indexed. Likewise with irisprints, voiceprints, signatures and visual light photographs. There are ways of indexing all these things, so they can be rapidly found in a computer search.

Not an invasion of privacy? How so? Because the databases would be strictly private. Even government officials could not search them. The identification databases would have only one use, and that is to verify that the person presenting a money card is the one who owns it. The card itself would have no picture or other visible information, except for a bar code across one end, and a 5 character sequence of any of the 256 different signs and symbols which may be generated on a computer keyboard. Those

5 symbols allow more than 1 trillion unique combinations, and yet, would be easy to remember. People would mainly identify their own cards by the 5 symbols. The person could not use someone else's card, if it is lost or stolen, unless they can also provide the correct fingerprints, irisprints, infra-red prints, signature, voiceprint and so forth, with a DNA print being the most conclusive. The bar code would be for low tech devices. All other information would be encoded by a secret encryption technique in holographic format. There might be only a very few places where one would have to provide all the proofs of identity, but many places where one would have to provide at least a thumbprint. Surveillance cameras could identify individuals in a crowd by doing an index of the face. An even better identification could be made in the dark, with an infrared image of the face.

Such an unforgable ID card could be used to make secure transactions. In other words, you could use it to transfer money or other property. Indeed, it is important that this be the only lawful currency, so that all monetary transactions are made with the card. Thus, every time someone buys something, or uses a telephone, or goes into or out of their home, or their neighborhood, or a place of business, or a mall, or a city, they would leave a trail on the location databases. Walls and checkpoints make it impossible to do otherwise.

Location databases would be the other half of this system. There would not be one central location database. Rather, every neighborhood or shopping mall would have their own location database, and it would be necessary to organize all commercial and shopping areas into open air malls. Individual stores or firms would have their own checkpoints for going in and out. So we would constantly be leaving tracks on location databases.

But how can that not be a violation of civil liberties? Because the location databases are private. Not even government officials or the military or the FBI or CIA could look through these databases. They would only be activated when someone was reported missing, or a crime was reported, with suitable uncertainties about place and time. All appropriate location databases simultaneously search for the missing person, or victim, as well as all those who could possibly have been at the same place at the same time. It would also track all those could-be-present people backwards and forwards in time. This would always provide a list of suspects for police. Studying the output would also allow police to distinguish a runaway from a victim of foul play in the case of missing persons. It is every American's right to run away, without notice to friends and family, and that right must be respected by the government. On the other hand, if a person's use of their card simply stops at a certain place and time, police must suspect foul play, even if no body is ever found. It is only the location database that can connect a serial killer to his victims.

Satanic terrorists could be kept out of the country if we were much more strict about who can enter the country, even as a tourist or student, and especially strict about ejecting them when their visa ran out. No one could come into the US without a visa and a money card. A tourist or student would have to get an ID card, with money deposited in an electronic account. They would have to give all the required indices as well as provide a paper trail of where they were born, where they have lived, or worked, or traveled, who can vouch for them, who knows them. All the information collected on them must be checked against police and other records. If they have ever left DNA or a fingerprint at a crime scene, this fact would become known before the money / ID card would be issued. As I write this, a prudent policy might be to deport all non-citizens of Middle-Eastern descent currently in the nation, who have expired visas, and bring the rest in for close questioning. But what about the 4th Amendment? Don't people have the right against unlawful search and seizure of their person or property? Yes, they do, unless there is some reason for the magistrates to issue a search warrant. And right now, being a person on a visa from the Middle-Eastern at least makes it possible that they are a sleeper member of a terrorist cell. Of course, people of Middle-Eastern descent who were born in this country, or naturalized citizens might be asked if they know any Middle-Eastern terrorists, but there would certainly be no search and seizure. In practice, Americans of Middle-Eastern descent have been only too happy to help if they can. As Americans, they are in danger from terrorists too.

How can we put walls around neighborhoods or "malls?" Or to be more precise, how can we guarantee that everyone would have to come in by the checkpoints rather than over the walls? A twenty foot stone wall with smooth surfaces would keep small children from accidentally wandering across. Pressure sensitive tiles on the top and sides could detect ladders. Heat sensitive infrared detectors on top could detect objects which somehow pass over without touching, and surveillance cameras could be rewound to see what it was. Sound detectors in the base of the wall could detect sounds of someone tunneling underneath.

Yet all these fortress-like innovations would in no way restrict the movement of ordinary citizens. If someone had a protection order against them, they could be kept out of the neighborhoods and "malls" where the victim lives and works. A community could decide who they wanted to allow in, and who they wanted to keep out. That is every community's right, according to the public/private ideal. Vagrants who refused half-way houses or shelters might be excluded from a metroplex, and so might all those convicted of felonies for violence. Naturally, the same rules apply to border crossings. So we might build a second border, away and out of sight of the actual border with Mexico, a border with all the protections of the wall described above.

Canada's long border presents a different problem, in more than one way. The simplest solution would be to persuade Canada to convert to the same electronic money as the US, as well as creating the location databases, and creating walls and checkpoints too. There would then be just one currency throughout the US and Canada. Perhaps someday we could make the same arrangement with Mexico.

No new principles or ideals have been introduced in this chapter. The ideals of justice and self-preservation govern these attempts to catch criminals and terrorists. Sometimes it is necessary to spell out the details, showing how an ideal is to be applied.

An Anthropologist's View of Morality

Murder and the Social Contract: The ideal of reciprocity (the social contract) lies at the heart of civilization, and finds many applications. It defines murder and citizenship. Reciprocity is the golden rule and the mosaic law, the basis of economics and marriage. Put more formally, it means something for me, if you want something for you. Pay for work. Profit for investment. You help me and I will help you. A person with a lot of good friends is a good friend to a lot of people. Hobbes and Locke recognized that the essential glue of society is a kind of social contract, that all those physically capable of committing murder make with one another. Each member contracts with the others not to kill them, if they won't kill him. This does not refer to any historical period preceding the social contract, nor to any formal ritual. It is a gedanken experiment, showing the essential logic of the social contract, or as I call it, the ideal of reciprocity.

The refutation of socialism leaves the ideal of reciprocity as the only known alternative for this class of problems. I base my analysis of morality, legality and virtue on reciprocity. We must make this analysis in order to make any headway on the abortion controversy. There is no solution which will completely satisfy fanatics, but I can make a proposal which may be acceptable to the moderates on both sides.

Murder: Every community's moral code contains an injunction against murder. But is abortion murder? If it is, we must execute the mother and the doctor in the name of consistency. A few dangerous fanatics have been doing just that. But such actions are repudiated by most anti-abortion groups.

So what is murder? I take a strictly anthropological view on this. In a general way, every community defines morality in the same way. It is murder to kill a full citizen of ones own community. In today's world, we are developing a global community, so except in time of war, there is no full citizen of the global community who can be killed with impunity, without being charged with murder. What is a full citizen? A full citizen is "full" of rights, responsibilities and capabilities.

We offer full rights and responsibilities only to those who are capable of reciprocating, and capable of assuming the full rights and responsibilities of a citizen. In other words, we answer this question with the ideal of reciprocity. As a thought-experiment, or as a teaching tool for moral precepts, we contract with everyone who could murder us but won't, if we won't murder them. It was the Renaissance English philosopher Thomas Hobbes who recognized this as the basic "social contract," the logical basis of the moral tradition.

Morality: Morality is the strongest, most important and most universal of the three "oughts". Anthropologists tell us the moral tradition worldwide is to ingrain a tabu against murder into a child from an early age, so it becomes psychologically impossible to commit murder. We call this personality trait "the conscience." It is not innate, nor divine, nor a universal natural law. It is simply a tradition, and different communities have different traditions. When this traditional socialization does not happen, the result is a sociopath, a wild animal, lacking the minimum requirement for entry into society, which is a conscience. A person lacking a conscience is the most dangerous and unpredictable wild animal. Thus, we should not allow a sociopath into house or city. It would be prudent to shoot him on sight, like a rogue elephant or a rabid dog.

The moral tradition has content, scope and strength. Content is whatever is tabu or required. While murder is always tabu, a requirement to defend the community to the death is also usually included in the moral tradition, and sometimes various sexual tabus.

Scope defines the group with moral rights. The moral tradition gives some people rights by means of a correlative obligation placed on everyone else. Who is protected by the tabu on murder? There is no known society where the scope is "everyone."

Finally, strength has to do with the degree of success of a community in giving everyone a conscience. The Zuni, for instance, have traditionally been quite successful. In modern times, there has never been a murder by a traditional Zuni. Clearly the larger American society has a much weaker moral tradition, much weaker than European society or some of the First Nations. We are not yet consistently successful in giving everyone a conscience.

Only a sociopath is capable of committing murder. A strong moral tradition is advantageous, because it means there are few or no sociopaths. It is better to live in a community with a strong moral code than to live in a community with a weak moral code. A conscience works all the time. It works even when a potential perpetrator gains something by murder, and even when he could get away with it.

Why Execution is not Murder: We can execute murderers without ourselves committing murder, because a murderer has demonstrated the absence of a conscience. He has proven himself to be a sociopath. He has clearly broken the social compact and thus, is not a citizen, not a member of the community protected by the tabu on murder, no more than insects or bacteria. Murderers can be exterminated like flies, or bacteria, or mad dogs, without breaking the moral code.

Why Abortion is not Murder: So why isn't abortion murder? It is because of the principle of reciprocity. A fetus cannot commit murder, and thus is not a party to the social contract. Up to the age of eight a child is not a full citizen, essentially because he is unable to commit murder, get a job, vote, drive, start a family and so forth. Until age eight, a child is the ward of its parents or guardians, almost their property, to be taught or disciplined as the guardians choose (within limits).

Thus, the ideal of reciprocity shows us that abortion is not the moral equivalent of murder, not the unforgivable evil calling for execution of the mother. And past experience shows us that making abortion illegal produces "coathanger" abortions, raising maternal mortality, essentially zero today. On the other hand we cannot regard abortion with complete indifference, a matter of personal choice as casual as trimming ones nails. Killing a fetus may not be murder, but it is not exactly a virtue either. We could argue all day about whether a fetus is a person, but certainly it will become a person unless we deliberately kill it. It has already passed all the major hurdles that could terminate it.

Fetus Vs Blastocyst: Incidentally, use of the "morning-after" pill is not abortion, because a fertilized egg is not yet a fetus, and has only a 30% chance of becoming one. The "morning-after" pill just lowers those odds. The subdividing ball of cells develops into a blastocyst. A blastocyst is not a fetus. A blastocyst is just a hollow ball of cells, with a small pile of stem cells inside. If a blastocyst attaches to the uterine wall, the ball becomes the placenta, while the stem cells inside develop into a fetus. Many encounter some mistake in differentiation and spontaneously abort and the woman simply has a late period. By the way, there should be no moral difficulties in performing scientific experiments on blastocysts and stem cells, which can be created in the lab, unlike a fetus, which cannot be created in the lab.

Without abortion, a fetus will almost certainly become a cuddly newborn, a charming toddler, a fascinating teenager and possibly the savior of civilization. So, I believe a fetus, unlike the ball of cells or the blastocyst, deserves some consideration from society.

Middle Ground on Abortion: At the present time, the conflict between the right-to-life people and the freedom-of-choice people is so acrimonious, even violent, it seems impossible they should ever come together and agree on anything. But wouldn't they both agree abortion is not a virtue? And wouldn't they both agree it is a virtue for the pregnant woman to carry her baby to term for the sake of a sterile couple, instead of killing it? Then instead of making abortion illegal, we simply change the law to give sterile couples a week or so to try to persuade the pregnant woman to carry the fetus to term and let them adopt it. Let childless couples interested in adopting a newborn interview every woman applying for an abortion. And, in a way, the pregnant woman is interviewing them.

If a sterile couple thinks the biological parents have good genes, and the mother is not drinking or using drugs, and is eating properly, getting prenatal care, they might offer to pay all medical expenses of the pregnant woman, offer wages for nine months of inconvenience and a few hours of hard labor, offer the woman a place to live, and throw in a cruise trip afterward. And other couples might do likewise. This must be done under the watchful eye of the magistrate, so the pregnant woman doesn't make contracts with more than one couple. These are binding contracts.

Such a contract is not the same as buying a child. It is simply paying the pregnant woman for her time and inconvenience.

The childless couples and the pregnant woman should not come face to face. No names should be exchanged, and no addresses. All information about genetic diseases in the baby's inheritance is disclosed to the childless couples. Adopted children should never be told they are adopted. The birth mother should not be allowed to see or hold the newborn baby, otherwise she will change her mind, and decide she wants to keep the child. It should instead be given immediately to the adoptive mother, to begin the process of bonding. Without such rules, the birth mother may feel guilty, and seek to track down "her" child. Or the child may try to track down the biological parents. This often winds up in the courts, which have usually ruled in favor of the biological parent. This is the wrong ruling, and such court proceedings would not be possible if the records were sealed. We should not forget that the biological mother was prepared to kill the child. Biology doesn't make someone a parent. The records should be sealed forever, and guarded jealously by the magistrates.

The solution to the abortion controversy presented in this chapter will not result in the production of babies for sale, because of the birth licensing requirement, necessary to bring population growth to a halt. We haven't discussed this yet. A woman who repeatedly gets pregnant without a birth license will lose her reproductive rights. I propose that no one can keep a child or repeatedly get pregnant without a birth license. The number of birth licenses will be scientifically set to reach a stable population in a century or so. Roughly, the same number of birth licenses will be given out as death certificates. Halting the population bomb is job one for saving the planet. The local magistrate will decide who gets a birth license and who does not.

We have taken two problems, put them together, and let them solve each other. On the one hand, we have the problem of sterile couples, and the desperate, expensive and usually futile struggles of heroic medicine to impregnate a woman whose biological clock has run out of time. It is also difficult to find a normal infant baby to adopt. The other problem is a woman who does not wish to be a mother (or a mother again in some cases).

Virtue: The virtue of carrying an unwanted fetus to term for the sake of sterile couples recognizes an element of truth in both the right-to-life position and the freedom-of-choice position. It recognizes that abortion is not like clipping your toenails, and can have serious long term consequences for society, and for the life of the woman who has the abortion. I shall give you a personal example.

When my mother was pregnant with me, she was diagnosed with cancer of the cervix and womb, and both our GP and the specialist advocated immediate hysterectomy, with the abortion of myself. But my mother was stubborn and heroic. She insisted on carrying me to term. After my birth, the doctors were surprised to find no sign of cancer on the cervix or in my mother's womb, and as I write this, she is now a spry 80, while I have so far been granted 58 years to try to save civilization. If my mother had permitted the abortion, then Utopian Analysis would never have arisen. It still may not. Creating a scientific discipline is a cooperative enterprise. But at least the idea has been planted.

A normal fetus means everything to a childless and sterile couple, even though it is considered worthless to the biological mother. And that is why it is a virtue for the pregnant woman to go through the embarrassment, inconvenience and pain of carrying the fetus to term and delivering it, for their sake. Birth licensing requirements would not allow her to keep the baby for herself, in most cases. The alternatives are usually abortion or adoption.

The Third Republic

Bureaucratic Absurdities: The Nuns of the Missionaries of Charity (headed by Mother Teresa) wanted to convert abandoned buildings in the South Bronx to homeless shelters. New York City was willing to sell Mother Teresa the buildings for $1 apiece. $500,000 of the Nun's money was set aside for the purpose. However, New York's building code requires an elevator in every new or renovated multi-story building, which costs $100,000 per building. There was no one with the power to waive this absurd requirement. Thwarted by a year and a half of going from one agency to another, Mother Teresa gave up. Even Saints are helpless before the massive roadblock of bureaucracy.

Ever wonder why it costs so much to get from the airport to Manhattan? Because an idiotic FAA regulation forbids building the subways out to New York City's three airports. Why? I don't know. It is theater of the absurd. Sick of "politics-as-usual?" Bored with political speeches, which promise everything and deliver nothing? Scornful of a government that can't even balance its books? Tied up in red tape and laws so complex that it is impossible even to do your own taxes? Your frustration is not pathological. We have finally arrived at total gridlock, or freeze-up, to use Lazare's metaphor. Our government is now perfectly dysfunctional.

If you want a detailed account of its dysfunctionality, I recommend *The Frozen Republic*, by Daniel Lazare, and *The Death of Common Sense*, by Philip Howard. But what is the alternative?

Parliament: Scrape off the ancient encrustations of Royals, Lords, Barristers, and a state religion, and the Parliamentary system in the UK would be a great improvement over the tricameral, judicial superior system in the US. Parliamentary elections are short and local, since the people only vote for their local MP (Member of Parliament), probably someone that they have met and actually talked to. Commons then elects the Prime Minister, who forms a government with a cabinet. Because elections are short and local, MPs wind up with no debt to the money men. In the US, the money men who finance very expensive elections must be satisfied if the politician is ever to be re-elected. One sign that Parliament works well is the high voter turnout in countries with a Parliamentary system. This is a normative particular, a point in favor of Parliament.

Aristarchy: A change to Parliamentary democracy would be an improvement, but a change to Aristarchy would be better. Aristarchy is a form of democracy suggested by the Classical Chinese Mandarin system of government, in which government officials are selected from a pool of candidates who have passed exams. It is democratic, because only the people can change or add to the original set of laws, by means of a petition signed by three-fourths of the full citizens of the relevant jurisdiction. The laws are broad statements of intent, which the Aristarchs are free to interpret as needed, following the spirit of the law, rather than the letter.

In our system, it is the attempt to predefine every nit-picking detail, and leave nothing up to the discretion and wisdom of the administrator that has given us 100 million words of law.

The magistrates, metropoles, governors and archons of Aristarchy are given all discretion. Like the Mandarins in classical China, the local magistrate has combined executive and judicial powers. He or she is judge, mayor, and chief of police. The metropole has the same sort of power over a metropolitan region, and is thus is in a position to hire and fire or transfer the magistrates underneath.

The equivalent of the President is the First Archon. The cabinet (and line of succession in case of sudden death) consists in the Second, Third, etc. Archons, each of whom replaces a vast bureaucracy in the present system of government. For instance, there is ONE Archon who decides when a drug has been tested enough to be marketed, thus replacing the entire FDA.

It has been said that power corrupts, and absolute power corrupts absolutely. Of course, the First Archon does not have such absolute power. Still, it is easy to imagine a First Archon with a Napoleonic complex. How do we get rid of him or her? No problem. First let us define "the electors," somewhat like the electors of the Holy Roman Emperor. They consist in all the Archons, all the governors of the major regions, and all the metropoles (chief aristarch of a metroplex). If a First Archon does not specify a Second Archon before he dies or retires, three-fourths of the electors can elect one. The First Archon can come from any level of the Aristarchy. Similarly, a vote by three-fourths of the electors can unseat a First Archon. So, we need not fear little Napoleons.

The Classical Chinese Mandarinate: The reader has to know something about the brilliance of the Mandarin system between the beginning of the T'ang dynasty (600 CE) and the end of the Ming (1644 CE) to get excited about Aristarchy. Unfortunately, our schools teach almost nothing about Chinese history. A pleasant introduction to the Mandarin system is found in the historical novels and translations by Robert Van Gulik about the exploits of Judge Dee, an historical mandarin from the middle of the T'ang dynasty. The first and best of the Judge Dee novels is a translation of Dee Goong An, a novel about Dee by an 18th Century Chinese author.

Although Dee was a real person, who rose to cabinet rank, and wrote many brilliant position papers which were studied thereafter by Mandarins, there is little real historical knowledge of his life as a local magistrate.

Instead, the Chinese author, and later, Robert Van Gulik,

simply made use of the vast number of stories and legends about the adventures and achievements of local magistrates. These local mandarins wrote poems, practiced martial arts, donned disguises and entered the underworld to catch criminals. Sometimes they retired as Taoist mystics, living in the mountains.

Since the exams were open to all, sons of peasants, tradesmen, and Mandarins could and did rise into power, so it was certainly government of the people. Because the exams were open to all, the Mandarins never became a hereditary Aristocracy. Think of the chaos produced by hereditary Aristocracy in Western Civilization. The Chinese experienced all that too, in the Shang and Chou dynasties, before they got rid of their hereditary nobility. Of course, we got rid of hereditary titles in our first revolution, the one of 1776, the one celebrated on July 4th.

The Mandarin exams were essay exams, based on the body of so-called Neo-Confucian literature, which were case studies of good and bad government. The Mandarins were the best and the brightest. They were often inventors, scientists, poets or artists, as well as magistrates.

The Mandarins created a marvelous and resilient civilization of great beauty and originality, which time after time rebounded from foreign invasion to re-establish the native empire, with the Mandarins as the civil servants. The Mandarins designed canals, dams and other waterworks and roads which kept a large population fed and informed.

They invented silk, paper, printing, the compass, gunpowder, the stern-post rudder, porcelain, tea-drinking, stir-fried cooking, to name a few, all borrowed by the West. It is unfortunate that we have not borrowed their most brilliant innovation, the Mandarin Aristarchy. When the West was sinking into the Dark Age, the Chinese were rising to their most glorious age, the T'ang Dynasty. And this was due in large part to the Mandarins.

Bureaucracy: The Mandarin system was efficient because it had no bureaucracy. Our system has nothing but bureaucracy. In fact, the typical way our government "solves" a problem is to create a new federal agency to do it, like the FDA, EPA, REA, CIA, FBI, OSHA, FEMA, IRS and all the other alphabet soup agencies. In time, every bureaucracy becomes the problem, rather than the solution. The FDA is the chief obstacle to medical progress. The FAA is the main impediment to safe air travel.

A bureaucracy is a giant social machine which usually only has to make decisions. All the elaborate layers of bureaucracy of the Social Security administration, for instance, has as its sole function deciding who gets disability (which takes them an average of two years), and who gets retirement. All the FDA does is decide what drugs doctors are permitted to prescribe. All the FAA does is set regulations for the airline industry.

The opposite of a machine is a person. The founding fathers tried to build machines that perform their service irregardless of the quality of the office-holders. The Chinese selected the best person, and then gave that person full power and held them personally responsible. For instance, if a magistrate executed someone for murder later shown to be innocent, he was himself executed.

A single individual could make these decisions just as well, and much faster. Furthermore, we would then know who to ask, who to blame, and who gets the credit. SS decisions, for instance, should be made on the local ward level, by the local Aristarch who knows the family and the individual in question, with the money to pay for it coming out of local taxes. In the Aristarchy, all taxes are paid to the local magistrate, who first takes care of local needs, and then passes what is left up the hierarchy. Much government could be conducted on a local level, in this fashion. A person can do in an hour or two what it takes the SS administration two years and thousands of bureaucrats. In the system I propose, a magistrate is in charge of no more than 10,000 households, which could be a small town, or even an entire county in rural areas, or just a local neighborhood in a big city.

Lawyers: Make the laws simple and the legal instruments simple, and we could put lawyers out of business. They would have no place in court, since the accused must speak for himself. The prosecution consists in presenting the facts uncovered by the investigation. The top policeman would do that, prodded by questions from the magistrate, if necessary. Before a decision is made, members of the audience (or the jury, if one is impounded, magistrate's choice) could raise whatever questions they like. The trial could be adjourned temporarily to investigate these questions if necessary.

Above all, simplify the tax laws. They are now a stack of paper one meter high. If it is doubtful if anyone knows every provision. In the chapter on economics, I introduce a one line tax law, so I will save further discussion until then.

Revolution: Thomas Jefferson thought every generation ought to cancel the public debt, have a revolution and create the kind of government that suited the new times. It is time to take his advice. Revolution! The very word clears the head, like smelling salts. Cancel the national debt. Padlock the FDA, EPA, REA, CIA, FBI, OSHA, FEMA, IRS, DEA and all the other alphabet soup agencies. Adjourn Congress permanently. Fire the Supreme Court and all the appellate courts. Eliminate state, county and city governments in favor of a single vertical system. It is only by giving particular individuals the power and responsibility that we can escape the endless "process," as in "due process," which has brought government to a halt. We are drowning in process. The EPA's regulations run to 10,000 pages, 17 volumes of fine print. Federal statutes and formal rules total 100 million words. OSHA has 140 regulations just regarding wooden ladders (all figures come from Howard, 1994, p. 26).

Revolutions do not have to be bloody. The French and Russian revolutions simply got out of hand, resulting in anarchy, until a tyrant came along to save them. When I think of "revolution" I have in mind the "glorious revolution" of 1688 in Britain, which made Parliament supreme. It was "glorious" precisely because it was bloodless. And I also have in mind our own unconstitutional but peaceful transition from the First Republic, ruled by the

Continental Congress, to our present Second Republic, with a strong Federal government. This was done in secret, by the Continental Congress of 1787, who made some vague noises about "the matter of the nation" and "improving government" and promptly threw out reporters and banned the taking of notes. They worked through a hot summer creating this new Constitution, and decided that a favorable vote by three-fourths of the states ratified it, as a clear indication of the consent of the governed. We could do something like that again, and create the Third Republic.

Differences between 2nd & 3rd Republics: In some ways, the Second Republic and the Third Republic are opposites. In the Second Republic, we don't get to vote on laws, but we do get to elect Presidents and the Congress. In the Third Republic, we don't get to elect the Magistrates or other parts of the Aristarchy, but new laws would come about only through the petition and initiative process, and a favorable vote by three-fourths of all qualified citizens. A "qualified citizen" does not mean "registered voter." Everyone "who has come of age" is a qualified person, unless they have committed a felony or been judged mentally incompetent by the magistrate and given a guardian.

Ending War Using Hierarchies of Community

Nuclear weapons add nothing new to the problem of war. Even in Neolithic times it was possible for a community to be totally destroyed in war, all its inhabitants wiped out, its buildings burned and leveled, its language and traditions utterly lost and forgotten. Nearly every "tell" in the Middle East tells us just such a dreary and dreadful story. War is not new and neither is total war.

Nor is there anything new about the strategies employed by communities for conflict avoidance or conflict survival. All the known strategies have been tried many times. There are consistent patterns in the success or failure of these strategies. The solution to the nuclear madness is the solution to the problem of war. The solution is known and has worked many times. This is the ideal of higher community. What it means is that two formerly warring communities combine into a larger community stronger than any of the factions. This is not an idealistic pipedream. It has happened many times.

Remember Romeo and Juliet? A true story from medieval Verona. The story of the young lovers is set against the backdrop of a clan feud between the Capulets and the Montagues. Every clan built its own tower, trying to build one taller than anyone else. These medieval towers still exist in some small Italian towns.

Medieval city-states were plagued with armed clashes between clans in some periods, and clashes between classes in other periods. For instance, the Guelfs and the Ghibellines were political factions in Italy who fought each another in the last 200 years of the medieval period. The Guelfs represented the free merchant class of cities like Florence, whereas the Ghibellines were the Imperial Vicars of Italian cities controlled by the Holy Roman Emperor, and their followers.

Stable city-states were finally achieving success everywhere in the time of Machiavelli. Naturally, he approved of this. Peace is always preferable to chaos. *The Prince* is part observation of the process at work and part prescription.

Of course, as soon as baronies and city-states became strong enough to keep peace between clans and classes, they began waging war on one another. Remember the war between Genoa and Venice, in which Marco Polo was captured? If he had not been captured, we would not have had the book of his travels. Genoa and Venice were always fighting. Florence, Siena and Pisa were often at war.

Hundreds of years of war between France and England make up their medieval history, retarding the Renaissance in both places. Crecy, Agincourt, the Hundred Years War, the Thirty Years War, the Napoleonic Wars are just a few names that swim up from the dismal history of France and England from the Norman conquest until World Wars 1 and 2. It is only now, with the Chunnel and the European Economic Union, that we can at last be sure that the various states of Europe have ceased their bloody and pointless feuding.

World War Two was the last of these global wars between states. The reason is the appearance on the scene of a larger political unit, the nation of states. For a time, there were two "United States," the United States of America and the United States of Soviet Republics. Now there is only one, the USA, since the USSR unfortunately came apart at the seams. This is always unfortunate, because the internal states are soon at war, as in

Chechyna. Soon, there will be two nation-states again, as the EEC and NATO evolve into a European nation of states. No individual state can stand up to a nation.

Not only is NATO and the EEC steadily growing more united, it has steadily gained new members, and it now appears that the former communist states of Eastern Europe will also join, and there will be a de facto United States of Europe, which may include all of linguistic and demographic Europe.

Dissolution of the USSR and of Yugoslavia as well as the US Civil war sounds a cautionary note. Just because a group of sub-communities is temporarily united under a single government does not mean they have formed one community. Sometimes it happens, and sometimes it doesn't. Before our own Civil war, we had one government, but two communities. Only recently can we really call the USA a single community of states. This unity could be challenged if individual states decided to repeal the tyrannical War-On-Drugs, root of half the violence in this country since Prohibition.

Moslem Mullahs have whipped up the ignorant and disenfranchised masses of the Middle East into a wholly irrational hatred for Israel and the United States. The events of September 11, 2001, were a wake-up call for the US. As I write this, the Taliban in Afghanistan have fallen, a new government is in place, but Osama Bin Laden and the Al Qaeda terrorist network have not yet been rooted out. This is a war the Mullahs cannot win. They want to turn back the clock to the 8th Century, when Islam was a great civilization, and the West was in a dark age. The US could easily turn the sands of the Middle East into radioactive molten glass, which glows in the dark for the next thousand years. Just as the Japanese made a huge mistake at Pearl Harbor, so the Radical Muslims made a huge mistake in bringing down the twin towers of the World Trade Center in NYC. Once aroused, the US is a persistent and implacable foe.

Peace will require bringing the Middle East into the modern world, with science, learning, liberty, and a clear separation of church and state. Clearly the actual terrorists must be rooted out, but that is only a beginning. In the Middle East, we have a string of failed states, and a people drunk on fantastic conspiracy theories and totally unrealistic dreams of the past.

Seeds of Hate

Nothing can justify the terrible evil of 9/11. It was a completely unprovoked attack on innocent victims, who never did anything against our attackers. Our actions since 9/11 are not acts of revenge, but of self-defense, since 9/11 showed us we are vulnerable to suicidal fanatics, domestic or foreign. We will do whatever we must to protect ourselves from additional attacks, short of giving up our libertarian ideals.

Why do they hate us so much? At first, we could only attribute it to the outbreak of some unfathomable new evil, like Fascism in the 1930s. But as we learned more about the terrorists, new hypotheses arose. It turned out that the terrorists were not the poor and downtrodden, not even people brought up in the fundamentalist tradition of pure Islam, where the only book read was the Koran. No, the terrorists were rich, urbane, well-educated men, who lived and moved without notice in the West. Some of them were born in the West, educated in the West. They begin to seem more like traitors from within, like the American Taliban fighter, than traitors from without.

Enormous rage is required to turn an intelligent and well-educated person into a suicidal killer. The presence of an Islamic background leads them to the Mosques of the radical Mullahs, who can give them a specific focus for their rage, and can tell them where to go and who to see to become a suicide pilot or a suicide bomber. Every religion has within it the seeds of violence and intolerance, so this chapter is not about Islam. It is about the West.

Western religion is not Christianity or Judaism, as you might imagine. It is the religion of science. The distinction between "science" and "the religion of science" is that the former refers to "anything learned by scientific method," while the latter refers to a specific set of articles of faith. Followers of the religion of science would probably not see this distinction. But it can easily be shown that the reality of such things as reincarnation, NDEs, OOBEs and UFOs are well-established by the same rules of scientific method that are used elsewhere. Here I use the term "UFO" not in its original sense, but in its popular sense as spacecraft piloted by humanoids from other stars. One can easily detect the followers of the religion of science by offering to show them the studies which establish the reality of reincarnation, NDEs, OOBEs, and UFOs, using scientific method. If they are not interested, if they simply laugh at you, then it is evident that you have stepped across a line into a forbidden zone. You are challenging a core set of beliefs which are resistant to empirical refutation. That is the definition of a religion. It has become the religion of the West, supplanting Christianity and Judaism among the educated elite.

Science is a seductive and powerful religion, draining the lifeblood out of all the older religions, and forcing its way everywhere. And the reason is, science is not called a religion, but confidently presented as "the truth, which only ignorant fools reject." Indeed, the high priests of the religion of science chart the spread of irrationality with polls testing to see how many people believe in reincarnation, ESP or UFOs. In the eyes of the high priests of science, belief in any of these forbidden doctrines is sufficient proof of irrationality.

Western religion is seductive in other ways as well. People in Pakistan or India or Saudi Arabia can easily see that many good things come along with the religion of science, including Western luxuries, high technology, democracy and wealthy economies. All it will cost you is the loss of everything sacred. In the religion of science, there is no soul, no divinity, no life after death, no immortality, no meaning to our existence. As Nobel Laureate Steven Weinberg said at the end of his book *The First Three Minutes*: "The more the universe seems comprehensible, the more it also seems pointless."

Once a sensitive young man recognizes the nihilistic character of the religion of science, he may begin to despise all the outward signs of Westernization, such as the growth of huge, impersonal boxes for architecture, or the spread of tawdry strip malls, or the cancerous spread of McDonalds and Wal-Mart, a cancer which destroys the distinctive *souk* or the small towns painted by Norman Rockwell. He may become frustrated that nothing seems capable of halting reductionist materialism.

I become pessimistic myself when I see the psi-cops, the high priests and Grand Inquisitors of the religion of science in *Scientific American* and on the Discovery Science channel on cable TV. Does no scientist object? Can't anyone see that this is the end of scientific method? You have to choose. Either scientific method applied to all things, known and unknown, or the religion of science. The psi-cops (CSICOP) want to close the books. No more new sciences to be allowed. Rationality is now defined as believing the textbooks, and irrationality is everything else. After three centuries the grand adventure of ideas is over and science becomes just another faith, another superstition. One can easily see why this leads to a desperate search for any alternative.

Islam provides an alternative, one that seeks to destroy the West. It may now be clear why the most Westernized of Moslems and the most intelligent are the first to raise the bloody flag of Jihad. They know better than anyone the cost to the soul of the soft luxury and gadgets of the West. A good example of the core terrorists is Ahmed Omar Sheikh, abductor of the Wall Street Journal reporter Daniel Pearl. Sheikh is Pakistani, but raised in a middle-class neighborhood in East London (*Newsweek*, 2/18/02/ p.42), educated in an elite private high school and the London School of Economics. So it would seem that merely educating Moslems in the ways of the West would be counter-productive.

It is we who must change, and offer kinds of spirituality which are compatible with science. No spirituality is compatible with the religion of science, which we must vigorously reject, as we reject all other religions, with some regrets, with some sadness. They have outlived their usefulness. They all induce sectarian intolerance, and they all teach fear, where there need be no fear. We need not fear death. It has no terror for those who have had an NDE. Death has no terror for those who know Professor Stevenson's *Twenty Cases*. We need not fear "the endtimes." This universe has lasted at least 15 giga-years, and will certainly last at least that much longer, without any discontinuities in time. It is odd that this is a common fear among the religious, perhaps because they do not understand why the sun comes up every day, or why one season follows another.

What is emerging is a new metaphysics, which shall be the basis for a renaissance of art and architecture. It will be rich in mysticism and symbolic revelation. Anyone can have a symbolic revelation. All they have to do is make a mandala. This new metaphysics will be open to all seven ways, and there shall be no credo, nor any social hierarchy. It will be open to ceremonial magick, and to every form of meditation, and to every kind of entheogen, as we party and frolic our way towards a brighter day. Freedom! Liberation from our Puritanical past, and a repressive and tyrannical present. Throw off the shackles! Begin the long journey. It will not be a hardship. It will be a party, as we live, and love, and express ourselves, and grow. Let spiritual evolution and the divine purpose be our goal. *Sic Itur Ad Astra*. The way to the stars—and to immortality.

Urban Gridlock

The hybrid gas/electric car is being touted now as the 21st Century car. However, the car IS the problem. It is the greatest killer of young people by accidents. 40,000 people die in ICV crashes in the US every year. At least another 20,000 pedestrians are killed by cars. ICVs are the sole cause of smog, acid rain and gridlock. They are the main cause of the national epidemic of obesity. We have stupidly created all these "labor-saving" devices, and then have to carve out another part of the day just for going to the gym. There would be no problem with obesity if we used our muscles every day to travel a few miles as part of our commute to and from work. There is no improvement to cars which makes the conventional automobile any part of the solution to travel around the 21st Century metroplex.

In any case, by 2010, all the smaller oil reserves will be gone (see the chapter, "Hubbert's Peak") and we will be utterly dependent on the mad sheiks and mullahs of the Middle East, who presently have 66.5% of all the oil reserves (*Newsweek*, November 19, 2001). That might be their ultimate weapon against the West. They could decide who gets oil and who doesn't. Thus, we must end our dependence on oil, and do it soon.

Do we love our cars? If we believe the commercials, owning a luxury sedan brings almost mystical joy. And in the commercials, the car is speeding far beyond the speed limit, on a narrow and winding road through the mountains, with no other traffic. Have you ever driven on a road like that in your entire lifetime? Only once in my case, while driving an MGB through West Virginia. Even if you find such a road, you will be stuck behind a logging truck, or an Airstream trailer, with no place to pass.

No, the reality of cars is choking gridlock, sitting idling, breathing the fumes of the car in front of you. It is an amazing sight to see all 8 lanes (each way) of a Los Angeles freeway coming to a complete stop on a sunny Sunday afternoon, when it isn't even rush hour. Why? An accident? No. No reason. When the carrying capacity of a freeway is exceeded, it suddenly gels and comes to a complete stop. Which would you rather have? Easy travel around the Metroplex or the "thrill" of owning a new Lexus. I drive a 1983 Buick myself, one with measles of gray primer paint. And it is just as good a car as that Lexus or Mercedes. My car always starts, always runs, and has never stranded me anywhere. And I can break the speed limit if I have to.

So get rid of the cars, and all other Internal Combustion Vehicles (ICVs). Banish them from the Metroplex if you value your sanity. What replaces them is subways and freeway trains. A train is the only way of transporting an unlimited number of people from A to B at rush hour. Simply add more cars to the train. Remember, these rules only apply to a metroplex which has excellent public transportation systems. It does not apply to 99% of the land area of the USA.

Freeway trains draw power from overhead lines, are rubber-tired, entirely robotic, and they break apart into individual cars which are also entirely robotic and spend most of the day and night going up and down one street. It is only at rush hour that they congregate on freeways into a train, either going to a suburb, or from a suburb. Where freeways cross, the trains will stop and people can transfer to a train going up or down one of the crossing freeways. As a train goes along a freeway, it sheds cars which take exits to streets, where it takes up its duty as a bus, going up and down that street until the next rush hour.

So will we have no mode of personal transportation? I have seen a tiny 1 person 3-wheel car which runs on batteries and also has a generator which one pumps like a bicycle. With advanced paper batteries, it should be light enough to go about 10 mph on a flat battery, and as fast as 55 mph on a full charge, with a range of about 50 miles, sufficient for commuters. This tiny vehicle would mix well with the mix of traffic I envision, and would contribute no pollution or noise, unlike the hybrid cars. So let us call this vehicle an "electric HPV" and not a "car," a term reserved for the conventional automobile.

One other thing. People should be allowed to bring their bicycles right on the freeway train. The combination of bicycles and trains works well in good weather. They are even feasible in the rain, so long as there are no ICVs on the roads. They are not good in snow. I suggest skis. Either way, using muscle power every day to get to work and back is a good thing, not a bad thing. It is the only way we will ever shed our huge load of fat. We are a nation of fatties. We don't get enough exercise. Exercise should be part of the daily business of getting to work and coming home again, whether it is walking, roller-blading, bicycling, or skiing.

Electric taxis can be part of the mix, but not on two-way streets that have a freeway train car-bus going up and down it, which will always be in the right lane, next to the sidewalk. And that is where the taxis need to be as well. If a street has enough lanes and is one-way, one side could have taxis and the other side could have the free-way train-bus. Otherwise, some streets would have taxis and other streets would have train-bus cars. A taxi would not be a car. Not anything like an ICV. It has to be all-electric, rather Spartan, and tiny. It should be no wider than two seats, and not much taller than a seated person, with the batteries under each seat. It could run on batteries, or it could merge into a freeway train lane, raise power pickups and travel at the same high speed as the freeway trains, possibly about 100 mph when on a freeway, 25 mph on a city street. On streets, the robotic freeway cars obey the traffic lights automatically. The taxis and electric HPVs and bicyclist or roller-bladers must obey the lights as well. When running on batteries, the taxi should be limited by law and technology to 20 mph, the same speed as a bicycle. This is necessary to make a safe traffic mix.

It is much easier to replace cars and buses than trucks. Our economy depends on trucks in numerous ways we hardly notice. The general rule, however, is that heavy traffic must go back to the rails. This will be supplemented with a modification of the freeway train. Where we now see 18 wheelers blasting down the freeway, we will then see a steady stream of freeway trains in the fast lanes. Some will carry passengers, but many will be carrying freight, and will have a driver. If an object needs to be moved that is so large and heavy that it must go on a tractor trailer, then the tractor shall be battery electric, with movement restricted to the wee hours of night, with that section of road and side streets temporally closed off (by setting the traffic lights to red). No diesel engines will be permitted in the Metroplex, because of the fine particulates (that ugly black smoke!) which they put into the air. Even freight trains must switch to overhead-wire electric locomotives before entering the metroplex.

Like passenger cars, freight freeway trains will be controlled robotically, by computer, when on the freeway train routes. Like taxis or private electric cars, the operator must get in the adjoining lane and request entrance to the train lane, just as the operator must request turns, and request exit from the train lane. Much of the time, the freeway freight trains will be creeping around side streets and truck routes on batteries alone. There is no reason for passenger freeway trains to have batteries. Made of high strength steel, they will be light in weight, low to the ground, and capable of 200 mph.

You may notice that I have left a loophole for semi-trucks, provided that the tractor that pulls it is electrically powered. However, they must stay off the freeways, and take prescribed truck routes into and out of the metroplex. Garbage must be handled in a different way—no more garbage trucks. Firefighting and police work must also be handled in a different way. No more firefighting trucks, and no more police cars. There are cities which have no garbage pickup. Everyone has garbage disposals and trash compactors. Everyone is responsible for taking their own compacted trash to a rail spur, where it is loaded onto rail cars. Buildings must be retrofitted with sprinkler systems to handle fires. Local policemen must "walk the beat" as they did before cars. Fast response teams may come by helicopter.

Some American cities already have the nucleus of an excellent subway system, only needing to be extended and improved. At the very least, they should be extended out to the airports and to distant suburbs. Freeway trains supplement the subways, going as far as the most distant bedroom communities along the freeways.

Now what about inter-city travel and commerce? For passengers and fast packages or freight going from one coast to the other, there is a choice between a 15-20 hour trip in a freeway train, or a 6 hour trip on an airplane, or a one hour trip on the tube train, to be explained later. Long distance express trains would have a bar-restroom car. They would have to slow down to 100 mph when passing through a metroplex.

Eliminate the frustrations of travel in NYC and Los Angeles, and we shall see an immediate improvement in mood. The LA basin is beautiful when we can see it, and the mountains that rim the basin will be visible every day, instead of one day in a year, once ICVs have been banned from the basin. And since most people will be riding bicycles or HPVs, we will all become fit as a nation and heart disease will disappear.

Because of the great distance between cities in the United States, I have not proposed any change to our present system of transportation, which is the airplane. There is a possible alternative, and that is the evacuated magneto-levitation tube train, or "tube" for short. Magneto-levitation eliminates rolling friction; evacuating the air from the tube eliminates air friction. The next limit to velocity is going orbital, so such tube trains could reach a velocity of 17,000 mph, at least on straight stretches. And the arrangement of the continents in our present epoch makes it possible to connect every coastal city to the tube, on every continent, without ever needing to place the tube in water deeper than about 600 feet. It is important to note that the tube mainly lies on continental shelf, for its flatness, and the great circle routes it allows. And it makes getting right-of-ways much simpler. There are no pre-existing buildings that must be purchased and demolished.

If we look at a globe which exposes the ocean bottom, we can see that the continental coast surrounding the Arctic Ocean can serve as a "roundabout" or traffic circle, connecting all of the continents. Suppose we start at New York City. A northern branch of the tube goes through the fabled Northwest Passage (only a seafloor tube can freely use this route) and divides off Point Barrow, with the West Coast tube dropping Southeast, cutting through a tunnel through the Aleutian peninsula, and then down the West side of the Americas. A southwest branch takes the continental shelf to the once fabled Orient, to Tokyo and Hong Kong, Singapore and Sydney (having to bridge deep water in one place). This Oriental tube might be buried in the bottom of the Suez Canal to take it into the Mediterranean.

Now go back to the three-way split at Point Barrow. One branch would simply continue around the edge of the Arctic Ocean, having stations at the mouth of each of the major rivers in Russia which feed into the Arctic, and cutting a trench to wind up at St. Petersburg, or Petrograd, or whatever they call it this month. This branch gains access to the Baltic, with stops at all the major cities on the edge of the Baltic. This branch of the tube might meet up with the Oriental branch at Amsterdam.

Building the tube would be a colossal construction project. I propose using voidless concrete, with micro-fibers to stop crack propagation. A tube of such stuff would have nearly the tensile strength of steel, and a much greater compressive strength. Of course, the weight of the water would provide mostly compressive forces on it, however, the rare earthquake might provide tensile forces. Riding the tube in airtight cars should be a pleasure. No need for any sudden accelerations, so no need to buckle into seat belts. No worry about weather or season. With a double tube, where trains run in opposite directions, it should be possible to travel from one sea-side city to another anywhere in the world in half an hour, far faster than any airplane on the drawing boards, with no pollution or noise, no danger from terrorists or weather or birds or pilot error or the breakdown of the air controller's system. Sounds pretty utopian, doesn't it? Well, utopian dreaming is my greatest pleasure.

Hubbert's Peak

In a book called *Hubbert's Peak: The Impending World Oil Shortage*, Princeton professor Kenneth Deffeyes predicts that global oil production will peak between 2004 and 2008 and begin to slowly decline after that. Such gloomy predictions have been made before, for instance, in the 1970s book by the Club of Rome called *The Limits to Growth*, and they were wrong. So why should we believe this one? Because Professor Deffeyes uses the same techniques as M. King Hubbert, a Shell geologist who in 1956 predicted that US oil production would peak in the 1970s and forever after decline. He was absolutely right. Hubbert knew that the oil production in any particular field follows a Bell curve. He also knew that when the rate of new discoveries does not keep up with the growth of oil production, the amount remaining underground begins to fall. Globally, there have been no new fields discovered since the 1970s, despite the heroic efforts of geologists to look everywhere.

A second problem is that the supply and demand curves for oil are like those for food; they are inelastic. Let me explain. If we plot the supply Vs price curve for any commodity, it is generally true that the higher the price, the higher the supply. It is also generally true that if we plot the demand Vs price curve for that same commodity, the higher the price, the less the demand. The point at which these two curves cross sets both the market price, and the production level. In the short run at least, the supply and demand curves are pretty flat, both for food and for gasoline. People who have no alternative to cars for getting to work or to go shopping will buy about the same amount of gasoline whatever the price. The demand declines slowly with price. Similarly, the availability of gasoline does not go up instantly when the price goes up. The supply curve increases slowly with price. The result is price volatility, which we have seen in 2001. Small shortages led to huge increases in the price of gasoline. Small declines in demand led to an equally dramatic fall in the price of gasoline.

What we must consider is a time not far off when no increase in price will increase the supply of crude oil. Only the richest nations will be able to afford crude oil at all. And as time goes on, even the demand of rich nations can no longer be met, and in one way or another, supply will be rationed. It is hard to believe that we are close to such a time, but according to the Hubbert analysis, expect it by the end of this decade or soon after. The Century of Oil will have come to an end.

If we assume that this Cassandra warning by Professor Deffeyes is ignored, and no efforts are made to create alternatives, then a global economic depression in the 2010s can be expected. Assuming world leaders were not distracted by the war on terrorists and decided to create alternatives, we must start now.

In the long run, we must have the Solar-Hydrogen economy, and we must have mass transit, run on electricity. But there are still some technological hurdles to be overcome to make that practical. It would be nice if water could be separated into hydrogen and oxygen by pure sunlight in the presence of a catalyst. Both the hydrogen and the oxygen would be shipped in pipelines and stored in vast tanks. It would be nice if we had affordable fuel cells to use that stored hydrogen and oxygen and convert it to electricity, in an efficient manner which only has water as its final product. No pollution of any kind. The final part of that equation would be mass transit and freight trains drawing electrical power from overhead wires, while some personal transportation of people and goods would operate on batteries.

If Al Gore had been elected President in the year 2000, perhaps a major technological effort would have been mounted to create the Solar-Hydrogen economy, with electrical mass transit and electrical trains. It is more likely, I think, that nothing will be done until the price of oil becomes astronomical, and it finally becomes clear to everyone that we are finally going to run out of it.

Assuming the US supply of natural gas holds up for awhile, it would be fairly easy to convert vehicles to run on Liquefied Natural Gas, or LNG. Modest pressures suffice to liquefy it. It would take up all of the trunk space on a car, but I suspect that a rapid conversion to Natural Gas and to LNG would be the first response. People who rely on oil fired furnaces for winter heating would have to convert to natural gas or to a large tank of LNG. However, the supply of natural gas is also finite. I have not seen a Hubbert analysis of natural gas, but I think this would only postpone the inevitable by a few decades.

Many countries, including China and the US, have vast deposits of coal. If a way could be found to use coal without polluting the atmosphere, that is likely to be the next option. I suspect that nuclear power will come back into favor as well, and I am confident that we now know how to avoid incidents like Chernobyl or Three Mile Island. Of course, a great deal of our coal will probably be exported to Japan, which has none. Even LNG may be exported to Japan, because they have no natural gas deposits either. Undoubtedly, Japan will increasingly resort to nuclear power. One reason for nuclear power is to use up Plutonium, a man-made element with a half-life of 100,000 years, if I remember correctly. I would put the plutonium reactors inside existing nuclear plants. No one wants to build any more nuclear plants. I would suggest a traveling factory for reprocessing spent fuel rods, so the plutonium in them can be used in the power plant, and there would be no danger of it getting loose and into the hands of terrorists. Highly radioactive elements could be used in the plant to heat water and make steam. What is left would be of little danger and could be vitrified and safely transported by rail to permanent storage facilities.

In the long run, over the course of this millennium, first uranium, then coal will run out. The supply may be large, but it is not infinite. And both are non-renewable resources. Those countries that convert earliest to Solar-Hydrogen and electrical mass transit will have the fewest bumps in its path. Eventually, all must do so.

The Beautiful City

Beautiful is not what springs immediately to mind when one thinks about Twentieth Century cities like New York or Los Angeles. No, the images are those of schizophrenic or alcoholic bums on the sidewalk, gangs as ruthless and barbaric as any ancient Vandal or Visigoth, and oppressive, monotonous monoliths that leave the streets in perpetual shade. The pungent aroma of ozone and diesel fumes attacks the nasal passages and makes the eyes water. Gridlock. Stress. Serial murder. Cannibalism. Conspicuous consumption next to burned-out, desolate wastelands. But we need not accept this condition. After all, we built it. We can build it anew.

A Theory of Aesthetics: Beauty is intelligible novelty. In order for there to be intelligible novelty, there must first be recognition, i.e., some level of familiarity and expectation. The information lies in the novel or surprising details within this overall pattern of recognition. The setup for a joke presents one expectation, which the punchline contradicts. It is the unpredictability in a relationship that keeps it going. If total predictability sets in, the friendship or relationship wanes. That is why our best friends are people who make us laugh, or think, even if we seem to have nothing in common. Most of us love sunsets, surf, forests, mountains, the Sonoran Desert, and clouds, because we all have a certain level of expectation and familiarity with these things, yet there is variety in the details.

Aesthetics is whatever we do to not-be-bored. Sex, food,

getting warmed up or cooled down, or coming in out of the rain, can all provide a moment of pleasure. But once the need is satisfied, we are satiated. We are never satiated with aesthetic pleasure. The First Law of Aesthetics is that Aesthetic pleasure is intelligible novelty.

Architecture: From the First Law of Aesthetics, we can immediately conclude that the endlessly repeated, identical, rectangular window treatments on 20th Century High-Rise boxes represent the nadir of aesthetic sensibility. Such buildings hold no more aesthetic interest than a shoebox. So city-dwellers hurry along, eyes on the ground. Only tourists look up at the forest of towers, impressed by their sheer size, if nothing else.

It may be hard to find rules for beauty, but it is not hard to find rules for monotony. The relentless application of any geometric rule (such as the rule of plumb and horizontal lines meeting at right angles, common to domestic architecture) must lead to monotony. Even with row houses, each house can be differentiated by color, as they are in Amsterdam. As Jane Jacobs has pointed out, row houses with a mix of offices, businesses, and walk up apartments along a curving street, with wide sidewalks, stoops, and trees . . . well, this is paradise for human beings. The front surface of each row house need not be flat. It could have a subtle "bay window" effect. While such apartments would have a freight elevator in the back (which many tenants would use), the height of such buildings will rarely exceed five or six floors, because that is as much as most people would care to climb. Surprisingly enough, this kind of architecture provides the maximum number of households per acre, 100-200, better than high rises, and of course, far better than the 3 households per acre in suburbia. A great city is designed for walking, which means it must be compact, and not allowed to sprawl all over the landscape.

The endless repetition of rectangular window units is not only boring, it makes it impossible to see the entire building as a single shape. Near the Battery Park, on the tip of Manhattan, there is a cylindrical skyscraper which avoids any window treatment and thus becomes a single sculpture. The reflective glass curtain wall has an attractive blue color. Unfortunately, more boxes have been built around it, somewhat hiding its beauty. The Dallas skyline features many "sculptural" skyscrapers, which make for an attractive skyline. I am not suggesting that skyscrapers are inherently bad, or that we should pull them down. But new cities may be built in a new way.

With the dawn of the 21st Century, we see a new kind of aesthetics being developed on computers, which really does succeed in escaping the box. See "The Sky Line; Building on a Computer Screen," by Paul Goldberger, *The New Yorker*, March 12, 2001. The new software not only allows the architect to freely create non-rectangular three-dimensional shapes, it also does the engineering. It was exactly this kind of software that allowed the engineering of Frank Gehry's Guggenheim Museum in Bilbao, which may very well be the forerunner of a whole new and distinctive 21st Century architecture.

Human Factors: Architecture should be restful; it should make solitude or gregariousness equally possible. Architecture has an enormous, unrecognized influence on social life. The pleasure we find in friends is aesthetic pleasure. It ultimately boils down to intelligible novelty. It makes one day at work different from another. In a happy office, there is a kaleidoscope of human relationships, which change from day to day. The difference between a happy office and one where people are sullen and glum often depends on the precise layout of each floor, and the positioning of break rooms, coffee machines, copiers, elevators, the use of glass walls (with shades), and the flow of human traffic. All these architectural details determine whether it is easy or hard to meet others, and whether it is easy or hard to have any solitude.

In some office buildings, there are whole floors of desks, without partitions. No solitude. In others, there is a maze of corridors, with nothing but closed doors and no way to orient oneself as to direction. No human contact. Such buildings are machines built for machines. But contrary to the Bauhaus school of architecture, we are not machines.

Urban Design: The principle of intelligible novelty can be applied to the layout of entire cities. At least until 1965, Paris consisted in row houses, for the most part. Only a few special buildings, such as the Notre Dame cathedral, were freestanding. Some features of Paris simply grew, without plan, giving us the narrow, winding streets that remain from Medieval times.

Some features of interesting cities were consciously superimposed on a chaotic Medieval pattern, for instance, the broad, tree-lined boulevards radiating from a central traffic circle that we find in Paris. The combination works beautifully. We want some order, and some disorder. We want some planning, and some things we want to leave to the accidents of time or topography. Seattle and San Francisco are interesting cities partly because they are built on steep hills, around irregular bodies of water. While freeways may go slashing through, ignoring topography, the ordinary residential street does not.

City planning produces brutally monotonous designs, but not if we made the Ideal of Intelligible Novelty our highest priority. It applies to the design of cities, to the design of buildings, and to the layout of offices. This is the Ideal of the Beautiful City.

Cars, Dogs or People: One can design a city for people, which gives us 1965 Paris, a city of row houses with interesting architectural details. Or we can design it for dogs, which gives us the typical suburb, three households per acre, to permit the backyards full of yapping dogs, bored, ignored, with nothing their breed was bred to do. Or we can design it for cars, which gives us Los Angeles, where no one walks, where no one knows their neighbors.

My suggestion about pets in a metroplex is that they have to stay indoors, although they could be taken for walks on a leash, and there could be dog parks where they could run freely. Not for defecation purposes, however. Dog owners must have indoor doggie toilets, with swinging doors that the dog can push through.

While in the dog toilet, an electric fan quietly vents odors out of doors. After the dog leaves, it flushes. Such a dog toilet would cost at least $1000 and must be installed by a plumber. Dogs could easily be trained to use it. Dogs would be taken out on leashes only for exercise. These rules are only for the metroplex. Out in the country or in small towns, they will probably have more relaxed rules.

Dangerous Dogs: Breeds of dogs that are known to have killed human beings I would ban altogether, not only from the enclosed metroplex, but from every town or city or suburb. They might be allowed in rural areas. I do not subscribe to the "vicious dog" theory or the "vicious breed" theory. The rules of behavior are exactly the same for all members of the canine species, whether wolf, coyote or dog. Every canine is friendly, gentle and tolerant with its own pack, but with any living creature not of its pack, if its anger exceeds its fear, it will attack. Dog owners never seem to understand this. They think just because it is gentle with its own pack (made up of humans and other pets), it will be gentle with everyone. Not so. A ferocious wolf will allow the puppies to step on him, pounce on his tail, or pull his ears. But let a stranger approach, and it is all fury.

The factors that influence fear and anger are also the same for all canines. Canines are territorial. Any living thing not in its pack which invades its territory makes it angry. As for fear, canines are more afraid of adults than of children, and they are more afraid of humans standing their ground than ones that run. Thus, the very first thing my Daddy taught me about dogs, was "never run from one." Even a child is unlikely to be attacked if it stands still.

So why single out certain breeds of dog to be banished from urban or suburban precincts? Merely because of their size and strength. These are the breeds that are large and strong enough to kill a human being, and that includes Rotweilers, Dobermans, pit bulls, bulldogs, and the larger breeds of Shepherds and Hounds. Miniature poodles are just as likely to attack a stranger child who runs from them. It is just that miniature breeds are too small to do much damage. I might mention that there are breeds of large dogs which have never harmed people, probably because they were bred to be retrievers, rather than hunters.

Civilization and Permanence: As Lord Clark said, "Civilisation has something to do with permanence." This leads me to wonder whether we have as yet built an American civilization. According to Lord Clark, we still live in wigwams in the US, which I take to mean, wood frame houses, with wood or asphalt shingles, paperboard sidings, plastic doodads on the windows, and everything else required to make a house unlivable in about thirty years. Civilization requires some confidence in the future, and some care about our great-grandkids great-grandkids. Perhaps we haven't achieved that. But we should. I propose to make it a law that everything non-consumable be designed to last forever, given the prescribed maintenance and repair. This is particularly necessary for buildings, roads and bridges. Thus, build houses and buildings out of galvanized steel, use galvanized steel sheeting, use brick, glass, bronze or stone for the exterior, and roof it in ceramic tiles, bronze sheeting, slate, or metal. There is a new type of metal roofing which looks like slate. This might make houses more expensive, but so what? They would last forever, and be passed down, generation to generation.

Great Cities and Metaphysics: I have one last point to make about the beautiful city and about utopian analysis in general. In this book we find a rational, non-metaphysical approach to social problems. However, no great civilization has ever existed without a great metaphysics to go with it. Nor has there ever been a grand architecture without metaphysics. Can we imagine the great monuments of Ancient Egypt or Medieval Europe without the spiritual beliefs and energy that went into them? Therefore, utopian analysis cannot answer all questions, and does not suffice for a peak civilization. For that we must turn to the science of metaphysics, based on reproducible mystical states and on symbolic revelation. We will get to that later.

Saving the Planet

On April 18, 2000, Nova and Frontline combined to present a thorough analysis on PBS of the complex relationships between poverty, energy and global warming. Let's start with the global warming. Since 1990, we have entered unknown territory, because our CO2 levels are higher than they have been in the past 350,000 years and continue to rise. On the other hand, there was 18 times as much CO2 in the atmosphere during the Mesozoic as there is now. This produced a global tropical climate, where tropical plants and animals lived in polar regions and there were no polar icecaps. Experts disagree about how much global warming there will be, if the amount of carbon dioxide in the atmosphere doubles, which it is expected to do in the 21st Century. Estimates of the increase in global temperature range from one degree Celsius to seven degrees Celsius. A five degree increase in global temperature would melt the ice caps and drown coastal cities and low lying countries.

The problem is complicated because there are positive feedbacks to consider, which would amplify the warming effects of more CO2 (low level clouds), and there are negative feedbacks which would dampen the warming effects (high level clouds). And everyone agrees that special rivers in the oceans, such as the Gulf Stream, have enormous effects on climate. The Gulf Stream is the surface part of a world wide flow which sinks to the bottom in the North Atlantic and after a global journey, connects again to the Gulf Stream on the surface. But no one has been able to model the effect on the Gulf Stream of increasing CO_2.

One significant fact which emerged from this program is that mankind now uses 10 terawatts of energy. This will certainly increase to 40 or 50 terawatts as China and India industrialize. Where will this energy come from? In the short term, almost certainly from fossil fuels, primarily coal. Why not biomass? It would take the world's entire arable land to produce the 10 terawatts we presently use. And the area of arable land is not likely to increase. Why not solar? If used directly to produce electricity, we would only have electricity for the day time. Wind power is erratic, and the world has already damned most of its rivers for hydroelectric power. Why not nuclear? There is no safe way of disposing of the radioactive by-products, including the nuclear plants themselves.

My proposal is a drastic increase in efficiency, coupled with solar-hydrogen. In other words, the solar farms would produce hydrogen, which can be stored, rather than electricity. Efficiency will often require replacement of existing technologies. For instance, in my "gridlock" chapter, I propose banning ICVs (cars, buses, trucks) from the metroplex and the super-highways which connect them, in favor of a combination of electric trains and bicycles. This would have multiple benefits. We would be in much better shape from walking or biking as part of our daily commute. No more smog or acid rain. Auto "accidents" are a major cause of premature death. No more gridlock. We would all be able to get to work on time. And it would be a much more energy efficient way of moving people around the metroplex than using cars. It might be ten times more efficient. Turn off the streetlights to cut down on light pollution, eliminate chemical fertilizers and return to the use of horses and oxen on farms (they live on hay produced on the same farm) and we could maintain the same standard of living on one-tenth the energy. This makes solar-hydrogen a feasible alternative. Finding and adopting the efficient green economy will take time, perhaps a Century, during which we will be burning fossil fuels. So, I propose that during this transition time power plants at least should be required to capture the CO_2, and sequester it underground.

The Solar-Hydrogen Option: "Green" means ecological, which means sustainable, not just for a lifetime, but for millions of years. The Green economy uses hydrogen or possibly both hydrogen and oxygen transported and stored under pressure in steel tanks, generated by solar energy farms in the Arid Zone (between the Rockies and the Sierras). This eliminates smog, acid rain, and the Greenhouse Effect, since the only by-product of burning hydrogen in an external combustion system, such as a gas / steam turbine, is water vapor. No hydro-carbons, no sulfides, no nitrides.

An even better technology is to combine pure hydrogen and pure oxygen in a fuel cell to produce electricity.

According to the Environmental Defense Fund (EDF)(see *Newsweek's* Periscope in the December 6, 1999 issue) we must quit burning fossil fuels and switch to solar power now. Computer models suggest that fossil fuel burning, methane production in rice paddies, in cows, and in termites, will all raise the Earth's temperature by as much as 10 degrees as early as 2200. That would certainly melt the ice caps, raise sea levels several hundred feet, and drown coastal cities around the world. What we do in the 21st Century will determine our climate for the next thousand years.

We do not quite have all the technology necessary for this. Ideally, sunlight is focused by double parabolic troughs to a quartz tube filled with a catalyst system which separates pure water into hydrogen and oxygen, which migrates' in opposite directions out of the tube. Such a trough does not have to track the sun. It only needs to change its angle of inclination each day to match the sun's angle of inclination.

Europe could make use of the deserts of Africa for their solar energy farms, making some kind of deal with the nations that own those deserts. China and Japan can make use of the deserts of central Asia. While I'm sure Solar-Hydrogen is the only long-term solution to mankind's energy needs, in the short term, America could first switch to an all natural gas economy. We also have the problem of getting rid of Plutonium, which is a man-made element used in nuclear weapons. It is possible that the only permanent way of disposing of this dangerous element is to burn it in tamper-proof nuclear power plants, which are simply abandoned in place when they run out of Plutonium.

Recycling: Garbage is my term for all the problems that come under the term "recycling." Do complex problems require complex governmental rules? Not necessarily. All we need to do is require retail stores to add the cost of recycling to the cost of the product. In effect, a store will buy its products from two companies, one which produces it and one which reduces it. And let there be full competition on both ends. Consumers DO wind up paying both costs, one way or another. If both costs are included in the initial cost of an item, the market itself will drive the economy to ecology.

Let's just look at a few examples. The cost of manufacturing those plastic 6-pack holders is pennies. The cost of retrieving them from the oceans is astronomical. Thus, 6-packs in plastic pop holders have an astronomical cost at the checkout stand, and cease to exist. The same thing is true of monofilament fishing line.

What shall we do with plain old garbage, the kind that big trucks pick up at your curb twice a week? Handle it a different way. Garbage trucks are the only kind of heavy truck regularly in residential areas. If we can eliminate the need for it, then the neighborhood can be enclosed with a impregnable wall, given a single checkpoint for entering and leaving, and the people will be able to sleep at night, knowing they are protected. Requiring working garbage disposals will help with some things. Every enclosed neighborhood will have a spur of railroad track and a door in the wall for the train to pick up full cars and drop off empties. There will be shredders for plastics, smashers for cans, fork lifts for dumping the result into railroad cars and even a huge community composter, which will take grass clippings, leaves, household refuse, and shredded limbs from trees. The cars will have bins for each separate type of plastic, metal, or toxic items, such as batteries or old cans of paint.

National Zoning: Conservation and preservation constitute another side of ecology. Major conservation of soils, trees, beaches, species and cultures could be achieved by national zoning. Zoning is a cheap way for a government to impose standards on an area, since it is not necessary to buy up land for the purpose. There should be a forest zone, where loggers could only log forests they had themselves grown. Make them live up to their advertising as tree farmers. This preserves remaining national forests and even old growth forests on private land. Also, we should never allow mining, logging, grazing or roads in our National Forests. But we could allow forest retreats to be built, if they could process and recycle their own garbage.

We could also require that all framing members in houses (studs, rafters, tresses) be made of galvanized steel. Steel is already cheaper than wood, and is in every respect superior. It's just not traditional.

There should be beach zones and flood plain zones, where any houses built are non-insurable. Given enough time, the weather will clear the beaches and floodplains for us. No more FEMA, no more bail-outs. Agricultural land should be zoned agricultural. This means it can never be turned into suburbs or industry, never flooded by dams, never crossed by freeways. It can only be used for agriculture. This will deflate the speculative value of this land, so farmers can afford to own it. It will also maintain the green belt around metroplexes and halt urban sprawl.

The two most interesting zones are the arid zone and the prairie zone. The prairie zone is triangle shaped, with the wide part at the top, and the narrow part at the bottom. It is bounded by the Rockies. The Eastern edge used to be near the eastern edge of Oklahoma, Kansas, Nebraska and the Dakotas. This region was originally tall-grass prairie in the east, shading into short grass prairie west of the 100th meridian.

The arid zone is the intermountain west, the vast, underpopulated region between the coastal sierras and the Rockies. This is a triangle shaped region, broad at the base, and tapering to a narrow neck in eastern Washington state. Embedded in it are several metropolitan zones, including Los Angeles, San Diego, Salt Lake City, Las Vegas, Reno, Phoenix and Albuquerque. All emigrants should be restricted to the arid zone exclusive of the metropolitan zones for two generations. This is where we need population. We must take immigrants, unless the promise of the Statue of Liberty as the "Mother of Exiles" is to be broken. But we can at least specify where they can and cannot live.

The arid zone needs population because it will become the source of the nation's energy. In addition, I wish to restore the 1830 desert ecology and prairie ecology in the name of preservation of species and even of cultures. To that end, herding and agriculture cannot be permitted in either the arid zone or the prairie zone. Furthermore, all domestic livestock (even those growing wild) must be eliminated, except on Indian reservations, which are sovereign nations.

The prairie Indians, such as the Lakota, have never done well on reservations. They could be given their beautiful prairie back, and the huge herds of bison, making a good cash income on the side hosting visiting safaris, and taking them on Buffalo hunts. Only Native Americans are allowed to hunt prairie game with anything but a camera, and they must use bows and arrows. The prairie zone becomes the world's largest animal preserve, cultural preserve, and tourist attraction for safaris.

The idea of a Buffalo common has been proposed before, by the Professors Popper of Rutgers, who point out the decline to near non-existence of human population on what was originally prairie. Like the original desert ecology, the prairie is fragile. Domestic livestock destroy both, and must be banned ruthlessly. Most parts of the prairie do not make good farmland. Indeed, large parts of the prairie seen by Washington Irving in the 1830's now consists in abandoned farm land grown up in scrubby, weedy trees like the red cedar and scrub oak. Other parts consist in a thin layer of soil over desert sand dunes, and could easily revert to sand dunes after a long drought if they continue to be grazed or farmed. Those parts of the prairie which are flat and have deep soils and make good crops of hard red winter wheat should be left as agricultural islands in the midst of the sea of grass. Towns and cities inside the prairie zone are also islands, not part of the prairie zone.

One strip capable of supporting cities and intensive agriculture lies over the Ogallala aquifer, which I propose to refill with water from the Mississippi, pumped across Iowa. The closest part of the aquifer to the river is in eastern Nebraska. By refilling it, it will overflow to those parts of the aquifer further south, passing more or less along the boundary between Colorado-Kansas and Texas-New Mexico, a region otherwise utterly desolate and devoid even of interesting desert vegetation. This is one of two massive waterworks I propose, the other one pumping water from the Columbia and other Pacific rivers over or through the mountains to the arid zone.

Prairie is an ecology born of fire. Prairie consists in all and only those plants and animals that can survive periodic burning. That excludes trees, weeds and brush, although stands of wild blackberries and sand plums can survive in the creek bottoms. These are favorite foods of black bears, if they can be re-established.

Few people living in the prairie zone have ever seen prairie. The rangelands sparsely populated by a few cows or sheep are not prairie, because domestic animals selectively destroy the higher grasses such as big and little bluestem, and the hundreds of flowering species, many of them legumes, leaving only wire-grass, broom-weed and buffalo grass. The only true prairie left are those patches of prairie called "meadows" which are cut once a year for prairie hay. These small fields have never been grazed or plowed, but we lose more of them each year, to agriculture, grazing, or to urban sprawl.

True prairie is incredibly beautiful. And it smells wonderful, unlike domestic lawn grasses. It is a complex ecology of hundreds of species, many of which bloom with large showy spikes sometime in the growing season. In fall, the tall bluestem turns purple (seen as blue in the distance by early visitors), while in winter it assumes various metallic colors of gold, silver and electrum. When it turns dull brown in late winter, it is time to burn it.

Throughout the arid region of the west, water is precious, though not always expensive. One of the first rules we should institute is a free market for water rights.

The next rule is no sprinkler irrigation, drip or soak only. This eliminates those fabulously wasteful alfalfa fields in the desert. Alfalfa can be grown back east. Let's not waste our precious water on that. Another rule is: no livestock. There is not much livestock as is, but there is some in river valleys of Idaho and Utah. Next rule: desert plants only. It is criminal to plant lawn grass in Phoenix or LA when the arid loving succulents and cacti are so much more interesting and exotic.

Many people originally moved to the southwest to escape hay fever. That only works if the eastern pollen producing (water intensive) plants are left behind. Indeed, they should be actively rooted out and destroyed, since pollen is pollution to those with hay-fever or asthma.

Arid zone cities must be required to recycle their water. Outflow from the sewage treatment system goes through special treatment and right back into the water treatment system as input! Or maybe it would be used for irrigating parks and golf greens.

· This can be done with artificial wetlands, which can double as a park, for the final processing of this outflow. The outflow of the artificial wetlands could be the purest water in the country. The outflow from modern sewage plants is already required to be of high-quality for environmental reasons. It is merely discolored and slightly odoriferous, being full of dissolved and suspended organic material. It makes wonderful fertilizer.

Algae and bacteria will grow on the organic material in the water, removing it. Tiny crustacea, insects, and fish will eat the algae and bacteria. Larger fish and other birds will eat the crustacea, insects and fish. Some of the larger fish will be caught and eaten (with perfect safety) by Sunday fishermen. The last stage is to put the water through ion exchange membranes which only allow water molecules through, no salt or viruses or bacteria.

The arid zone can be a beautiful and varied place, with its numerous mountain ranges, canyons, deserts and arid flora and fauna. All that is needed is a little bit of infrastructure to make it economically viable as a place to live. The federal government must provide this. Chief among the requirements is water. One possible source is the Columbia river. If half of the Columbia could be pumped to the east side of the coastal range, and then brought down into and throughout the Arid Zone, finally dumping into the Colorado, the water needs of the region could be met, so long as everyone shows proper reverence for the value of water. Some of the water is feedstock for the solar energy farms.

Who builds and maintains these solar farms and all the other infrastructure of pipelines and roadways? Immigrant homesteaders, of course. It is run like the Habitat project, except here we are dealing in adobe and Mexican saltillo tile. Homesteading is done a village at a time. The immigrants learn various specialties and help one another to build a village from local materials, and then create a network of pipelines and roads extending outward from it, connecting to the master network built by the federal government. Within each large region to be served by a village, (which should include both mountain and desert) the villagers pick their own spot for their village.

Once established, each village has a cash crop export in the form of hydrogen piped to the nearest major collector line, and make use of drip irrigation to establish local garden crops, to make themselves fairly self-sufficient.

Green Farming: My last point of ecology could be called conservation of the soil, except it is much more complicated than that. It is more complicated because fertilizer and pesticides and other "icides" washing off industrial agri-business kill lakes and rivers and even seas. And the residue on the product is slowly killing us as well, since it is all carcinogenic. Welfare programs are involved, since farmers have been on the dole for fifty years, and it is an important part of our economy. Like so many other problems, this one appears insoluble to Washington bureaucrats. It is not so complicated. First ban ICVs on the farms as in the cities, and return to horses and oxen. Secondly, ban all non-biological commercial fertilizer, pesticide, herbicide and fungicide, all made from fossil fuels.

Horses can reproduce; tractors cannot. Fuel for horses can be grown on the farm as crops or by-products of crops which humans cannot consume. Horses and oxen not only do useful work, they produce fertilizer. Oxen can survive quite well on straw, cornstalks, corncobs, and even paper or sawdust. Horses require a somewhat richer diet, but they also eat hay. This is not a proposal to return to the backbreaking labor of the 1930's, when my father worked sunup to sundown all summer with a team of mules to plow a quarter section of wheat. The oldest technology can be combined with the newest, to create the robotic farm.

Plowhorses are not expensive. They are not like the thoroughbreds that fetch fabulous prizes because they can run fast. Plowhorses can reproduce cheaply, and live on grass and hay. A farmer can have many teams of horses, all hitched to implements controlled by a computer program, which opens and closes gates, pulls reins or steers a wheel by radio control. The robotic farm implement will have electronic sensors. Motive power and fertilizer is provided by livestock. Because it is robotic, one farmer can run a dozen teams simultaneously. Every morning and evening, he has a production line process of harnessing or unharnessing, feeding, watering, and in general, animal husbandry. No doubt he goes out from time to time during the day to check on his teams, just as if they were hired hands.

The farmer receives the same number of dollars for a bushel of wheat now as fifty or one hundred years ago. The same number of dollars. Yet, the land, the tractors, the fuel, the fertilizer have all gone up ten-fold or a hundred-fold since the mechanization of the farms. It is not surprising that farmers are going bankrupt, blindly following the advice of the county extension agents of the local land grant college. How do we eliminate the ruinous surpluses which have made grain and milk dirt cheap for a hundred years?

The answer is grower's associations, as found in the citrus business. It should be the law that wholesale farmers have to belong to the grower's association for their commodity. Otherwise, the government stays out of it. The association decides exactly how many acres each grower will plant, and how many bushels he will sell on what date. In other words, the grower's associations carefully regulate supply so that it just barely meets demand. They are also given full control over exports and imports, and full power of attorney to sell the product. So the producers set the price, not the miller or butcher. Wheat or beef farmers could decide to stay out of the international market, if they wished, since the international commodities market is always dirt poor. They can prevent fast-food places from importing cheap Brazilian beef, which will help preserve the rain-forest as well as keep domestic prices high. The Japanese and the French also wish to keep their agriculture sector out of the international free trade market, and we should too. This is all part of conserving the soil, and preserving rural culture.

Won't this increase consumer prices at the supermarket? Not as much as one might expect. If the farmer simply gave the miller the wheat that goes into a loaf of bread, it reduces the final price by a nickel. Thus, a ten-fold increase in wheat prices adds fifty cents to the price of bread.

By banning the use of grain and supplements to "feed out"

livestock and pork, we could instantly make all our domestic beef and pork a health food. It seems an ecological crime to feed grain to an animal that can prosper on paper, or sawdust, or acorns, or alfalfa. It seems almost an insult to that species of animal. And if the result has to go in a pot roast, or a true pit barbecue . . . we're going to have to ban those backyard charcoal grills anyway. They pollute the air. And once again, we may be just in time to save or resurrect a culture, that of the family farm and the rural communities, along with saving the land and our own health. And this is done without creating a bureaucracy (at least not a government bureaucracy) and with no red tape.

A Social Safety Net

Social Safety Nets: The platform programs include Freeway Trains, MakeWork, Old Hotels, Soup Kitchens, Free Clinics, Underground Villages and educational vouchers (discussed in another chapter). This is like a platform or safety net. No one can fall below this level of well-being, no matter what their difficulties. The subtle difference between these and welfare programs is that anyone can grab a meal at the Soup Kitchen, or a place to stay at the Old Hotel, even if they are as rich as Bill Gates. These programs are not based on the socialist ideal of "from each according to their ability, to each according to their need." The platform programs are free and available to all, no matter how wealthy. I fully expect everyone to use the freeway trains, one of the platform programs. And at least at some time in their lives (possibly in youth, or in old age) most people will make use of the Soup Kitchens and the Old Hotels. The ideal behind these programs is reciprocity. Most of us are two paychecks from being homeless. So we can at least imagine ourselves in need of the Platform Programs, if we have a run of bad luck.

The Homeless: The ragged homeless that clutter our streets by the thousand in the US accuse us of all of a lack of empathy or bad planning. Addicts and alcoholics could be sent to the addiction sanitorium, where people spend six months under fairly monastic conditions, with some psychiatric treatment. Schizophrenics will go first to state mental hospitals, where some will stay, but most will go to half-way houses, much like boarding houses, except that everyone has to produce a urine sample on demand. A good many homeless are merely homeless, so give them a home, in the Old Hotels, and something to eat in the Soup Kitchens, and a job in MakeWork. Old Hotels are often abandoned schools, hotels, monasteries or almost any type of large public building.

Old Hotels provide shelter for all comers without qualification (unless there is a restraint order against an ex-husband whose wife lives in the Old Hotel, or similar situations). It is a goal of all platform programs not to compete with private enterprise, so no effort will be spent making Old Hotels luxurious. Safe and attractive, but not luxurious. In some climates, they are not airconditioned. If the carpet is in bad shape, and there is good hardwood flooring or ceramic tile underneath, the carpet will be removed. The important thing is to run such places with humanity, preserve their natural beauty and make them welcoming communities to all who need them, run by people on MakeWork.

By the way, how can an Old Hotel always have an open door, no matter how many show up on a given night? Most travelers will stay in dormitories with triple bunk beds. The rooms will mostly be reserved for permanent residents. If the dormitories fill up, cots and sleeping bags will be brought out. An Old Hotel will redirect some travelers to nearby Old Hotels, but the system as a whole will never turn people away.

Guaranteed Employment: MakeWork is designed firstly to give a guaranteed job to anyone who needs one, and secondly to accomplish tasks that are of value to society which cannot easily be accomplished by the market economy. Public artworks, for instance, such as the tiling of all the gray concrete surfaces in urban environments. Or creating and maintaining public parks, and keeping everything picked up and clean. And it includes running the Old Hotels and the Soup Kitchens.

One kind of MakeWork is tending to community orchards and gardens and vineyards and berry brambles and asparagus beds to provide fresh fruits and vegetables to nearby Soup

Kitchens in season. Nothing is served out of season, except for crops that go into the cellar, i.e. potatoes, onions, garlic, beets, squash, apples and pears. An overflow of fresh cabbage is turned to sauerkraut. An overflow of fresh tomatoes is made into tomato stock, suitable for soups or sauces, or sun-dried. Nothing is purchased at a supermarket. Corn on the cob is served on the day it is picked, and likewise with tomatoes and melons.

MakeWork is sometimes Make-An-Entrepreneur. In particular, with the cars gone, I wish to re-introduce the pushcarts to city streets, as the easiest way for a person to become his own boss. MakeWork can help and try not to meddle. I can imagine pushcarts that make handmade shoes to a last made from a cast of a person's foot and ankle. Hand-tailored clothes could be done with pushcarts, i.e. measurements could be taken and materials chosen. People too disabled to be on the streets could work in the sewing shops that make the clothes. Most of us have trouble finding clothes or shoes that really fit "off the rack." It also sometimes happens that a particular style that we like is discontinued. The MakeWork artisan can duplicate anything, or design an original to the customer's specifications. These are just a few examples of the kind of unmet needs which MakeWork could satisfy.

The first requirement of both the Soup Kitchens and the food pushcarts is that no one is made sick by eating there! Workers must scrub up like surgeons, put on clean clothes and a hairnet, wear surgical masks and rubber gloves and use tongs to handle food. We must rule out any possibility of Salmonella or E. Coli or viruses being spread from raw food to the finished product, or from a worker to the finished product. Thus, all workers must be carefully checked for infectious diseases before being allowed in the kitchen or behind the serving line. Soup Kitchens should confine themselves to foods thoroughly cooked, such as soups, chilies, baked goods, casseroles, or pickled items.

No One Should Go Hungry: What is on the bill of fare at a Soup Kitchen? A variety of hearty soups, such as potato soup or vegetable stew, many kinds of fresh bread, such as corn bread, and a variety of flavors of pickled eggs, and catfish served in a variety of ways, and cheddar cheese in large wheels. Raw fruits and vegetables, in season. Sauerkraut, beets, winter squash and potatoes in the off season.

Except for farm fed catfish, no meat or seafood is served, as a way of reducing competition with ordinary restaurants. Soup kitchens are cafeterias. Bags of raw coffee beans are not expensive at the dock, so I suggest that each soup kitchen roast, grind and brew their own coffee. Barley and hops are not expensive either, so I suggest a micro-brewery for every soup kitchen, with a limit of one liter per customer per day. This is a hearty and robust brew. No wine, and no milk, and no more milk subsidies. (Infants should be breast-fed, and the rest of us can get calcium in many ways, from tofu, for instance).

Eggs are pickled on intensive five acre farms, given out as MakeWork. The eggs are delivered in five gallon jars. Cheese is cut from a large wheel of cheddar. Catfish are steamed, skinned and deboned at the catfish farm. So the Soup Kitchens get catfish in cooked, sterilized, boneless pieces each about the size of a lamb chop, to be dried and smoked, barbecued, batter fried, deep fat fried, broiled with dill and lemon juice, pickled like Herring, or served as is with malt vinegar.

Low Cost Housing: Next on the list are Underground Villages, my form of low cost housing. How can a traditional frame house be built for two or three thousand dollars? It can't! Too much hand-labor, requiring skilled craftsmen. It requires an unconventional design and the labor of those who will live in the Village to build housing for a few thousand dollars per dwelling.

The parts for the Underground Village that come out of a factory are all doubly curved, stackable pieces of heavy PVC. This is the same plastic chosen nowadays for waste systems because of its durability. Some of the ideas that have gone into space-station design are applicable here. Many of the surfaces discovered by soap-bubble research are double curved and stackable, and can be combined to form strong structures. They need to be strong to support the tons of dirt we are going to cover them with. They need to be air-tight and water-tight to prevent soil microbes from entering the living space, because most of these soil bacteria produce diarrhea.

But why put them underground at all? To avoid both heating and air-conditioning expenses. Normal underground temperature is about sixty degrees, about the temperature of a typical British summer. So neither heating nor air-conditioning is required. Just sweaters by day and blankets by night. Each home is a ring or a stacked ring of rooms around a central atrium which goes all the way to the surface. The homes themselves are linked to a large central space, with more atria and skylights.

This central space is just like a mall, and the rooms facing the mall can become a Mom and Pop store or workshop of some kind. Each room has an individual skylight above, reflecting the sun to a large diffuse surface. Naturally, the amount of light could be controlled. On the wall away from the central family atrium, each room has a camera obscura, i.e. a large piece of ground glass displaying a scene from the surface above, a scene which may be changed by turning the surface mirror or tilting it. This has the psychological effect of looking out a window. The central atrium is roofed with a flat transparent lid of lightweight, flexible but hard material, i.e. not easily scratched. Such a material may not yet exist. In winter, it seals the atrium, which becomes a closed ecology. In summer, it may be raised a foot or so to allow ventilation. What do we put in our atria? Waterfalls, and orchids, and every botanical delight known to man. After all, an atria is just a kind of recessed greenhouse.

Affordable Universal Health Care: Last but hardly least among the platform programs are the Free Clinics. No Band-Aids will make health care affordable. In particular, simply putting pencil-pushers in charge (the basic idea of HMOs) will only result in a decline in the quality of medical service. We must rethink the whole medical system. Let us begin with an attitude adjustment.

Just what do we want from our medical care system? Most Medicare expenses are incurred in the last months of a person's life, when the prognosis is terminal. Western scientific medicine does little to comfort or ease the patient or the family through this terminal phase. Patients become habituated to opiates, which then lose their pain-killing power. Western medicine denies death, and fears it, fights it to the bitter end.

Do we want our lives to be dragged out for another year or two, in agony, sometimes out of our heads, with tubes running down our nose and needles in every arm, at vast expense, as if death were the enemy? And do we want life to be prolonged in nursing homes, when we no longer recognize relatives or have any idea where we are? Do we want to try to preserve one and two pound newborns, knowing that fifty percent will die and fifty percent of those that live will be permanently brain damaged, when all it takes to prevent underweight birth is a little proper nutrition and prenatal care by the mother? Our answer to all these questions may depend on our metaphysics.

Later on, I provide evidence for immortality, and many already know this—those familiar with the literature on Near Death Experience or Ian Stevenson's studies of young children who spontaneously recall former lifetimes. Death is a wonderful experience, nothing to be feared. It is not the end, only the beginning of another phase in our infinite journey.

If we strive to make an honest terminal prognosis as early as possible, we can stop treating the disease and begin treating the person, with palliatives in hospices or at home, and with alternative therapies, such as Chinese Herbalism, acupuncture, Tai Chi or the remedies of Edgar Cayce. Hospices should have books, videos and roundtable discussions about Near Death Experience and other witnesses to immortality and the actual act of dying.

Hospitals should not be places to die. Half the beds now are filled with terminal cancer patients, for whom our expensive care is doing nothing but running up the bill and prolonging the agony.

Death is not the enemy. For those in agony, or those in a vegetative state, death is a friend.

Dr. Kervorkian's Doctor Assisted Suicide should be an option for Living Wills, for those who do not wish to be sent to nursing homes, mentally and physically incompetent. His method is very similar to execution by lethal injection and produces an easy and certain death, which is not true of most methods of suicide. Everyone should have that choice, by means of a Living Will, created with the help and advice of a doctor, setting forth the conditions in which the patient would rather die in peace than suffer. Dying in peace, or dying when ready, can mean "no resuscitation," or "turning off the respirator," or "shutting off the feeding tubes," and in some cases it means Dr. Kervorkian. This is the humane treatment for patients. It is also the only way we can afford medical care for those who can use it, for those who have many good years left of life.

The Free Clinics are bound to be controversial, because I propose staffing them entirely with MTs, instead of MDs. Medical Technicians have one year of training and a salary of $20—$50,000. Many of them come from the ranks of emergency room nurses or surgical scrub nurses. MDs have eight years of training and an income of $200,000 and up.

Using optical fiber and video, there will be MDs "standing over the MT's shoulder," so to speak, whenever he or she needs help. This will be particularly true of trauma cases, remotely overseen by a trauma surgeon. Surgery in the Free Clinics will normally be laparotomy, under minor anesthesia. If a procedure cannot be done that way, the patient is sent by helicopter to the hospital trauma center, after stabilization. But if that is not possible, the MT may have to plunge in with scalpel and rib-spreader, following the instructions of the remote trauma surgeon.

Much of the training of MTs will go into learning how to use all the high technology to be found in all Free Clinics. He or she will practice the laparotomy techniques for removing diseased or damaged organs and tumors. He or she will learn how to set fractures, close cuts with superglue and butterfly bandages and all the routine stuff. The MT will spend no time learning diagnosis, and will learn anatomy from plastic bodies one can take apart, name, and put back together. MTs will not dissect a cadaver, because a scalpel will be a little used tool in the practice of an MT.

Diagnosis will be done by computer programs written by Doctors and researchers at the Mayo clinic, or similar places, or by the MD "looking over the shoulder" of the MT. As input, we have the results from the standard tests run every time, e.g. temperature, BP, heart rate, respiration, urine analysis, and a statement of complaints, if any. The programs will ask a series of questions, which the MT relays to the patient. Sometimes the program requires additional tests, such as throat cultures, MRI scan, PET scan after drinking radioactive antibodies or a plain old x-ray, or immediate transport to the hospital.

There is one Free Clinic per ward, with the MTs living in that ward, and every Free Clinic is open all the time. This is always the closest and best place to go with trauma, heart attacks, poisoning, drowning, sudden high fevers in children, and all those things that go wrong in the middle of the night.

The Free Clinics should have two pieces of high technology that have so far been expensive. I propose to put them on an assembly line and bring their costs down and their quality up. One of these is the general purpose MRI, PET, and CT scanner for telling where there is a tumor or infection. These could be inexpensive if they used powerful permanent magnets, like those made by the Russians.

To tell what, laboratories presently have an array of devices for separating and identifying molecules or fragments of molecules in the blood or urine. New techniques have been developed to identify molecules, so far used to identify molecules in a Martian meteorite. (See the May 1997 issue of *Discover* magazine, "The Light on Life," by James Shreeve, p. 50 ff. about the work of Richard Zare with lasers.)

Clearly this work has a medical application. Most diseases can be identified by molecules excreted in the urine. Antibodies to viruses, bacteria, parasites and cancers can be used to identify diseases. Computerized systems can count red cells and white cells on a microscope slide. Combining all such systems so they can work automatically on a single drop of blood or urine, and then mass-producing the equipment to do it, that is the challenge.

Preventions (e.g. vaccination) or early interventions are much cheaper than crisis surgery. For instance, we now know that a program of counseled exercise, diet (ten percent fat), and meditation can reverse the effects of arteriosclerosis. Doctors should look for early signs of heart disease and treat it vigorously with such programs, run by nurse-practitioners. What shall we do with a heart patient told to enter one of these diet-exercise-meditation programs and give up smoking, who does neither? Shall the taxpayers pay for coronary bypass operations or heart transplants for such a person? I don't think so.

The Free Clinic system has three tiers. At the top are the Mayo Clinics and other hospitals with demonstrated expertise at a particular treatment. In the middle is the Free Clinic, where everyone is an MT. Everything is done by MTs, from mopping the floor to greeting patients or keeping electronic charts updated. The Free Clinics are places of gleaming tile and a fanatic emphasis on antisepsis. Today, one out of three hospital patients picks up a bug during their stay, often one resistant to all antibiotics.

The Free Clinics and associated hospitals must be designed so that all surfaces can be sterilized daily, and the air system must filter out all viruses, fungal spores, dust particles and bacteria. However, we may want to follow sterilization with spraying surfaces with a mixture of benign bacteria that can out-compete deadly varieties. Otherwise, our elaborate efforts may just create bacteria that are antiseptic proof, just as we are gradually creating antibiotic-proof bacteria. How do we avoid that? Perhaps by spraying the antiseptic field with benign bacteria!

On the bottom tier are nurse-practitioners, trained and

supported by the local Free Clinic. These include midwives, since by far the best place to have a baby is at home. No nasty disease-resistant bugs lurking at home, and no baby-stealers either. Skilled midwives can even turn the baby to the correct position before birth, if they are in the wrong presentation. Home births have only about 1/3 the neonatal mortality rate or maternal complications as hospital births. If you don't believe this statistic, read the book *Spiritual Midwifery*, which I also recommend for all couples about to have natural childbirth at home with a midwife. This book is published by a Tennessee commune called The Farm, and they compare neo-natal mortality with those for Tennessee hospitals and several other groups of hospitals. My own children were born at home with standard pre-natal care, and with the assistance of an experienced midwife, and me as Lamaze partner.

The Free Clinics make housecalls, if there is a relative or companion that can provide some basic care, such as meals, bedpans, diapers, dressings, and sponge baths. Visiting nurses, portable monitors and drug injection systems, could allow many people to go home.

Quality medical care is not always cheap. Where a large expenditure is worth it, as for the MRI-PET-CT machine, I'm all for mass-producing it, or redesigning it so that it uses permanent magnets.

Often the best medicine is conservative. For instance, no one believes our health is better than Sweden's because we do ten times as many births by C-section. No, this is an indictment, taking a routine procedure (birth) and turning it into hazardous major surgery. Why do American ObGyns do this? Because they are afraid of being sued? Or because they can charge thousands instead of hundreds?

Service-for-fee provides a strong economic incentive to cut, to prescribe, to conduct tests, i.e. to do something rather than nothing. The MTs and MDs in the Free Clinic system are all on salary. They have no financial incentive to do more than is necessary. If you will recall from the Justice chapter, there are no torts in the new law. No suits for damages. No mal-practice suits, or suits of any kind.

Conclusion: The platform programs are the third major piece of the green solution, the union of economics, ecology and social welfare. The homeless shall be sheltered, and the hungry fed. Those with no medical insurance shall have Free Clinics. There will be no more acid rain, gridlock, foreign oil dependence, economic depression, inflation, and the fat and flab that afflict our sedentary population. That is what it means to "think green." Think of the whole while thinking of the part. This is the material foundation for the renewed civilization of the third millennium.

Learning Versus Indoctrination

The Electronic University: Certainly one of the things wrong with college education today is that it has been priced out of the range of many middle class children, including my own children. My own Alma Mater (which shall be nameless) charges at least thirty times as much for tuition today, as it did in the late fifties. Middle class incomes have risen by less than a factor of ten. Fortunately, with the invention of the Web, and VHS and DVD and all the other media miracles of our times, it is possible to create an Electronic University, with mini-campuses in major cities, but without the huge overhead of the traditional school. And the quality of the instruction would be vastly improved, for a variety of reasons. Real production values could go into the creation of each series of lectures. Think of Lord Clark's "Civilisation" TV series, or Carl Sagan's "Cosmos." Interaction between student and course (a computer program) would be one-on-one, and would go at the student's own pace. At the beginning of each course, the student would be told how many points it took to make an A, how many for a B and so forth. One would make points (or lose them) by taking "exams," which could be thought of as similar in some ways to a computer game. Do a good job and get points. Do a lousy job and lose points.

But what about campus life? What about the intellectual

stimulus of conversation over coffee? How would you meet girls? The answer to all these questions is university districts. Here would be the labs for science classes, with Teaching Assistants. Here would be old apartment buildings bought up by EU and rented out solely to EU students. Here would be the bottomless cup of coffee or tea, for EU students in coffee houses also owned by EU. Continental breakfast (a basket of hard rolls with butter and jam) and inexpensive bagel sandwiches and soup, for EU students. Possibly such pockets of EU-dom could be established in places that are already student districts, such as the left bank in Paris, or University hill in Seattle.

EU would have advantages for faculty as well. Since a faculty member of EU would be paid a royalty for each copy of his class sold, creators of popular classes could become rich. And having the class on tape or DVD means not having to teach the same subject over and over for years until one is dead tired of it. Just update it occasionally. It might not even be necessary to change the filmed lectures, just the texts and exam-programs that go with it.

Now that I have your attention, there are a number of deeper issues that affect all levels of education, not just colleges and universities. Just what do we want our schools to do? Unfortunately, most people would say "indoctrination" and then argue about which courses should be required. But I am a libertarian, who always found it easy to learn on my own, and difficult to absorb "required courses."

Indoctrination: Just as "faith" is another name for "dogma," so "education" is another name for "indoctrination." One reason it fails is the old adage "you can take a horse to water, but you can't make it drink." Similarly, with students and learning opportunities.

Away with compulsory education after the age of seven. Away with any kind of "education," if that only means indoctrination. Let us live up to our libertarian ideals and inaugurate a new age of learning. Students start school full of curiosity and creativity, soon killed by indoctrination and repetitious homework. The few learned people I have met somehow avoided repetitious drudgery. If we wanted to instantly double the quality of our classes, we only need to repeal the compulsory education rule, at least for those eight or older. We must provide many alternatives, to be paid for with the vouchers.

Traditional schools follow a lockstep, cookie-cutter approach, which forces children to sit quietly at their desks all day. But not all children are alike. Some children need to be physically active, running back and forth between chair and blackboard as they give their answers. Some children need to develop their physical coordination, or their musical and linguistic skills, before they are able to absorb traditional school subjects. Some children do better if everything is made a game, preferably a game involving music and dancing. Apprenticeship to a trade at age eight should also be an allowable alternative.

Vouchers: Part of this revolution, and one suggested before (by John Holt, for instance) is the use of vouchers. We need to bring free enterprise to learning. That's what vouchers do. I say give vouchers to everyone, and let them be fully transferable, salable or savable for any number of years, but redeemable only by a teacher given a license by the local magistrate, and not redeemable by a school. This is a way of implementing the Ideal of Freedom of Information for students over 8. Another thing vouchers do is provide equal opportunity. It means that everyone at least has a chance to go as far as their talents and ambition will take them, without being discriminated against on the basis of race, religion, sex, tribe, age or family.

If a student qualifies for a high priced teacher or high priced school, the whole family can chip in vouchers to make it possible. Let vouchers be used for child care, if the child care facility correctly expands the mental and physical horizons of the children. This can actually be measured, in terms of the number of words spoken directly to a child per hour. Indeed, it begins to appear that the first three years of life are the most important in the development of linguistic, social, musical and mathematical skills (*Newsweek*, Feb. 19, 1996, p. 54).

Let vouchers be used for apprenticeship in the skilled trades. Let them be used for religious schools, even those of new or alternative religions or spiritual paths. Let them be used for therapy. Let them be used for enrichment programs for the elderly, and classes on Near Death Experience and other transpersonal knowledge in hospices. It is never too late to learn, and it never ceases to give pleasure. But learning is a pleasure only when it is voluntary.

Liberal Arts: I went to a "liberal arts" college myself. I didn't quite know what that meant, but it sounded good to me. It turned out that the faculty and administration had no idea what it meant, either. I have thought about the meaning of "liberal arts" over the years, and I can now define it as "knowing everything important about everything important." This is a challenging goal, but not impossible, since the growth of knowledge in all fields occasionally produces a new theory or organizing principle, such as the theory of plate tectonics in geology. It is far easier to learn plate tectonics than to memorize the piles of unrelated facts that used to constitute geology.

This is true in all fields. If there is no theory or organizing principle, it would not be included in our list of "everything important."

In order to teach the Liberal Arts Introduction to physics, it is first necessary to learn higher math. This can be done, if math is taught as the language of number, rather than a proof system. Engineers or scientists teach this course, rather than mathematicians, since they are the ones who use the language. Mathematicians don't consider math a language and don't care whether it has any use. For them, it is a mind game. But for the rest of us, the only mathematics of significance is that part which is used as a language of precise logical relationships and careful measurement.

I shall give a brief description of this language. Higher math has a single sentence form, the equation, and it has five parts of speech, three kinds of number, and two kinds of operator. The five parts of speech are numbers, constants, variables, operators and functions. The three kinds of numbers are real, complex and array. The two kinds of operator come from algebra or calculus.

Algebraic operators are like addition and multiplication, which work on anything, including other operators. Calculus operators work on functions, transforming them into other functions. There are equations, operators and functions for each of the three kinds of numbers, using both kinds of operator. Learn all the permutations, and you have mastered higher math.

As a language, the emphasis is on learning to read it and write it. This is never taught in conventional math classes.

Start off with a little plane geometry. Here proofs can be easily and quickly shown visually, since they are all constructed with a compass and ruler. Tell the students that some of these rules will be used in Newtonian physics, to resolve vectors into those in the direction of free motion, and those at right angles to it. Introduce trig, devoting time to topics in proportion to their importance. Clearly, the sine and cosine definitions and functions and usages are the most important. One needs to know the tangent, in order to understand the arc-tangent. This is also a good place to introduce the infinite series definition of the exponential, the sine and the cosine, and to demonstrate the connection between them, by using an imaginary number for the exponential. Tell the students this will be very important in Ordinary Differential Equations (ODE), and many laws of nature are expressed as ODE. Give the example of exponential growth and decay.

Some review of algebra is then introduced, leading up to the quadratic formula, which will again be useful in solving second order ODE. Show how it becomes an algebraic second order equation for the constant B, if $Y = A*\exp(B*T)$. Use the quadratic formula to obtain a complex number, which then resolves into a combination of exponentials, sines and cosines. Practice making figures where X = F(sin(t)) and Y = G(cos(t)) where t goes from 0 to 2 PI. Why such strange units they will ask? Because of the definition of these functions in terms of infinite series. Introduce a few more such definitions, such as the one for the inverse of the exponential, the natural logarithm.

As in any language, it is good to immerse students in it, without drowning them. Provide foreshadowings of events to come, where simple examples can be given. Never do anything in N dimensional space. Avoid the cumbersome terminology of the professional mathematicians. Make everything practical and concrete, with the maxim that no topic is understood until one knows how to get down to actual numbers.

This might be a good place to introduce coordinate systems and the multiplication and division of units. Point out that in the real world there are very few pure numbers. Most numbers are measures or counts. Also, it might be a good place to suggest that math is a language with one sentence structure, the equation, five parts of speech (functions, operators, numbers, constants and variables), and three types of number (real, complex, array). Give examples of equations using all three kinds of number. Show that "solving an equation" is an experimental, trial and error process, where the goal is to get the thing wanted on one side of the equation and everything else on the other side of the equation. Give examples. Point out that there is only one rule for manipulating equations, and that it works for all kinds of equations. You can do anything legal to one side as long as you do the same or equal thing to the other side. Give examples from calculus and linear algebra.

From here, plunge directly into calculus as a way of introducing two new operators on functions that yield other functions. At first, stick to simple functions, like X**2. Assume that all functions describe things that change, and mark the fundamental difference between the ancient math of statics and the modern math of dynamics. Give a plausibility argument that integration is the sum of the accumulation of change, while differentiation is the velocity of change. Give a plausibility argument that these are inverse operations. Introduce the constants of integration set by initial conditions. Do the horizontal cannon shot example, at first neglecting wind resistance. Add wind resistance. Do the simple harmonic oscillator, with and without friction. Teach them to divide or multiply through an equation with an infinitesimal, just as they have learned to do with units. Have them do the exact solution for the pendulum by direct integration, and show that the pendulum really isn't very good for time-keeping, since its rate of swinging depends on how high the mechanism swings. Have them calculate the force on a dam as a function of the depth of water. Throw at them a mixture of integral and differential problems. Teach them how to create new equations using differentials on a problem. As in any language class, we must learn to read and to write. Leave proofs for the professional mathematicians.

There are a finite number of rules for differentiation. Learn them. There is not a finite number of rules for integration. Have them learn to integrate polynomials. Beyond that, introduce them to the math handbook, and have them solve a variety of problems by looking up the solution in the handbook. Next introduce them to the program "Mathematica" or something similar. Emphasize that this will be their chief tool from now on, just as the calculator is for lower math. Have them learn to search for closed form solutions when they can, and numerical solutions which are plotted when they can't.

It will be natural to go on to ODEs at this point. Emphasize that this is just part of calculus, not a different subject. Have them do electrical circuits, first determining the natural decay or oscillator properties of unforced systems, then tackle systems forced by an input oscillation. Spend some time resolving force vectors and solving the resulting ODEs for the free variable, using Newton's laws with simple force functions. Here they will get to apply stuff from plane geometry and trig. Then go on to problems of the solar system, using the inverse square law. Do the one body problem, two body, and three body problems, with the aid of Mathematica. Solve in elliptical coordinates.

This would be a good place to revisit coordinate systems, looking at the way everything is transformed in accelerated coordinate systems, such as a Cartesian coordinate system fixed on the Earth, spinning with it. Show how such things as precession, nutation and coriolus forces arise simply from the accelerated coordinate system. This is never done in ordinary math books.

Introduce linear algebra by looking at systems of simultaneous equations, first algebraic, then ODEs. Teach them how to do it with pencil and paper, and then with Mathematica. Introduce Partial Differential Equations, PDE, with boundary conditions, and let Mathematica solve those. Study the theory of musical instruments thoroughly, introducing such concepts as eigenfunctions, eigenvalues, and "quantum numbers" as integer indices for the overtones. These can be investigated as simple PDEs of pressure waves as a function of X and T. Introduce the Hamiltonian and Lagrangian methods for investigating musical instruments.

They are now ready for systems of simultaneous PDEs, such as Maxwell's equations. Have them solve for a variety of boundary conditions, plotting the resulting force fields, using Mathematica, of course. First plot the boundary condition, then the effect on those initial equations of Maxwell's equations. Show that Special Relativity can be derived from Maxwell's equations.

The next topic is tensors. Make sure they know how to write out all the terms. The compact notation hides a great deal of complexity. Introduce them to the tensors for General Relativity, showing some solutions obtained by setting time to a constant, and reducing all space variables to R. Revisit electro-magnetism and rewrite electric and magnetic force fields in terms of tensors.

Finally, I would use the last half of the second semester just on chaos theory, which is also the theory of non-linear systems. Show how a space orbiter can save energy by using chaos theory.

Consider that all real systems are probably chaotic and nonlinear. The linear, mechanical solutions are just first approximations. Of course, Mathematica will be invaluable for calculating and plotting the world lines for chaotic systems.

One good reason for learning a language is to learn the great literature in that language, which, in this case, consists in the great equations of physics, engineering and economics. So, the second semester of the math class is the literature. After that, the introductory courses in the sciences are easy, even though they include the equations, which are usually left out of beginning classes. No graduates from traditional universities could match the skills and vast knowledge of a Master of Liberal Arts from EU.

Discrimination and Tribalism

The ideal of Equal Opportunity and Responsibility says we can neither discriminate for nor against someone on the basis of arbitrary characteristics. "Arbitrary" means "having nothing to do with suitability for the task in hand." If we were casting the part of Abraham Lincoln in a play, no one could accuse us of arbitrary discrimination if we limited the choice to skinny and tall white males. In such a case, race and gender become relevant.

Discrimination against blacks is called racism, and is a bad thing. But many blacks (not the more serious black intellectuals) think it is quite all right to discriminate in favor of blacks. This is called "affirmative action." In truth, discrimination FOR some group is far more widespread and insidious than discrimination AGAINST. This is particularly true when it comes to tribal discrimination. I use the term "tribal" in a broad sense. Of course, we are familiar with the idea that the Native Americans were tribal, and Native Africans still are tribal. I also categorize Kurds, Basques, Serbs, Croats, Bosnians, Palestinians and Jews as tribal peoples.

Tribal people always want a homeland, where they are sovereign, and no other tribe may be given full citizenship. When a tribal member gets into a position of authority, it is assumed he or she will use that power to further other members of the tribe at the expense of everyone else. In just this way, a business, profession or industry may be taken over by one tribe. No others need apply. There are many peoples in the world who are tribal in their behavior, including many African tribes, Afghani tribes, and Balkan tribes. The law should not have special rules for particular peoples. Rather, there should be a general rule against tribalistic discrimination, whoever is doing it.

When people immigrate to America, they must give up their tribalism, and with it, their nursing of old grudges and hatreds. That is the real meaning of "the melting pot," a phrase one doesn't hear much anymore. It never meant a melting together of all races and ethnic groups (although that inevitably happens). It mainly means a melting down of all the cultural baggage from the Old World, so ones first allegiance is to the new American People. That is not the first allegiance of tribal people, which is always to their own tribe. Indeed, that is the very definition of tribalism. Middle America now finds itself excluded from Hollywood, and discriminated against in academia, on Wall Street, and in the higher rungs of the professions. I say that reluctantly. Utopian analysis often turns up results which are not "politically correct."

Stability and Instability of Families

In the 40,000 years of the existence of Homo Sapiens, this is the first time that we have had no sexual specialization, beyond those imposed by biology. As a result, there is no particularly good reason to get married. It brings no economic or material benefits to either man or woman. So there is no particularly good reason to stay married, especially not "in sickness and in health, for better or for worse, till death do us part." Are you kidding? If one partner gets fat and ugly, the other is gone. If one partner becomes permanently disabled, the other is gone. The children are the ones who suffer.

If a man thinks he will get home cooked meals, child care, and housekeeping, he will have a rude awakening. He will only have home cooked meals if he cooks them himself. He will only have child care if he does it himself. The house will be cleaned only if he does it himself. He would be much better off hiring a housekeeper. And it would cost a lot less too.

If a woman thinks she will get to stay home after marriage, she too is in for a rude awakening. Her husband will insist that she go to school, get a job and have a career, so they can afford paid childcare, housekeeping and takeout food. Bon appetite!

No one is very happy with the result. Parents miss out on the formative years of the childhood of their children, when everything they do seems miraculous and wonderful. One good thing that has come out of this disappearance of gender roles is that at least a few men have chosen the stay-at-home role, and enjoy it. And are good at it. We men have been missing out on a lot.

Still, the root problem with this new unspecialized marriage is that there is no glue to bind man and woman together. If they are interchangeable, then it doesn't make much difference if one or the other decides to leave. Reciprocity is the glue, and it seems difficult to make that work in this unisex view of marriage. So marriage has become as fragile as glass. Children worry that their parents will break up, since this happens to all their classmates. And sooner or later, it does. One reads that half of all marriages end in divorce. I suspect that if we confine ourselves to the baby-boom generation and later, the fraction that will stay married "till death us do part" is much less than half, maybe only a fourth, or a fifth.

The ancient religious and legal institution of marriage is not geared to this new situation. The trouble is, everything is either black or white. Nothing in between. Either two people are joined at the hip, and must do everything together, or they divorce, which always ends up in bitterness and alienation between the former lovers. And, of course, untold psychological damage to the children.

Assuming we cannot go back to traditional marriage, I propose a different sort of joining. We won't even call it marriage. If there is a ceremony, we will have to invent it anew. The bond will not be so tight, nor separation so absolute, as in marriage. Let us imagine all degrees of closeness and separation between men and women. At the very least, men and women should retain their pre-joining circle of friends, and there will be a boys night out and a girls night out, every week. From the beginning. And many activities involving both man and woman and the children. That was certainly the best part of marriage for me. We should not insist that men and women sleep in the same bed, the same room, the same house, or the same city. Let us assume that both man and woman will change, and that this in turn may cause a change in living arrangements. This should not be regarded as failure. Nor should we insist on "fidelity." Both men and women will be attracted to other people. It could be a casual fling, or it could lead to another joining. This does not supersede the old joining. All joinings are forever, so that children know that neither of their parents are ever going to go away and never come back.

The key to joining is flexibility. Let the children in on decisions. Maybe they would prefer to live more with one parent than another. When they go through the changes of adolescence, maybe they would prefer to go live with the other parent. And at all costs maintain the framework of the extended family, of cousins, aunts, uncles, nieces, grandparents. In my case, this is mostly done by family Email or Long Distance phone calls, with only occasional visits. Modern economic trends have a way of flinging the members of a family all over the map. Still, connection can be maintained over the Web. It should not be considered unusual if children go live with cousins or grandparents for a period of time. The one iron rule is that if two people (really two families) are joined, nothing can ever sever that tie. Family consists in all those people who will help you when you are down, help you no matter what, give you a place to stay, and help.

So instead of the black and white of marriage and divorce, we have the infinite variations of closeness or separation without regret or bitterness that is the joined family. There will also be cycles in the relationship. Once attracted, always attracted, at least through the child-bearing years. So there may be cycles in the intensity of relationships between members of the family, and this should not be considered a failure. Yes, it is a radical solution, but the only way to preserve the family is to get rid of marriage.

At the very least we must think about family and joining. So much of what we do as parents or as spouses is what we have seen other people do. The minutiae of everyday life are impossible for each person to invent anew for themselves in every generation. There are countless strains between intellectual dogmas and cultural tradition. Just to take one example of that, no man is good at cooking or housework unless he has grown up in a household where the dominant male did all the cooking and housework. And was good at it. So men, at least unconsciously, expect the woman to take that role. And if she doesn't, it just doesn't get done. They live on takeout food, and the house is a pigsty. Men who live alone learn how to clean their houses and prepare nutritious food. Their houses are clean and tidy, their diet simple and reasonable.

When it comes to dealing with conflict, we all resort automatically to the mechanisms employed by our parents. For men, this usually means silence, which women interpret as withdrawal, coldness, or a lack of emotional expression. However, for countless generations, men have reacted to an angry wife by getting out of the house. Not permanently. Perhaps just for the day. Go off and have a few beers and play cards with the guys. They won't get mad at you for leaving the toilet seat up.

People expect too much from marriage. In particular, they expect happiness. Women even expect entertainment. But that was not the original function of marriage. Originally, it was for survival, of the individuals, of the extended family, and of the genetic stock. Pioneer families would have starved if they depended only on the hunting or farming prowess of the man. So women had a kitchen garden, and worked hard at drying and storing food for the winter. Further back in time, the men went out to hunt or scavenge meat. The women stayed closer to the hearth and gathered roots, nuts, berries, grubs and similar reliable but low fat foods. They needed each other to survive. Happiness and entertainment probably depended more on the stories told, sung and danced by the old men and old women of the clan. And that is why our species, almost alone among birds and mammals, allows for the survival of the grandmother generation. Some of them anyway. That is why we have menopause, unique among mammals.

Does this chapter offend your sense of the meaning of love?

What is love? Do you think love is forever? Love conquers all? Romantic nonsense. There was no romantic love in the traditional families of the past. Some of the married women of my father's generation had tongues like knives, and never missed a chance to slash their hapless mate to ribbons. Yet, this did not result in divorce. The men of my childhood always had an escape. They could go out and putter around in the shop, or go to town and have a few beers and play cards in the smoky, beer smelling saloons of the 1950s. Modern men don't seem to have any such escape. And maybe women don't either.

Romantic love does not exist. Or if it does, it exists only in the minds of virginal adolescents. Nonetheless, it is the basis of Western culture, especially movies. Consider movies to be fairy tales. There is nothing wrong with fairy tales, so long as children are told at some point that Santa Clause and Prince Charming do not really exist. Remove all romance from relationship movies and what do you have left? Woody Allen, Bergman, and Kurosawa.

And who will take care of the scutwork of home cooking, housework, and changing the baby's diapers in my utopia? Whoever chooses that role. And if no one in the extended family wants that role, hire quality childcare and good housekeepers. Maybe we need to revive the bracero program. These are people from other countries who would be willing to work for a dollar an hour, with housing, food, transportation, clothing, medical care, everything provided by the host family. The unions are wrong to oppose this. The bracero program does not take away jobs from American worker, because no American is willing to work this hard for so little. Yet, compared to what they have back home, it is riches for the bracero. And the children will be raised bilingual.

In the long run, the solution to homecooking and housekeeping may be robotics. The robotic kitchen and the robotic cleanup station would take up some floor space, but less than a room for a bracero housekeeper. True robots look nothing like those of science-fiction. They do not require any Artificial Intelligence, even if AI were a possibility. The necessary robots could be built now, at the beginning of the 21st Century, and manufactured and sold at a reasonable price for a kitchen appliance.

The kitchen robot would resemble a large cabinet. All the user needs to do is keep the bins full and use software on the home computer to select a menu and a serving time. The user also schedules the pickup robot and the cleanup robot from the computer menu. The computer would communicate with the robots via radio commands. Chef-programmers would create the code to run on the home computer for fixing meals. The kitchen appliance would have no smarts. It would respond to radio commands for each step, such as "pull out a 3 quart pan, put 2 quarts of water into it, bring it to a boil, drop 6 ounces of pasta into it, bring it to a boil, cook for 10 minutes, and dump into a strainer over a sink. It would then clean and dry the pan and return it to the bin, while announcing "The spaghetti is ready." Each family member would take a plate, dish up some spaghetti out of the strainer with a pair of tongs, and hold it under a nozzle which instantly heats the sauce for one serving. Push the button for the sauce, sprinkle on some parmesan cheese and take the plate to the table.

The kitchen robot does not serve the table. It is not much trouble for the customers to clear the table and put the dishes in the dishwasher, which itself adds detergent and runs when ordered to do so by the main computer. The human customers would have to put the dishes away. The kitchen robot does not have to do everything. Just enough so that fixing supper is not a chore.

As for the pickup and cleanup robots, they would have to be guided on their appointed rounds by a human the first time, or whenever there is a major re-arrangement of furniture. This would be like steering a radio controlled toy car. This would program the linear part of the robot's code, which could be contained on a cassette tape on the robot.

This robot is no more than an appliance, able to respond to simple commands from its linear program or from the home computer via radio. The first task is to pickup and drop objects into a pull behind cart. When the cart is full, it unhooks and reverses course to the pickup station, where the objects picked up are sorted and put in the appropriate bin. Simple sensors could measure things like the heat conductivity of something to distinguish books/magazines, plastic objects, metal objects, and ceramic objects, each being deposited in its appropriate bin. The pickup robot waits patiently. The cart retraces its route and hooks on again and the pickup robot continues. It would have wheels, of course, but the wheels could be extended vertically perhaps two feet, so the pickup robot could climb or descend stairs. Doors would have to be left open. If the door to a room was shut, the robot would skip ahead to the point in its linear program when it goes to the next room.

Naturally, the robot would stop if it encounters an obstacle. If the obstacle emits heat, it might be a cat or a human leg. Wait a minute and try again. If the obstacle does not emit heat, it might be a chair out of place, or toys, clothes, books or magazines which need to be picked up. So the robot will try to pick it up. If successful, the object will be deposited in the cart behind. If not successful, the robot calls for help from the main computer, which will invoke a program for avoiding the object and getting back on its linear track at a later point on the tape.

The cleanup robot would be just like the pickup robot, except that when programmed, it would be told whether to use the carpet vacuum module, the carpet "rug doctor," the tile mopping module, the tile waxing module, or the vacuum module. When the cleanup robot passes over into a new space, it would retrace its path, deposit one module at the cleanup station (which would empty dust chambers or dirty wash water) and latch on to the module required next. Human customers would still have to dust, vacuum drapes or blinds, cleanup the cobwebs in corners, and clean the bathroom. But these are jobs that do not have to be done every day.

Science fiction raises false expectations. If it were not for science fiction, we would probably already have robotic kitchens and robotic housekeeping, since they only require simple engineering. As long as everyone is waiting on AI to develop, nothing will happen. We will be waiting forever. Would I hire a Bracero or buy the robotic maid? No. My children are grown; my pets all died, and I have not replaced them. Once clean, it is easy to keep my house clean. I live on a simple yet nutritious diet which does not require elaborate preparation.

To summarize, nothing is more important than family. A person without family can hardly be considered human, alone in an urban jungle. Family is forever, or it is nothing. The closeness or distance between one member or another will naturally go through cycles and changes. The eternal stability of family must be preserved. And the only way to do it is to avoid the legal and religious strictures of marriage. If there is no marriage, there can be no divorce. No marriage means no expectations. We don't fall into the unconscious trap of being our parents. The only place the law need intervene is to insist that all full citizens have equal right to the care of their biological offspring. Of course, a person can be declared an unfit parent and lose that right. When a child is in your custody, you pay the tab. When not, you don't. No child support payments or alimony. That is where the law needs to be changed. Eventually, if this experiment works, we can just abolish marriage.

The Full Keynesian Economy

Taxing and Spending: I define "economics" as "anything that has to do with our physical well-being, whether it involves an exchange of money or not." Academic economics is only concerned with money transactions, something which may be measured and counted. I have little to say about this side of economics, other than to advocate the full acceptance of John Maynard Keynes. No more "voodoo" supply-side economics, which quadrupled the national debt during the Reagan-Bush years. The 1997 tax bill is more voodoo economics, claiming to be able to cut taxes while balancing the budget. Politicians will always tell us whatever fairy tale we want to hear.

No administration has ever tried what I call the full-Keynesian counter-cyclical policy of making taxing and spending adjustments to prevent depression and inflation. It's not so difficult. It doesn't require a Ph.D. to understand this. It is taught in every beginning class on economics. To even out the natural bumps in the free enterprise business cycle, the government should raise taxes and reduce expenditures (sounds paradoxical doesn't it?) during the boom part of the cycle, running a surplus, something not seen for many years, although here at the turn of the millennium, we are about to enter an era of surplus. During the down side of the cycle, government should lower taxes and raise expenditures, thus running a slight deficit.

There is nothing wrong with a deficit, so long as it is balanced in the average by the surpluses. It is only this full Keynesian policy, scientifically rather than politically applied, which can prevent depressions, reduce the depth of recessions, and eliminate inflation. To learn more, take economics 101 (something President Clinton clearly understands, since he has halved the deficit in his first administration).

Opening or Closing our Market: The second matter of academic economics has to do with trade deficits. In the economic textbooks, it says that unlimited free trade is better for all consumers. The trouble is, we are not just consumers. We are also workers and owners. And unless everyone plays the game of international trade by the same rules, we may still gain as consumers, but this will be irrelevant, since all the good jobs and the ownership of our businesses and property will migrate to the more closed markets.

Our market is our own. We are not obliged to open it to anyone else. Those allowed to trade in our market should consider it a privilege. And if a trading partner has a market partially closed to us, we should close our market to them in exactly the same degree, without negotiation. It does not matter how they close their market; the Japanese have shown considerable ingenuity in this regard. The last twenty years have shown the Japanese a way to become world dominant without even possessing a fleet. Of course, at the end of this century, the Asian economic powers all appear to be paper tigers, beset by corruption and bad loans. They are not supermen.

Intellectual Property Theft: The government must also take a much more aggressive stance regarding theft of intellectual property. We should feel free to steal intellectual property from those who steal from us. Turn about, fair play. As long as there are no negative consequences, we will keep inventing things, like the VCR, and the Orientals will keep stealing the technology, flooding the market at a loss until all our own factories have gone belly up, and we will have gained nothing from our own creativity. We should be quick to develop a new invention, so inventors will not have to turn to the Japanese. And such developments should be safe-guarded as if it were military technology. We should then protect that market, until the industry is robust. Patents and copyrights are not sufficient in a world where the Chinese, Japanese and Koreans ignore the rules regarding such things. In short, the government should take a strategic interest in new technology, as if the fate of the nation depends on Digital High Definition Television and optical fiber, because indeed it does.

Watchdog Role for Government: Free enterprise varies from country to country and from one time and place to another. Theoretically, competition and the free market will keep it all running automatically. But in practice, it doesn't. In the 19th Century, huge monopolies developed, which then set their own prices (high). It was necessary for the Federal Government to step in. In the 1980s, corporate raiders ran rampant, buying corporations with junk bonds, which were then paid off by dismantling the company, and selling off the pieces. Eventually, most of these corporate raiders ran afoul of the law. In the 1990s, the fad is corporate downsizing.

There seems something obscene about 40,000 workers in one corporation losing their jobs, usually workers in their fifties and unable to find a similar job, all to the self-congratulation of management, which votes itself huge pay raises. Speaking of management compensation, why is it that American corporate executives make two or three times as much money as their Japanese or European counterparts? The general conclusion is just that the Aristarchy (see the chapter on "Revolution") must keep an eye on the corporations. Occasional intervention may be required.

Preventing Burnout: I have a proposal to make about vacations and holidays. This may seem a trivial matter, but in fact, it has a lot to do with the productivity of a nation, and a lot to do with preventing early burnout. In most middle class jobs, there are 15 days of vacation and 10 days of paid holidays. Five working weeks. Libraries, the post-office and government offices take off an additional 5 holidays the rest of us don't get. So they have 6 unproductive weeks. If that all came together at one time, it would be long enough to get totally out of the work frame of mind, allowing the total relaxation that staves off burnout. But unfortunately, it doesn't. People seldom even take their 3 weeks of vacation together.

What I propose is to make August a paid national holiday, while cutting the number of paid holidays to five, and reducing the optional vacation time to 8 working days. So instead of 5 weeks off we now would have 7 weeks. It is much more efficient just to close down the plant, so that everybody is off at once. For one thing, that would be a good time to retool or renovate the plant or office. For some businesses, the fact that everyone else is off means that they must work all the harder. Obviously any business connected to travel or recreation would have their biggest month in August and couldn't close down. So they should close down in February.

What holidays do we keep and which do we toss? I am in favor of moving to weekends all Hallmark holidays that do not have any deep tradition, such as Mother's day, Father's day, Valentines day, Easter and Good Friday, St. Patrick's day, Memorial Day, Labor day, and Thanksgiving. Provide 2 days off for Christmas and New Years day, since these are ancient festivals, pre-dating Christianity. Make Halloween the fall-fest, not Thanksgiving, which is only a day for stuffing oneself with food, which seems obscene given the fact that we are all too fat already. In America, the Fourth of July would be the summer-fest. Now what about spring-fest? I suggest Carnival, which would fall on the first day of good weather, suitable for outdoor activities, ranging from Fat Thursday before Lent in sub-tropical parts of the country, all the way up to May first for the Great Lakes and Northeast. Carnival is something we will have to more or less re-invent, borrowing traditions from both East and West.

What would we do if we had August off? Go some place cool, such as the Pacific Northwest. I imagine there would be a good business in summer cottages anywhere near Puget Sound or the Pacific, from Eureka to Anchorage and Homer, on Canadian Islands on the Inside Passage, and even in Vancouver or Victoria. A month off in the woods, prowling the beaches for crabs, clams and driftwood, watching the whales migrate, and possibly getting out in a boat and fishing for salmon, would restore the soul of the most compulsive work-a-holic.

Flat Taxes: Finally, I cannot leave the realm of economics without a tax proposal. I believe in the KISS principle. Keep It Simple, Stupid. Make it simple enough, and there will be no possibility of cheating, and no such things as tax returns. But can we make the tax laws fair? "Fair" is highly relative. Usually, what someone means by "fair" is something to their advantage. Every lobbyist in Washington wants to stick something into the tax code that will help their bosses. And that is why we have a tax code so complex that no one fully understands it.

I say tax every financial transaction somewhere around three percent. That's it. A one line tax code. After we convert to an all electronic monetary system, the tax will be deducted and put into government accounts automatically. Notice that this is like a combination of a VAT with a tax on gross income, which applies equally to institutions and individuals. VAT stands for Value Added Tax, and is a sales tax which also applies to wholesale. Property could be transferred with no deduction. This one line tax code ends and replaces all sin taxes, such as special taxes on liquor or tobacco. No more death taxes, also known as estate taxes. No more fees for licenses. The actual amount of the tax would vary day by day in accordance with the principles of the full Keynesian economy.

A Philosophical Breakthrough

I have done one original thing, one thing which everyone said was impossible. I have extended the essence of scientific method to all those questions heretofore left out of science, such as: How do we build beautiful cities? What about capital punishment or abortion? Is there life after death, immortality, divinity? Are we immortal? These questions are neither meaningless nor unanswerable.

Extending scientific method to new realms requires two things. One is the separation of the essence from the accidentals in the existing sciences. The second thing is to see all epistemology as problem solving. Then it is easy to see that the problems to be solved in Utopian Analysis or Metaphysics are very different from those of the physical sciences, and are based on different kinds of experiences. We can still be scientific, however, by insisting on reproducible particulars with veridical details, and by ruling out the alternatives, until we have only one well-established result remaining. See the chapter on scientific method.

The function of philosophy is the founding of sciences. At any rate, that is the only historical achievement of philosophy. Such philosophical breakthroughs are rare, but they do occur, when a subject which was formerly philosophical becomes scientific. It is not that a scientist comes in and cleans up the subject. No, there must be a long philosophical evolution of the subject, one which proceeds by fits and starts, sometimes trapped in a blind alley by false assumptions, sometimes languishing for centuries or millennia without any progress. The last philosopher of a subject ceases to be called "philosopher" by future generations, and becomes known as the founder of a discipline. The books used to teach philosophy consist in collections of the work of failed philosophers, ones who failed to graduate to the status of "founder of mathematics," or "founder of physics and astronomy." Reading this "philosophical" literature is tricky. What is most important is often an unstated (and false) assumption.

The last philosopher of mathematics was Euclid, building on earlier work by Plato, Zeno, Pythagoras, Thales and the Babylonians. The last philosopher of physics was Newton, who said he stood on the shoulders of giants. He didn't name them, but we can imagine it would be Kepler, Galileo, Copernicus, Ptolemy, Hipparcos and Thales.

In a way, the creation of a science is the solution to a group of philosophical problems. But they might not all be solved right away. It wasn't until the invention of the calculus that mathematicians were able to resolve Zeno's paradoxes. The point is, they were set on the right path, one which produced reliable results. Euclid's methods have been used by mathematicians from that time forward, just as physicists continue to follow the example of Galileo and Newton.

The new science which is mostly my own work is the new science of Civilization, also called "Utopian Analysis." I became a utopian dreamer at 15 after reading Plato's *Republic*. I got the idea for Utopian Analysis when I was 19 and a Sophomore in college. My professors told me to forget it, that what I was attempting was impossible. I got the same message from my graduate school advisor and other professors, and later from my colleagues in what is erroneously called "philosophy." It took me 30 years to solve these "impossible" problems and another 10 years to find a way to publish them (the invention of the Web).

In the creation of science out of philosophy, precise definitions replace vague or inconsistent concepts. For instance, "ethics" is a vague and useless philosophical concept, because it does not distinguish values from obligations, nor community concerns from personal concerns. Please note that the science of civilization is concerned only with community values and community actions, including those which create obligations and rights. "*De Gustibus Est Non Disputandum*" when it comes to personal values. There is no accounting for tastes. Which is one reason why liberty is better than "big brother" because no one can decide what is best for you, other than you. In particular, "ethics" confuses morality and virtue. While morality, being an obligation created by a community action, falls into the scope of utopian analysis, virtue does not. There are many different ideas of virtue, which depend on family, class, nation. There are no universal truths about virtue, nor about individual values. Medical ethicists are simply giving opinions. Yet, utopian analysis may be applied to their issues. I leave that to others.

Sometimes it is best to leave a term undefined, or at least, it is best not to engage in debate over the "proper" definition of a term, such as "utopia." For me, any effort to improve society and take the correct community action is utopian, and this does not mean "hopelessly idealistic," nor does it mean "perfection." The US is a utopia, created by the Founding Fathers. The UK is a utopia, created by the "glorious revolution" of 1688, which established the supremacy of Commons over Royals, Lords, and Justices. Communism turned out to be a dystopia, because it was based on false ideals, such as socialism and authoritarianism. We know both to be false because of their failure whenever tried. So the idea of utopia incorporates the use of correct and well-established ideals.

I call the new science of civilization "utopian analysis," because it always begins with an analysis of a controversy into consequences of underlying ideals which the two sides may not have made explicit. Also, if you consider such issues as abortion, world peace, beautiful cities, traffic jams, and so forth, the term "ethics" is just woefully inadequate. But the solution to all these problems can very properly be called "utopian," and that is why I prefer to use "utopia" instead of "ethics."

Utopian analysis does not begin with me. It can be traced back to Plato, Aristotle and the pre-Socratics. The last philosophers to make significant contributions to the science of Civilization were Hobbes and Locke and they lived in the 17th Century. I consider "utopian analysis" to pick up where the "moral sciences" of Hobbes and Locke left off. They discovered an essential idea in the science of civilization, and that is the "social contract," a kind of thought-experiment which reveals the underlying logic, not a description of any phase in human history.

Why the long dry spell? Why didn't the moral sciences continue to develop to keep pace with natural philosophy? It could have. I can easily imagine civilizations that have a highly developed science of civilization, yet no physical sciences, just the reverse of our situation. Hobbes and Locke did have a great effect on Voltaire and Thomas Jefferson and on the utopias of the US and the UK. Their efforts were not wasted. But their work was not picked up and the investigation continued, what we mean by a science. Why not? For the answers to that, I refer you to a chapter on sophistry. I can only hope that my own investigations will be picked up by others and continued, for there remain many issues in need of utopian analysis, such as those which plague the medical ethicists.

As you will see from the Sophistry chapter, I can show that nearly all academic philosophy after Locke is sophistry. I am the last, best and only living philosopher. But there is no competition for the role, so this is not quite the vainglorious boast it appears.

The only academic philosopher of the 20th Century who has had any influence on me is a British philosopher, whose last name is Austin. He said two things which are both true and worth repeating. (1) The function of philosophy is the founding of sciences. (2) Values are guides to action, not properties of things. Thus, values are relative to the actor. There is probably nothing which is of value to every person. However, I have found a number of community ideals which prove true for every community. I list them in the chapter on "Ideals."

Sophistry

The naturalistic fallacy is the logical inference of value from fact, for instance the inference of value from a policy which as a matter of fact does or might provide the greatest pleasure for the greatest number of people. This may sound plausible, but it really is a logical fallacy, and I do not commit it anywhere in Utopian Analysis. Ideals are tested by pursuing them long enough in a political experiment. In this way, the Soviet Empire gave the socialist ideal ("from each according to ability; to each according to need") a pretty thorough test, which it failed. Therefore, we know the socialist ideal is false. The failure of the Soviet Empire is what I call a normative particular, which is a particular matter of value discovered by experience. "Failure" is a normative term. It is a matter of history that the Soviet Empire collapsed; a normative particular that it failed. I shall not analyze a normative particular more than this. We learn things from political experiments, both matters of value and matters of fact. Let's leave it at that.

But notice, the failure of socialism does not imply the truth of the ideal of reciprocity and its corollary, the ideal of free enterprise. It is just that free enterprise is left as the only surviving alternative. That is always the way of it in science. As Sherlock Holmes said, "When you have eliminated the alternatives, whatever remains, *no matter how improbable*, must be the truth." When there is only one known alternative, all others having refuted, we call it well-established. That is the rule in physics, and it is the rule in utopian analysis. Ideals play the role of theories. Scientific theories are never proven. They are merely well-established. Why then should we believe in them? Well, it is up to you whether you believe in them. But if you wish to make any progress in your field you had better make use of them, since they are the only known solution to a set of problems.

In the creation of utopian analysis, the avoidance of the naturalistic fallacy was the least of my problems. But why were my professors and colleagues so adamant that it was unavoidable? I believe it is because academic philosophers after the time of Newton and Locke no longer understand the epistemology of our time, which is scientific method. They are stuck in the epistemology of ancient time, which was mathematical method.

The only knowledge-discipline known to philosophers before Galileo and Newton was mathematics, put in its rigorous modern form by a Greek philosopher working in the great library of Alexandria, a man named Euclid, building on a long tradition of mathematical philosophy. In mathematics, justification is proof.

However, Galileo and Newton invented a new kind of justification which we call scientific method, logically rigorous, but not based on an inference from facts to theories. In scientific method, justification is not proof. Hume never grasped the nature and significance of scientific method. He, and all the sophists who follow, remain in the Euclidean framework. They think justification is and must be proof, a logical inference from fact to theory. They call this inductive logic.

So how did Hume go so wrong? Perhaps he went wrong because science is "paradigmatic," as T. S. Kuhn pointed out in his famous book *The Structure of Scientific Revolutions*. Galileo and Newton never stated the essence of scientific method in abstract terms, and neither has any scientist since. Scientists learn their craft by example, master to pupil, Nobel prize winner to postdoc.

Or Hume may have been fooled by the form of Newton's *Principia*, where Newton sets forth his revolutionary new physics.

The *Principia* is cast in the form of a Euclidean proof from three axioms and one force function. This makes the *Principia* virtually unreadable today. But that may be why the philosophers never made the turn, and remain in the Euclidean framework.

In the entire history of mankind, there have been very few philosophers. Jesus, Buddha, Confucius, Lao-Tse, and Mohammed are creators of guru-disciple traditions, not philosophers in the western sense. If the function of philosophy is the founding of sciences, then only those who have contributed to that task are philosophers: Thales, Pythagoras, Aristotle, Euclid, Galileo, Kepler, Newton, Hobbes, Locke, Harvey, Adam Smith, Hutton, Darwin, William James, C.G. Jung, Toynbee and me. Fewer than two dozen.

So what are all these thousands of people who teach philosophy in the universities? I shall make the same complaint about them that Socrates (a stonecutter) made about the professional teachers of philosophy in his day, who called themselves "sophists." Thus, "sophist" just means "professional philosopher."

Our sophists (like those Socrates attacked) are only interested in "raising questions." When is a question not a question? When one has neither the ability nor the desire to attempt a solution. The sophists transform real problems into abstract "puzzles," incapable of solution when taken out of the rich loam of human experience. The sophists don't want to solve them. That ends the game and puts them out of business. This is my definition of sophistry: "mind-games, where it matters not which side you take, but only the wit shown in the word-play." Perhaps this is why I despise "mathematical recreations," chess, bridge or any sort of mind game, since I automatically suspect the players of a tendency towards sophistry.

How did philosophy become sophistry? Philosophy was certainly a serious business in the 17th Century, when the natural philosophers Galileo and Newton were struggling to figure out the motions of the heavens and the earth, and the "moral" philosophers Hobbes and Locke were earnestly working out the basis for a sound community. These efforts by Hobbes and Locke guided the social revolutions of the 17th and 18th Centuries. Their work was not wasted. Yet, philosophy had taken a wrong turn by the time of Hume. For 300 years, philosophy has been an irrelevant backwater in the university, where no one expects breakthroughs, or progress of any kind.

This farce has continued down to the present day. Sophists still put the Euclidean deductive logic in the first half of their logic texts, and then contradict it with the totally invalid inductive logic of the second half. Think on this. If scientific reasoning were really inductive, how is it possible to refute one long established theory and raise another with a single decisive observation, as Eddington did early in this century?

Newton's theory predicted that star light grazing the sun should be deflected by a certain amount, and Einstein's General Theory of Relativity predicted a deflection of twice as much. Eddington measured the deflection of a grazing star during a total eclipse. The result was closer to Einstein's prediction than it was to Newton's, so down went Newton and up came Einstein. If one test can refute a theory which has had millions of confirmations over centuries of time, then inductive logic is hogwash.

Perhaps sophists have confused inductive confirmation with the utterly different notion of reproducibility. We require results to be reproducible, since this is the chief means of weeding out hallucination, bad experiments and outright fraud. We want to see what results different scientists get, with different apparatus and perhaps a different approach. In most cases, the irreproducible result is quickly found out, and sometimes the source of the error is explained. In other cases, it may take decades to weed out an error, as in the case with the fraudulent Piltdown man.

We must totally reject Hume's rule that extraordinary claims require extraordinary proof, such as proof that fraud could not possibly occur. Such a demand is itself impossible to fulfill. If

Hume's rule had been applied in the 17th Century, we would still be burning witches and heretics at the stake. So you see, Hume is almost an anti-philosopher, since his ideas spawned the metaphysical nonsense of Kant and Hegel, as well as the obstructionist views of the Psi-cops today, who use Hume's rule rather than scientific method. Indeed, even scientists are apt to think scientifically only in their own specialties, and are often just as irrational as everyone else on other subjects.

Hume and the sophists were convinced that Newtonian physics was justified, yet they never understood the concept of a well-established theory. Neither has Sir Karl Popper, a contemporary academic philosopher-of-science of some repute. There is nothing difficult about scientific method. It is the normal problem-solving technique of Western civilization, used by gardeners, backyard mechanics, and mothers with a crying baby.

Because they are stuck in the Euclidean framework, sophists believe any empirical study of values must involve some kind of inference between fact and value, which they know to be invalid. The effect has been a halt to any further development of the "moral" sciences of Hobbes and Locke, thus allowing the dangerous sophistry of Karl Marx.

The existing sciences solve only a single kind of problem (finding explanations), with a single kind of experience (visible and tangible matters of fact). If the problem is not like figuring out how a watch works by taking it apart and seeing how the components move one another, then it lies outside the reach of the physical sciences.

In this book, I have shown that it is possible to extend scientific method to problems other than explanation, and to realms of experience other than matters of fact. This is the way we solve philosophical problems, by creating knowledge-disciplines. I have solved a philosophical problem thought to be impossible since the time of Hume, namely, "how do we determine the good, the right, and the beautiful from experience?"

Elsewhere I have solved the classical theological problem of evil. Elsewhere, I have given empirical content to the concept of free will.

For each philosophical question, there is some relevant realm of experience that can provide an answer, whether it is a question about immortality or divinity or free will or the nature of mind. It is not necessary to invent a new method for each problem. The method invented by Galileo and Newton suffices. It is only necessary to find the equivalent of a theory, a fact, and a test in this new realm of inquiry. Questions that had been matters of ideology and religious dogma can now be answered scientifically. Knowledge replaces faith. Science replaces philosophy. Religion becomes irrelevant. The eternal questions are neither meaningless nor unanswerable, even if our answers must be forever tentative, and subject to refinement by future scholars.

Funetik English

English is the easiest of all known languages, except for its spelling. It has by far the largest vocabulary of any language, more than three times as many words as any other language. It also has the simplest and most flexible grammar, since words do not have inherent gender (which just doubles the difficulty of learning German), nor does the vocabulary change depending on the relationship between speaker and listener (this makes learning Japanese a nightmare). English is already the international language of air traffic, international business, and international science. If it were only phonetic, then it would be as easy to learn to write, as it is to learn to speak.

English is phonetic, in one sense. The problem is that we have borrowed words from so many different places that we have multiple rules for translating the same phoneme into written English. With one or two exceptions my phonetic English simply selects a rule already in use, and standardizes it. My first meta-rule is to create a phonetic English which can be read without training by those who know standard English. Any choice of pronunciation rules is likely to produce some "rogue" words. By that I mean words which the standard English user wants to pronounce one way, while phonetic English says it should be pronounced a different way. My second meta-rule is to minimize the number of such "rogue" words, even if it means picking a fairly obscure rule of pronunciation over one that is more common.

My third meta-rule is to make phonetic English as similar to

Standardized English as possible. Thus, a great many words in English will go unchanged into Phonetic English. The more, the better. However, the cost of this is to make the rules of Phonetic English more complicated, with more special cases. The following paragraph is written in Funetik English.

English iz awlredy funetik. The problem iz that wee hav barrode wurdz frum so miny diferent placez that wee hav multipl rules for translayting the same foneem intu writn English. With wun or tu exceptshuns, my funetik English simply selekts a rule awlredy in uce, and standerdizes it. My ferst meta-rule iz tu kreat a funetik English which kan bee red withowt trayning by thoz hu no standerd English. Eny choyc uv pronunceashun rulez iz likely tu produce sum roge wurdz. By that I meen wurdz which the standerd English yuzer wants tu pronownc wun way, while funetik English sez it shood bee pronownced a diferent way. My sekund meta-rule iz tu minimize the numbr uv such roge wurdz, even if it meens picking a fairly ubskure rule uv pronunceashun over wun that iz mor kawmun. By studying this pairugraf, yu kan lern awl uv funetik English withowt looking at the rulez.

To distinguish homonyms, or for that matter, all the different meanings of words, subscript numbers will be used. These are the same numbers we see now in dictionaries, giving the different meanings in order of popularity.

Consonants are not a problem; we merely have to stop and think how we actually pronounce a word. For instance, "is" is iz, and "was" is wuz so that is how we will spell it in phonetic English. When we think about it, we find that many finial uses of "s" have a "z" sound, and some have a "c" sound.

The problems arise with the vowels. We have far more vowel phonemes than we have vowel letters. In school we were taught that every vowel has a long and short form. But the letter "A" is used for at least 3 distinct phonemes. They are: flat, as in the word "rat," short as in "bark," and long as in "rate."

Now back to the rules of phonetic English. To repeat, it's the vowels that cause trouble. One sticky problem is a vowel sound for which there is no consistent rule at all, and that is the phoneme shared in common by "soot, put, wood, should, good." I choose the double "o."

Expect different rules for (1) a vowel standing alone, (2) vowels which end or begin a word, and (3) different rules depending on the form of the word. In particular, we will look at different rules for the three short word forms: consonant-vowel, vowel-consonant, and consonant-vowel-consonant. And then we add rules for compound words, and finally, for polysyllabic words. Note that for each case, we first select the "natural" pronunciation, for the letter without adding any auxiliary letters (y, w, h, e are common silent auxiliaries) and without doubling the vowel or the consonant. Then, to make a naturally short vowel long, or to make long into short, we use an auxiliary letter. Here are my rules of phonetic English:

Vowels Standing Alone: Every vowel standing alone as an entire word is long. Examples: I, O, A. Thus, "oh" becomes O. This "O" usage is already found in English literature, but is rather archaic.

Special Cases Involving R: Special cases involving "r" might as well be introduced early. They are the combinations "er," "ar" and "or." The first two are always short and the last is always long, wherever they are found and in whatever type of word, and need no auxiliary letters. In this special case, to make the "a" long before the "r" sound, we follow the "a" with "i." Thus, hair, air, fair, fairy. To make the "e" long, we follow it with "a" as in ear, tears, fear.

Special Cases Involving CK: The letter "i" is naturally short anyway in the middle of words. But somehow it just doesn't look right in words that use "CK," such as "picking, kicking, licking," so I propose just to make this handful of words special cases. In other words, we will just have to memorize this handful of words where the "k" sound is made with a "ck."

Consonant-Vowel Words: A finial "a" will not occur in phonetic English. To make "a" short, we use the auxiliary "w", as in: saw, maw, thaw, raw, and add y to make it long. If there were a short "a," it would be spelled with a "uh." The letter "e" is naturally short in this kind of word, as in "the." When we pronounce "the" by itself, we sometimes make it "thee," but listen to it in a running sentence, and you will realize it is a short "e." To make "e" long, add another "e." To make the finial short "u" sound, we end the word with an auxiliary "h." Example: duh, datuh. This assumes that the first "a" in "data" is flat. If it is long, we must write daytuh. The remaining possibilities do not exist.

There is no consistent pronunciation for a consonant followed by an "o", as in "so" and "to." I choose to make a trailing "o" or "u" long. The long "u" rule is found in slang, such as "snafu, thru", and is a common rule in Germanic languages. To make it short, add the auxiliary "h" as in "duh." As mentioned above, to make a finial "a" long, we add the auxiliary "Y", thus: may, say, tray. To make a finial long "i" sound, we use "y," as in my, by, fly, cry, dry. Except for this one word type, a final "y" has a long "e" sound. And except for "my, cry, sy, dry, fly", all the rules apply to trailing vowels in any type of word.

Vowel-Consonant Words: The rules for words which begin with a vowel are not the same as the rules for words which end in a vowel sound. The natural form for "u" is short, thus upset, until, unlike. The natural initial "a" will be flat. Examples: atitude, ax, adz, algebra. Note that in ubout, artikls, ardvark, the last two are covered by the special rule on "ar" and are thus short, rather than flat. In the first case, we have been using "a" for the short "u" sound. "I" has a natural short sound when it begins a word as in itself. An initial "e" is naturally short, as in ever. Note that we use "g" in two different ways in Standard English. There is a hard "g" and a soft "g." I choose to make the hard "g" the natural form, and use "dg" for the soft "g," as in judg. There is no need for the auxiliary "e" in "judge," because the "u" is short, not long. Standard English is full of inconsistencies like that.

To make an initial "a" short, we use the auxiliary "w", just as in finial short "a". Thus: awful, awl. These happen to be Standard English. But consider the sound of "ought." It is apparent it must be spelled awt.

To make any of the initial vowels long, in a simple vowel-consonant word, we use an auxiliary "e" after the following consonant, except for "e", which doubles. Examples: ate, ale, ode, eek, ike.

Consonant-Vowel-Consonant: The natural pronunciation for "A" is flat, as in rat, fat, fad, sat, spat. These are identical to Standard English. If the vowel is "e", "i", "o", or "u" the natural vowel sound is short as in met, wet, set, sit, hit, tit, tot, rot, shot, not, rut, smut, grunt, long again all identical to Standard English. But there are also many cases where Standard English differs. Consider the words "bomb" and "tomb." Each has this consonant-vowel-consonant form, yet each follows a different rule. In phonetic English, these become bom and tume. Notice where two consonant letters are used together as in "nt", "mb", or "rt," it is considered a single consonant sound, for most purposes.

A special rule for one syllable words ending in "ight:" This shall simply be another way of making the "i" long, and making phonetic English more like standard English. Examples are right, sight, might, tight, fight.

The vowel in consonant-vowel-consonant words shall be made long by adding an auxiliary (silent) "e" at the end of the word, except for "e," where the auxiliary "e" immediately follows "e." Examples: fare, tale, rate, like, bike, strike, rode, mode, fore, rude, nude, prude, need, seed, feed, all cases where phonetic English is exactly like Standard English. This will not always be the case. Consider: seet, meet instead of "seat" or "meat", rute instead of "root."

Consonant-Vowel-Consonant-Vowel: The natural sound of "a,e,i,o" for the first syllable will be short, and for "u" it will be long. We shall use "y" as the long "e" sound in the second vowel. A terminal "i" shall be long, as in semi. I cannot think of any other examples of vowel sounds ending a word of this type.

Remember, that "o" preceding "r" is long, and the "a" before "r" can be made long by adding "i." Examples: gory, hairy, duty, pity, pithy, smithy. The first "i" will always be long in two special cases, one where the "i" is followed by the "t" sound (to signal this special case, we will use the auxiliary letters, "gh") and the case where the second consonant is "nd." Thus, mighty, kindly, rind, find, bind. This is another illustration of the fact that if we make the rules complicated enough, we can produce a consistent phonetic language which closely resembles standard English. And that is my policy.

Dipthongs: A dipthong is a vowel sound that changes as it sounds. "Vowel" and "sound" both contain dipthongs. In fact, it is the same dipthong, spelled two different ways. Which one shall we pick? I pick "ow" for the "wow" sound, "oy" for the "soy" sound. See how this affects common words, such as "wound," "sound," "voice" and "vowel." They become wunde, sownd, voyc, vowel.

When we find two vowels together, where the first vowel is "e" and the second is some other vowel, both vowels are naturally long. Thus, kreativ = "creative." A useless final "e" is found on "creative." This is not uncommon in inconsistent Standard English. The vowel in "tiv" is naturally short, but with the auxiliary "e" it would be long, as in endive. Also note that in Funetik English, "c" is never used for the "k" sound. The letter "c" is one of the three sibilants, "z,c,s" which are progressively more open and voiced.

Compound Words: Compounding words does not change the rules for the individual words. We must distinguish compound words from true polysyllabic words.

Polysyllabic Words—Middle Letters: In the middle of a polysyllabic word "u, and i" are short, "a" is flat, and "e" is used for the "neutral" vowel, written with an upside down "e" by phoneticists. For the neutral vowel, my choice is just to omit the neutral vowel altogether, and just pronounce the consonants on either side of it, unless there is a separation between the two sounds. For instance, "vowel" is unchanged because there is a distinct vowel sound between the "w" and the "l". Standard English is quite inconsistent with "o." In "polysyllabic," the "o" is short. In "phoneme" the "o" is long. In the word "inconsistent" the "o" sounds like a short "u". And, "polysyllabic" is really a compound word, which makes the "o" short. How about "following?" Here the "w" is sounded; it is not an auxiliary letter. The rule I choose is that an "o" in the middle of a polysyllabic word is naturally short, but can be made long by immediately following it with an "e." "Follow" becomes folloe. There are two "l" letters, because we pronounce them both.

Immediately following the vowel with "e" makes it long, except in the case of "a" where we follow it with "y" to make it long. A "y" standing alone will produce the long "i" sound in the middle of a polysyllabic word, where "i" would normally be short, for instance, fryday for "friday." The terminal "y" will produce the long "e" sound at the end of a word. Recall that "mighty" is mighty in phonetic English because of the special rule of the long "i" followed by the "t," written with auxiliary "gh."

Remember that "A" in the middle of a polysyllabic word is made long with the auxiliary y, as in sityuwayshun. Do you recognize this as "situation?" In a polysyllabic word, "u" is made long by immediately following it with "e." Note that "u" is sometimes pronounced with a "y" sound preceding the "u," and this "y" sound is written out in phonetic English. The "yu" is always long, without requiring an auxiliary "e."

Polysyllabic Words—Initial Letters: An initial "i", "e", "a," or "o" will be naturally long. To make it short, we follow it with two consonants. Thus "identical" becomes identikul, "emit" remains emit, "omit, only, onto, and omission" become omit, only, ontu, omishun. "Only" makes use of the rule that the standard way of ending a word with the long "e" sound is to use "y". "Elephant" becomes ellefunt, since we want the initial "e" to be short. Obsoeleet is an example where the initial "o" is made short by being followed by two consonants. "Immediately" becomes immeedeeutly.

Polysyllabic Words—Terminal Letters: The rules are the same for polysyllabic words as for consonant-vowel-consonant-vowel words. It is only the simply consonant-vowel word form that has a different rule for a terminal "y," being long "i" in that special case, and otherwise the long "e" sound.

There, I believe I am finished. This is my proposal for phonetic English. It would be possible to come up with a simpler set of rules, but the result would not resemble standard English as much as the second paragraph in this chapter.

Wil the wurld ever akcept funetik English? No dowt it looks like hilbily English tu English profesers. That iz beekahz the semi literut person wil natcherly revert tu funetiks. Are my rules kunsistent? Email me if yu katch inkunsistencies or kases not kuverd.

Mysticism and Revelation;

A Science?

The meaning of the terms, "illumination" and "enlightenment," derives from mystical experience, since both refer to light. Light is not just a metaphor for the mystic. In every mystical state, one is literally filled and surrounded by light, of different colors depending on the mystical state. No one knows why. Maybe this is the "uncreated light," which many mystics talk about. Today, "illumination" and "enlightenment" both refer loosely to the acquisition of any kind of knowledge. In some oriental guru-disciple traditions, one can supposedly acquire enlightenment suddenly, perhaps by nothing more than understanding the real meaning of a koan. But that is just sophistry. Just because something is part of Oriental Philosophy does not mean that it is true, or valuable. It takes years of "carrying wood and water" even to achieve the lesser mystical states which lead up to Cosmic Consciousness (also known as the illumination of fire).

Today, we acquire knowledge by the application of scientific method. And, I have worked to expand the application of scientific method to new problems, and new parts of the spectrum of experience, giving rise (maybe)(I hope) to a renovated Psychical Research, to a science of metaphysics, and to Utopian Analysis, a science of civilization. Yet, even that is not enough.

It takes doing as well as knowing. We shall never gain the kind of control over levitation and apportation exhibited by our humanoid brethren in their UFO spacecraft without spiritual evolution. Maybe I should say we shall not be allowed these higher powers without spiritual evolution. The spiritually evolved are open to many paths. Science is only one.

Spiritual evolution is not something I can define. But I know it when I see it. Lord Kenneth Clark made a similar remark about Civilisation. A society which takes care of its homeless and jobless is more evolved than one which does not. Knowledge is more evolved than ignorance, especially knowledge about things that matter, such as Psychical Research, metaphysics and utopian analysis. A cultural peak with many geniuses is more evolved than a dark age, no matter how necessary an occasional dark age might be. Arts which uplift are more evolved than those which incite to murder and riot. All forms of prejudice and discrimination over trivial matters is primitive. Our persecution of people just because they enjoy different recreational drugs is primitive.

On the other hand, the grand ideals of the Enlightenment are very evolved, if only we could learn to follow them, and recognize violations. The life of the Seeker is more evolved than a life of greed and brutality. Not that everyone must cease productive work. One can still meditate, one can still seek to erase hatred and greed in oneself, even with a job and a family. Still, the highest state of spiritual evolution may develop in those Seekers who do withdraw from the world to devote full time to spiritual evolution.

There are a important revelations which agree with one another, which can guide us into the new age. My favorite is the *Revelations of the Nameless One*, which has given us a new tarot, which contains an encyclopedia of wisdom, in symbolic form. I don't use it for fortune-telling.

Spiritual evolution is possible only when a person understands and applies the divine purpose, which reveals itself in the illumination of fire. It will take lifetimes of spiritual evolution before we are ready to undertake whatever spiritual exercises may be required to gain conscious control over levitation and apports.

Technophiles are so proud of the technological progress we have made in the past two centuries. But on the whole, the past few centuries have been a dark night of the Soul. One symptom of this is the decline of the arts in the 20th Century.

Turn on the local classical music station. What do they play? Museum pieces, mostly from the 19th Century. If it is a good classical music station, it will also play music from the Early Renaissance up through the Baroque. Professional musicians will go broke if they play more than a smattering of contemporary "classical" compositions with their aimless tone rows. Are we supposed to believe this is music because the composers say it is? Like rap, it lacks some of the essential ingredients of music, such as melody and harmony.

Consider painting. We have gone from the highest peaks, in the paintings of the Impressionists and Post-Impressionists to minimalism and conceptual art, where anything is art if the artist says it is. Have you ever been through the Hirschorn museum in Washington, DC? Junk. Room after room of junk. This is not art. This is the Emperor's New Clothes, a con game played for fun and profit by artists, art-dealers and collectors. The art-dealers provide the "artspeak" to convince the puzzled public why this pile of junk really isn't a pile of junk. And once the price can be jacked up enough, it becomes an investment for collectors, no matter how ugly they may regard the piece.

The worst example of spiritual devolution is architecture. Over the centuries, we have gone from the ecstasy of Gothic architecture to the brutal boxes with endless rows of identical rectangles that define the characteristic buildings of the 20th Century. Brutal arts breed brutality in the hearts of man. And the 20th Century saw the greatest mass murders, the worst pogroms, holocausts, purges and ethnic cleansing of any time or place. This is not progress. What science and technology have done for us is to allow us to build bigger boxes and more effective killing machines.

How do we restore the higher arts to a Civilization which has lost them? This is not an easy problem. My proposal is to bring a spiritual basis back to the arts, by means of the mandala technique, as it was developed and Westernized by C.G. Jung. Jung's approach to the mandala is described in the Afterword of the book Mandala by Judith Cornell, Ph.D. The Afterword is written by Michael Flanagin, Ph.D. and it includes full color reproductions of some mandalas made by Jung and by his patients. The medium appears to be watercolor or poster paint.

My drawn mandalas are made on typing paper with kindergarten supplies. Cornell's mandalas require a trip to an art supply house, because she uses 19" by 25" Strathmore charcoal paper, and Berol white and colored pencils. Get the book first, because she specifies the colored pencils by number. She takes her clients through a series of directed exercises, each producing a particular kind of mandala. The advantage of her technique is that the mandalas that result are invariably beautiful, though not as beautiful as those made by Jung and his patients. Cornell uses a particular Yogic meditation with each session, but I imagine any relaxation technique would work.

My contribution to the subject is to extend the mandala technique to all media, in other words, to music, dance, architecture, drama, and clothing. The trick is to balance form and technique. The circle and the square play a role in all forms of mandala. And so does the improvisational element, so no one has a preconceived idea of what will happen.

I hope someday to see mandala buildings, hear mandala music, participate in mandala drama, wear mandala clothing or use it as wall-hangings or bedspreads, and finally, to see mandala paintings on my walls. But this requires the cooperation of professional artists. I am quite happy to pay an artist to turn my scrappy looking mandala on typing paper into a larger canvas, painted with acrylics. But are there professional artists willing to do this? I don't know. The same distinction between composition and performance can apply to all the arts.

But mandalas are not just pretty. They are symbolic revelations from the deep, written in the little known and lost language of Jungian symbolism. Who can interpret them? You can if you are willing to learn the alphabet of symbolism. That may start you on a lifelong study of symbolism, which is the language of the deep, the language of the gods, the language of mysticism. Mystics always have a hard time describing their experience in English. But things can be said symbolically, that cannot be put into words.

Spiritual evolution is not just a matter of knowing. It is also a matter of doing. Participating in mandalas is a way of doing, alone, or in small circles, or the entire community, when it comes to erecting public buildings designed by the mandala technique. Another necessity is meditation. Indeed, for the serious Seeker, years of solitude in the wilds of nature are necessary. But how can anyone afford that? The chapter on the Seeker shows how freedom is paid for by simplicity. This chapter does not go into the details of meditation. It simply shows how a person can live for a year on $50 without begging or prowling around in trash dumps. The form of meditation which leads to mystical states is sometimes called "carrying wood and water." I experienced it by accident. Or by cosmic plan. Who knows? But the path I followed would be impossible to duplicate. The Seeker shows us a different way of following the same path.

Of course, this is not the only form of spiritual exercise. I do not know what exercises are required to develop conscious control over levitation and apports. Metaphysics is in its infancy. I only know that such talents will only come with spiritual evolution. We have a long ways to go. Murder and war must disappear. Theft and greed must go away. Compassion must flower, so there are no more homeless sleeping in the streets. The irritations of modern life must disappear, including gridlock on the streets or in the air. We must make peace with the planet and the creatures on it.

I suppose you are eager to learn the powers of levitation and apportation, so you can travel the stars like our brethren humanoids from other stars in their UFOs? Should you study Yoga? Huna? Shamanism? Well, you can if you like, but these studies are no more likely to give you levitation than a study of Christianity is likely to make you able to walk on water.

I do have a suggestion. We know from NDEs that the mind has two powers which come into operation automatically when we go Out-Of-Body (OOB), at death, or near death, or OOB from lucid dreaming. Let us work on developing those same two powers while In-The-Body (ITB). You will recall that these two powers are the de Broglie powers and the apparitional powers (which includes telepathy). Once we have evolved spiritually enough to be allowed these powers ITB, then we can see the chakras and nadi, and see what effect our exercises have upon them. And once we all have the apparitional power, then a teacher can telepathically convey to the student exactly what it feels like to levitate or apport. The teacher will not have to rely on ordinary language, which was developed for practical and earthly purposes. This will enormously speed up our pace of progress.

Mysticism—A First Hand Account

The first Samadhi is nature mysticism, which I shall introduce with a longish quote from Wordsworth's "Tintern Abbey."

"And I have felt / A presence that disturbs me with the joy of elevated thoughts; / a sense sublime / Of something far more deeply interfused, / Whose dwelling is the light of setting suns, / And the round ocean, and the living air, / And the blue sky, and in the Mind of man; / A motion and a spirit, that impels / All thinking things, all objects of all thought, / And rolls through all things."

As a child and a young man, I knew this state. Nature mysticism shows us that the Soul is distinct from the Mind, since nature is inanimate, and thus has no Mind, but nonetheless has mood and feeling, although not words or ideas. Nature Mysticism is the first step towards the Illumination of Fire.

The second Samadhi is "advanced daydreaming," or more poetically, "oceanic consciousness." It is sometimes called "bathing in the waters," and baptism probably was a symbol for this state.

Those who enjoy solitude are day-dreamers, and find their inner imaginative life richer than the pedestrian everyday conversation of their peers. I had plenty of opportunity for daydreaming as a child, in monotonous farm chores which required no concentration, such as plowing. Monotonous and repetitive physical activities which require no concentration are perfect for finding this ecstatic state of reverie. The best ideas come, unbidden, when doing something mindless, monotonous, and repetitious, such as driving to work, shaving, or doing the dishes. It is when the hands are busy that the Mind is free. Many mystic traditions had rules of silence, and emphasized "carrying wood and water" or other outside chores that require no concentration, freeing the Mind to roam where it may. I call any such situation "work-meditation."

In a state of reverie, one enters a trance-like, luminous state of creative exaltation, the state of genius, even though inspiration can pop up from the unconscious in more ordinary states of consciousness. When "bathing in the waters," one has entered the collective unconscious, the source of the universal language of symbolism, a realm of consciousness that underlies all ordinary consciousness.

Why don't all day-dreamers enter the oceanic consciousness of genius? Perhaps it is no more complicated than this: few people are allowed to day-dream for at least part of the day, from childhood to late middle age. I always volunteered for the really boring tasks on the farm, those which required no concentration. Plowing, or herding cows. As an adult, I made my lunch walk my meditation time. I never permitted friends to accompany me, gently explaining that this was my meditation time. At school, I was reading high school books in 4th grade and most of my teachers were smart enough to just leave me alone. I could lose myself so completely in a book that I only gradually returned from the great depths when I realized the class was laughing, and had been laughing for some time. The teacher had asked me something. I found that I could rummage through my short term memory and recall the question. I gave the answer, and then it was back to the book.

Day-dreaming is the opposite of concentration. Work-meditation as an approach to meditation is opposite to those schools of meditation which require constant repetition of a mantra or focusing on a single point or idea. Work-meditation is complete freedom of Mind, without worries or mental tasks, where the Mind is not forced into any mental routine. School's out when daydreaming. Those other forms of meditation are necessary for people whose Minds automatically fixate on some worry, fear or tragedy, when turned loose.

Many years of "carrying wood and water" are necessary before one can experience the illumination of fire, the third Samadhi, the one that shows us the meaning of life. All mystical states are ecstatic and luminous, in that one feels almost as if a spotlight were turned on you, without consciously being aware of any particular color of light. It is unmistakable in the illumination of fire. I had the distinct impression that I was filled and surrounded with fiery orange-red light. I was thirty-one years old.

The illumination of fire is often called "cosmic consciousness," for instance, by Richard Bucke in his book *Cosmic Consciousness*, one of the classics of Empirical Metaphysics. It feels like a god's eye view of one's own life and knowledge. The Illumination of Fire is concrete, a single gestalt, the way we take in all the details of a familiar face and recognize them as a whole.

What I saw is that a single pattern runs through all things, the meaning of life, the divine purpose of spontaneity, creativity, innocence, joy, love and grace. This is the divine purpose, not a divine plan. There is no one word for it in English. It is the glow of innocence of a state of grace. It is the first crisp evening of fall or the first warm day of spring, with the Mockingbird singing ecstatically and the first flush of green on the trees. It runs through all things. It is the spontaneity of a child playing alone in her sandbox, inventing the game as she goes. It is the grace of a flower, far more beautiful than it needs to be.

The illumination of fire not only shows one the meaning of life, it shows in particular why difficulties are put into our path, and why loss and destruction are a necessary part of the divine purpose. Without obstacles, there would be no creativity. Without renewal, there would be no freshness, spontaneity, youth, innocence, grace. So, the mystic can view the destruction of civilizations with equanimity, knowing that without the Dark Ages there would not be the youthful Western Civilization that we presently live in.

The mystical path does not require schools and classes, much less gurus. Meditation is not necessarily concentration. Meditation can be "carrying wood and water." It is when the body is occupied with monotonous and automatic activity that the mind is free to grow in its own way and to find ecstasy without giving up scientific method or the critical mind that distinguishes the West. If you want to know about meditation which allows you to sit, here is a good source: www.puresilence.org.

The mystical path does not require gurus, although teachers and schools may be useful. Two thousand years ago we gave up our western critical mind and took up a guru-disciple tradition from the East, and a Dark Age resulted. I would like to avoid that this time. This time let us have a brilliant old age, as did the Chinese, who were contemporaries of the Greco-Roman Civilization. It is quite possible to be both a scientist, a philosopher and a mystic, and this is attempted in the academic discipline of Transpersonal Psychology. It would be a good thing if this discipline were to become part of the curriculum of universities. I would not call it a science, exactly, because it makes use of transpersonal techniques from all 7 ways, from Shamanism, Yoga, Native American Medicine Path, African Voodoo, Buddhism, Taoism, and even scientific method. Mystical states are reproducible, as William James discovered. Symbolic revelations from the depths of Self are reproducible as C. G. Jung discovered. So, William James and C. G. Jung have laid the groundwork for a possible spiritual science. We shall just have to wait and see if anything comes of it.

Creation

A letter to Ben: I think the universe came into being, with everything so perfectly fine tuned to lead to stars, galaxies, life and humanoid intelligence, because you created it. I created it. This is perhaps the radical thing about the mystic's view of divinity. You are god. I am god. The terrorists of 9/11 have deep within them a soul which is never sullied, never evil, even when deeply buried inside a body and a mind which is twisted, and ignorant. I have read that some people can remember being galaxies under LSD. I think that is right. We were the soul of the galaxy, and the soul of this solar system and the soul of this planet and many other things before we became Ben and Chris. We are all ocean, though some times we become lakes or snowflakes, only to eventually return to the ocean, in a billion or trillion years. That is why I object to Buddhism. They want to return to the ocean and quit reincarnating immediately. There is no hurry. We live in a rich but also confusing place where the divine purpose is often forgotten and mankind has to remind us again by mystics, who come into this world in every Century, in every part of the world.

The mistake of Judaism-Christianity-Islam is to personalize the Ocean. That is wrong. Divinity is the sum total of all souls over the entire universe and maybe other universes as well. God doesn't kill children. God doesn't crash airplanes. People ask, how could god allow this? It was god in the form of 29 crazy suicidal stupid terrorists who allowed this. They were inflamed by alleged men of Allah, the Mullahs, who have forgotten the great mystics of their own tradition, people like the Poet Rumi. Yet these 29 hijackers are also god. Do not blame the ocean for the stinging pellets of sleet. It is also ocean, and to ocean it will eventually return.

The Problem of Evil

If there is divinity and a meaning to life, why do bad things happen to good people? This is not just a medieval conundrum. Scott Peck and Rabbi Kusher have tackled this question in our own time.

There is a divine purpose, and therefore a meaning to life. The trouble is that humans must have creativity and free will to express this divine purpose. And there must be challenges and renewals, which we do not always welcome.

Death is not the ultimate evil; death is renewal. Death is the way a crotchety old fart becomes a happy toddler once again. Pain and frustration are but challenges to jolt us into a creative response. It is a cruelty and not a comfort to say to someone who has lost a child that it is God's will. There is no God, and there is no Will. There is only a divine purpose. The future is what we make of it. There is no God because "God" is a name, as is "Jehovah," "Allah," and "Brahma," but One is nameless. As soon as we give divinity a name, it becomes divisive, an excuse for "ethnic cleansing," because it becomes attached to a particular historical and religious tradition.

Instead of saying divinity is good, we should say divinity is purposeful. The divine purpose that runs through all things is this spontaneity, creativity, grace, joy concept for which we have no English equivalent.

Also understand the absolute continuity of existence. Our existence merely goes through various phases and stages, which go by such names as sleep and waking, life and death, human existence and non-human existence. Life and history are full of both positive and negative experiences. Pain, discomfort, obstacle, and stagnation are usually perceived as negatives. They should instead be welcomed as challenges. How could there be creativity without challenge?

And how can there be spontaneity without renewal? Renewal sometimes requires death and destruction, of lives, societies, ideas, species, worlds, and universes. If things merely accumulated, if human lives merely lengthened without end, if there was never decay and destruction, everything tends towards a sameness, a stagnant old age, without freshness, newness and spontaneity. There are three handles on the chalice from which we drink the waters of life: creation, preservation, and destruction. Each may serve the divine purpose. We cannot say that this is the best of all possible worlds, yet it is surely better with grace, joy, spontaneity and creativity than without them. The evils are not as absolute as we think, and they serve deeper purposes than we know.

"Omniscient" cannot mean the ability to foresee everything that will happen. Free will and creativity imply that brand new things and ideas and expressions are and always will be springing into existence, for that is the purpose of all existence.

The medieval idea of omnipotence is also incorrect and incompatible with free will and creativity. The higher Self may put challenges, opportunities and coincidences in our path, but what we do with them is up to us. We may rise, or we may fall. Some accidents are just accidents. All actions have consequences. If a child or a dog runs in front of a speeding car, it will be killed. This is just a law of nature, not anyone's plan. It is wrong to say that everything that happens is some god's will. Only preachers talk of God's will, as if they knew anything about it. What they know is a convenient and legal way to fleece the suckers.

So what is the answer to the medieval "Problem of Evil?" I have already given it. Life is better with innocence, freshness, spontaneity and creativity than without. And this is only made possible by animacy and creativity, things quite impossible under the dreary religion of the scientists, where we are all just soulless machines. They would also be impossible in the world of medieval theology, where God wills all things and knows all things. The new age begins when we have liberated ourselves from both dogmas. All religions are evil, but the most evil is the religion of the scientists, because that is the most pervasive, and the one they put into textbooks.

Animacy, Free Will, Challenge-And-Response

A typewriter will never turn itself on in the middle of the night and begin clacking out the "Great American Novel." However, a cat will wake itself up in the middle of the night, find a ball of yarn, and bat it all around the living room, leaving a tangle of yarn around the legs of chairs. There, in a nutshell, is the difference between all machines and all life. It is odd that the behaviorists, alleged students of behavior, do not seem to have noticed this difference.

We know that no real car will ever behave like "The Love Bug" in some Disney movies, partly because we have at least some crude knowledge of how cars work. The great humbug of AI (Artificial Intelligence) is made possible only because most programmers do not become fluent in assembly language, and never learn the physics of a logic gate. It's just a dumb machine, and like any other machine, it does only what we tell it to do. If we don't tell it to do anything, it is just an expensive paperweight.

We have to push the buttons on machines. Living things, on the other hand, may initiate action without anything pushing their buttons. The first attribute of animacy is initiative. Our ordinary everyday experience is that machines and living creatures behave very differently. Hollywood writers instinctively recognize this difference. When they want to show us AI, instead they show us animacy. Herbie the Love Bug starts by itself and goes where it wants, regardless of the operator's inputs. Hal 5000 has to be cajoled, and the crew is nervous about its decisions.

When a computer program is run with the same inputs, it always produces the same outputs. This is still true if the program includes a random number generator, so long as it is provided with the same "seed" number. But in the same environment, cloned life forms take different actions. Thus, the second attribute of animacy is choice.

A virus may attack a cell immediately, or it may lie low and hide for years. Don't blame this on quantum mechanics. Viruses are far too large to be affected by quantum mechanics.

The third attribute of animacy is strategy, such as the strategy of a virus which decides to hide out in some unusual host while it rearranges genes until it can survive some new antibody to it. See Kilbourne's book *Influenza*. Strategy is a combination of purpose and creativity.

It is this combination of initiative, choice, and strategy that is animacy, which gives empirical content to the empty philosophical term "free will."

AI is a belief in magic. It is an age-old dream, one we find in Pinocchio, for instance, the dream of bringing an inanimate object to life with some magic spell. In the case of AI, the "magic spell" is a computer program. AI enthusiasts believe if they can just make the program big enough or smart enough, the computer will suddenly "come to life," like Number-5 in one of those Disney movies ("Short Circuit"). It will never happen. There are no essential differences between computers and other machines. If a computer can come to life, why not a car or a screwdriver? Ally Sheedy says "I'm a machine, and I'm alive." In what factory was she built?

Reductionists just assume that living things can be explained in terms of heredity and environment. The truth is, reductionists have ignored animacy. They haven't explained it away, any more than they have explained away consciousness.

Another way of looking at animacy is in terms of challenge-and-response, which may really be opportunity-and-response. The great historian Arnold Toynbee found repeated patterns of challenge-and-response in human affairs, although no one has ever found an example of cause-and-effect in history that could stand up to close scrutiny.

All living things have animacy. How do I explain this? Soul. Soul provides the coherency and continuity of perception, the overall organization of the organism, and animacy in behavior. The nervous system is only a pre-processor. Viruses, bacteria, fungi and plants display animacy and coherent behavior without a trace of a nervous system. And as Aldous Huxley learned on Mescalin, divinity is immanent in all things, animate and inanimate. Thus, even storms and mountains and oceans have free will.

I give two examples of coherency. If we watch bacteria under a microscope, we see all the internal parts jiggling around, doing the dance of life. At cell death, all cease simultaneously. There is no ripple of failure that spreads out from one place or another. Another instance of unexplained coherency comes from the study of neurophysiology in higher animals. A certain stimulus causes certain columns of neurons in the cortex to fire. But there remains an inexplicable quantum jump from that fact to the coherent field of perception.

This gap is finally being noticed in the scientific community. See "The Puzzle of Conscious Experience," by David J. Chalmers, in *Scientific American*, December 1995, p. 80. Physiology can never jump that gap. It is Soul that gives ordinary perception its coherence and continuity. All living things have animacy because they all have Souls. Thus, the detailed behavior of living things can never be predicted, even if we are talking about trees, fungi or viruses. But if this idea is correct, earthquakes, volcanic eruptions, tornadoes, and similar phenomena are also subject to free will. Anything in nature which is not strictly deterministic, anything subject to the mathematics of chaos, may be said to be subject to free will. In that case, it may make sense to pray to the gods of the mountains, or the gods of the winds. But what could you tell them that would make any difference to them? As a nature mystic, I know that they are really not much aware of human beings. They do not think in terms of words or concepts, but of emotions, which are old and cold and nostalgic. Perhaps the nature mystic could convey an emotion to them. I never tried.

The Desert Religions

It is well known that all the desert religions are closely related. The best known of these are Judaism, Christianity, and Islam. We know from the *Dead Sea Scrolls* that there were a variety of forms of Judaism in the first Century CE, and Christianity could be considered one of them. Judaism did not start as a mystical religion, but developed a mystical slant in the middle ages, giving rise to the Kabbalah and the *Book of Splendor*. Islam also had a mystical side, the Sufis, who were actually Christian Monophysites (monotheists) and desert saints who liked this new, simple, decidedly monotheistic religion, one which rejected idolatry much more decidedly than Christianity, which was torn by the battles over icons for centuries. So they converted, when the southern half of the Byzantine Empire was overrun by Islam. All three religions have run out of steam. Most cultural Jews are not religious Jews. Only about 2% of the members of the Anglican Church in England ever go to church. Judaism and Christianity mainly function today for the great transitions of life, birth, coming of age, marriage, and death. It is likely that all three religions will have disappeared before the end of the 21st Century.

So what did Jesus teach? I leave it to you to verify this for yourself, since it is not hard to find copies of *The Gospel of Thomas*. This Gospel has been preserved from ancient times in the dry desert of Egypt, and was only discovered in 1945. It was part of the library of a group of desert "Saints" (the same word is "Essene"). Only one copy of the *Gospel of Thomas* has ever been found and it is written in Coptic, the language of Ancient Egypt. Say what you will about the corruption of the traditional *New Testament*, caused by pious fraud and mistranslation over the millenia—this copy of the Gospels comes straight to us from Ancient Times.

The *Gospel of Thomas* could equally well be called "The Sayings of Jesus." There are no miracles, no Messiah complex, no Sermon on the Mount (but the Beatitudes are all there), no entry into Jerusalem, no Crucifixion, and no Resurrection. Indeed, there is nothing internal to the book which would date the time of Christ. He arguably could be the "Teacher of Righteousness" in the *Dead Sea Scrolls*, a man who lived about 100 BCE. If you want to know what Jesus actually said to his disciples, get this book. Most of these sayings are also found in the "canonical" gospels, Matthew, Mark, Luke and John, but there are a few crucial differences. Then there is also the question of just what he meant. In my opinion, certain crucial metaphors have been mistranslated.

Most of the teaching of Jesus consists in parables and metaphors about reaching a state of "the X of Y" where X is a word usually translated as "kingdom" but could also be translated "realm" and Y is a word for "sky" usually translated as "heaven." Translating ancient metaphors is a tricky business. We have to put ourselves back into that time, and try to imagine how people of that time would understand this metaphor.

From the time of Aristotle (300 BCE) to the time of Galileo (1600 CE), nearly 2000 years, the worldview, the background of all thought, was that of Aristotle and Ptolemy. It made a large distinction between the heavens (i.e. stars, the moon, the sun, and the planets) and earth. Earth was made of four elements, earth, air, fire, and water, and was mutable and perishable. The heavenly bodies were made of a fifth element (quintessence) which was immutable, imperishable and eternal. Thus, the correct translation of this metaphor is "realm of the imperishable," or "realm of the quintessence."

Given that meaning, it makes perfectly good sense to say "The realm of the quintessence is within," a saying found both in the *Book of Thomas* and the canonical gospels. Fundamentalists are sometimes rather taken aback when I point that out to them. And, it makes perfectly good sense to try to enter the realm of the quintessence while one is still alive. Although Yoshua clearly believes in an afterlife, he gives no details. But he does make it clear that the search for the realm of the imperishable must be done in this life, if the seeker is to find ONE. And that is exactly what the Saints were doing.

Desert Saints: Like mystics of all ages and all cultures, they found it necessary to withdraw from the world, to obtain solitude, for years at a time. The Yogis found solitude in the forest, the Taoist mystics found it in the mountains, and the Saints found it first in the desert, and later on remote islands off the coast of Ireland and Scotland. It is clear to me, someone who has experienced the illumination of fire, that this is what Yoshua bar Josuf had himself experienced, and this is what he wanted his followers to find.

The illumination of fire gives one a vision of life and history as a whole, with a single divine purpose running through it. This is what makes one whole (holy). Clearly, this was the original meaning of "holy," which has a common root with holistic, holographic, whole, hale and heal. Both men and women withdrew from the Saturnalia of the Roman empire to become pure and holy, and sometimes they returned as great witnesses to their experiences.

Martyr As Witness: The word "martyr" means "witness." This is something the legalistic Romans could understand. They had no science, but they had law, and they knew the value of a good witness. Since Christianity was periodically persecuted, these pure and holy witnesses to illumination were often put to death. But they went fearlessly, which really impressed the materialistic Romans. Such people were called Saints. The more Saints the Romans created, the more Romans became Christians.

Early Christianity: During the period of persecution, Christianity was also organizing itself as a religion, with priests and bishops. Peter went to Rome, as did Paul, while Thomas is alleged to have gone to India. James evangelized in Jerusalem among the Jews. So, there was a formal, hierarchical organization being developed, i.e. the church, but there were also the Saints, who were completely outside any such organization, yet, who provided the main impetus for the growth of Christianity. One of the strengths of the early church is that it was open to men and women, rich and poor, and it practised charity. It also opened the first orphanages, the first hospitals, and the first hostels. Even in the middle ages, pilgrims and travelers of all kinds stayed at monasteries along the way, which continued to be the centers of learning and even of innovation, until the rebirth of trade and of cities and of a middle class.

The first wave of pagan barbarians rolled over the Western Roman Empire, but stopped short of Ireland, Wales, and Scotland, possibly because of a Celtic war-lord whose name was "bear," i.e. "Artos" thus giving rise to the Arthurian legends, all of which first appeared in the Celtic Fringe in the 8th and 9th Centuries. The monasteries there created a brief golden age, an age of marvelous manuscripts and fine jewelry. For about a century, they were the only people in Europe who could read and write, both Greek and Latin, and who still had a taste for the classics in those languages, and still had libraries and scriptoria. Thus, they made copies, which wound up all over Europe. It was also a culture rich in Saints, some of whom began to evangelize Anglo-Saxon England, Frankish Gaul, and Lombardian Italy. This is how the Irish saved civilization, as described in Thomas Cahill's marvelous little book, *How The Irish Saved Civilization.*

One of the last of these Hibernian scholars was Alcuin of York, who started a school and scriptorium for Charlemagne, which was never extinguished, and eventually became one of the first European universities. Most of the ancient books that have come down through the middle ages are Carolingian copies, the first to separate words with a space, and the first to use the Carolingian minuscule, father of "lower case." It is a wonder the Ancients could read their inscriptions, since they were all upper case, all the words were jammed together, and they were very fond of allusions and abbreviations, just as today we are very fond of acronyms.

How Did Sunday School Christianity Arise? By pious fraud and forgery. The Popes themselves know this. And some Popes have admitted as much. In her book, *The Christ Conspiracy*, Acharya S introduces us to a vast, little known literature by people who challenge every part of Sunday School tradition. According to the skeptics, the Bible has been under more or less continuous revision from about 170-180 CE (when the oldest parts of the New Testament were written down, according to her) down to the dawn of printing in the 15th Century. The skeptics doubt the huge drama of the passion of Christ, because historians of the time, such as Josephus, make no mention of it (actually there is a mention of Christ, but scholars assume this is a later interpolation. It does not occur in all copies.). Nor do they think the life of Jesus could possibly be set in Galilee of around 30 CE, because Galilee at that time was a rich Roman province, with great cities under construction that are not even mentioned in the Bible. Nor could he have been from Nazarus, which did not exist in 1 CE, or 30 CE. In addition, the early church fathers, such as Justin Martyr and Marcion make no mention of the four canonical gospels, so they could hardly have been written in the First Century CE. In the letters of Paul, he makes absolutely no mention of the teachings of Jesus. He quotes no parable, no beatitude, none of the teaching about the Kingdom of Heaven. Indeed, no book in the New Testament makes any mention of any other book in the New Testament. Acharya and many skeptics conclude that the Jesus legend is pure myth, and has no historical basis.

At the very least, Acharya and other skeptics should teach us to doubt Sunday School tradition. That is why I confine myself to modern philological and archaeological discoveries that were not transmitted through the Church. Thus, I think the catacomb art is interesting for what it shows and what it does not show. And, the archaeology done under the Altar of St. Peters in Rome during WW II is also very interesting (see The *Bones of St. Peter* in the bibliography). Neither supports the extreme position of Acharya. Under the altar a First Century tomb was discovered, near Nero's Circus. The bones of a robust man of 70 were found, missing feet and head, wrapped in purple cloth veined with threads of pure gold, hidden inside what has been called "the graffiti wall," a part of a small, disguised church, with a baptistery, in the middle of a pagan cemetery. Why not the head? Another church in Rome claims that relic. Why no feet? If Peter really was crucified upside down by Nero, the easiest way to get him down would be to chop off the feet. Maybe not all the traditions of Christianity are pious frauds.

Whether Yoshua bar Josuf was crucified or not is debatable, because it isn't mentioned in the Book of Thomas. It would be an unusual punishment for heresy. Usually, the Jews stoned heretics to death, as they eventually did to James. In the Koran it says Yoshua was not crucified. The Jews keep a record of the several hundred would-be or accused messiahs between 100 BCE and 100 CE, and it includes one Joshu bar Josuf, whose mother was Mary, who was stoned to death. We find no crucifixes in the catacombs, nor any Last Supper, much less a Last Judgment. The earliest crucifix in Christian Art is a crude and obscure figure on the door of the church of Santa Sabina in Rome, dating to the 5th Century CE. Crucifixes did not become a common symbol until the Tenth Century. What we see in catacomb art is not the crucifix, but Christ in Orisen, which is the T gesture, standing with arms wide open. Do that to a person, and they will come give you a hug. Do that to the world, alone on a hilltop at dawn, and gain a wonderful epiphany of the wonder and beauty of the world, despite the pain and struggle. So, it could very well be that the T gesture came first, and was eventually given historicity by the process of myth-making, followed by ignorant Centuries which took these myths literally.

The oldest copies of the New Testament that have survived are the Vatican Codex, and the Sinai Codex, both dating from the 4th Century CE. There seems such a distance between the "Sayings of Yoshua" and even the short version of Mark that one suspects many decades or even centuries had to pass, decades of syncretism and mythologizing. It is not unusual for religions to begin with the mystical teachings of the founder to a small circle of disciples. As the religion develops it is not unusual for it to absorb elements from other religions over the centuries (syncretism) and to incorporate fantastic fairy tales, which may incorporate some symbolic truth (mythology).

The Books of the New Testament as we have it were selected from a vast variety of "gospels" at the Council of Nicaea in 325 CE, under pressure from Emperor Constantine, who brought Christianity out of the catacombs and built it fine basilicas. He was even prepared to break all sorts of taboos to do so. For instance, the Basilica of St. Peter was constructed over a pagan cemetery (which is still down there!), just so the altar could be placed directly over the tomb of St. Peter.

Constantine meddled in religion primarily for state reasons. He needed an all-embracing (Katholos) state religion to end divisive strife, and to make the Roman Empire more defensible. In this he succeeded, so that at least the Eastern part of the Empire survived for another thousand years.

Conclusion: So, are we to reject the Bible altogether? Did these miraculous events really happen? Was Christ resurrected? Did Paul have a transcendental vision on his way to Damascus, wherein he beheld the risen Christ? This might explain the eventual success of Christianity.

Here is a second possibility. Yoshua experienced the illumination of fire, and his teachings on the way to enter the "realm of the imperishable" (Kingdom of Heaven) worked. Those followers who gave up worldly concerns and went off into the desert as Seekers of the illumination of fire often succeeded, and when they returned to the world (or when the world came to them), they were not only holy and wise, but they also had "miraculous" powers, such as healing, or walking on water. The miracles of one age are the science of the next. The age of faith passes, and the age of spiritual science begins.

I feel I should say something about my own beliefs. I am not religious at all. Psychical and mystical research replace religion. Why accept anything on faith, when we have reproducible scientific knowledge? The issues discussed in this chapter are pure intellectual puzzles, like those about the historical basis of the Iliad or the Odyssey or Moses.

The god of the Christians is no more alive for me than Jove or Mithra. One thing I am sure of. The popular legend of Jesus is false, as is the legend of Moses, and the legend of Mohammed. It is possible that the Moses of legend was Ah-Moses (son of Ah), who drove the Hyksos back to Palestine and defeated them at Sharuhen (the Vale of Sharon). It was the Semitic Hyksos who were the tyrants, and the Egyptians who were the slaves. Ah-Moses liberated his people, true enough. But his people were the Egyptians. This event happened in 1550 BCE, about the same time as the volcanic eruption of Santorini, which could easily account for all of the 10 plagues which are part of the legend of Moses, as well as the parting of the Reed Sea. (Yes, that is what it says in the Hebrew Bible, Reed, not Red.)

Religious fervor is the root of all evil in the world, the background of all wars. The history of Judaism, Christianity, Islam, Hinduism or Buddhism is made irrelevant by the rise of scientific method, and its application to psychical phenomena, beginning in 1892 by the British Society for Psychical Research. The scientific study of mysticism and symbolic messages from the depths of Self has only begun . . . well begun by William James the philosopher and by C. G. Jung the psychoanalyst.

Current evidence may change, and my speculations could easily be proven false. That wouldn't bother me. I rely on Ian Stevenson and Raymond Moody, not on the Bible or Koran.

I would be remiss if I did not point out that current evidence leaves open the possibility that Yoshua was crucified and then transubstantiated. This idea could also easily be refuted by science, so I personally would not put much trust in it. Here is my current reasoning. There was a first Century tomb under the Tropaion which is under the altar of St. Peter's Basilica in Rome. The bones of a robust 70 year old man, wrapped in purple cloth with threads of gold was found hidden in the graffiti wall, part of the Tropaion, an early church hidden in a pagan cemetery. The head and feet are missing. Another church in Rome claims the head of St. Peter. The missing feet suggest that Peter might have been crucified upside down in Nero's circus, which was nearby. The easiest way to get him down would be to chop off the feet. If he chose to be crucified upside down, then surely Yoshua was also crucified. Countless would-be messiahs rose and fell between 100 BCE and 100 CE, 256 by Jewish count. All were forgotten except Yoshua. Why? Maybe he was transubstantiated in a flash of energy, leaving the faint traces of scorched fiber on the very top micro-fibrils of the Shroud of Turin, which form the image. Could the Shroud of Turin be authentic? At this point in time, it could be. The Carbon 14 tests did not take into account the microbial film on all the fibers. The same laboratories have an average error of 1200 years when asked to date ancient linen from mummies of known age, presumably for the same reason.

It is interesting that the transubstantiated Yoshua was often not immediately recognized by friends and disciples. How exactly does a pure energy body look? I don't know. Perhaps it glows in some strange way. But these visions could not be apparitions, which are always recognized. Of course, further scientific tests could easily show the Shroud of Turin to be a fraud, and a peculiarly cruel one. Someone was definitely crucified, scourged and made to wear a crown of thorns. And given the spear thrust in the flank. And then wrapped in that linen. Who it was, we may never know for sure. But in the end, it doesn't really matter.

The Sayings of Jesus

Jesus said: "I am the Light that is above them all, I am the All, and the All came from me and the All attained to me. Cleave a piece of wood and I am there; lift up the stone and you will find me there."

This saying (#77) may sound utterly egotistical. Certainly it is quite contrary to all Jewish tradition. But consider it in the context of the mystic's view of divinity :

"When you come to know yourselves then you will become known, and you will realize that is you who are the sons of the living Father."

Any of the disciples or any enlightened person could say the same thing as saying #77, for they know that all of us partake of divinity (consciousness), which is found in all things. If there is only ONE, which is ALL, then you are divine, I am divine, the stick of wood and the stone are divine. It is like the dance and the dancer; they are not separate. When the dancer stops, so does the dance.

Nonetheless, this is a teaching which is easily perverted. For instance, it can be taken to mean that we are each responsible for our own illness, or that we can each be rich and powerful just by believing it, or indeed, that anything can come true just by having faith. Thus, people can be made to feel guilty for being ill, or guilty for not being rich and powerful. This is a tragic misunderstanding.

If the TOTALITY creates nature, it is only in the sense of

creating space and time and the laws of nature. Sometimes the Higher Self can impose a pattern on random events. This is called synchronicity or divination, depending on the context. But on the whole, the individual cannot change even his own condition without full knowledge and remembrance of why his higher Self chose these challenges in the first place. And then he may realize there is a reason for this condition, a challenge to overcome, a lesson to be learned, karma to be worked off. In general, it requires the difficult and slow acquisition of knowledge and skills to change the reality that we experience as Nature.

"Men think, perhaps, that it is peace which I have come to cast upon the world. They do not know that it is dissension which I have come to cast upon the earth: fire, sword, and war."

Jesus said: "I have cast fire upon the world, and see, I am guarding it until it blazes."

Like everything Jesus said, this should be taken metaphorically, not literally. The "fire" is the "illumination of fire" while symbolically a "sword" means "decision" while the "war" is within ones own heart, a battle against conventional motives, which in the Roman Empire, led to greed and violence. Of course, this is not at all what the conventionally pious would expect to hear from Jesus, yet these sayings are in the New Testament.

Most of the sayings of Jesus in the New Testament are also found in the Book of Thomas. For instance, the beatitudes are here, but scattered through the book, not all in one place, nor delivered at one time. And there are a few more of them, such as "Blessed are the solitary and elect, for you will find the Kingdom. For you are from it, and to it you will return." But one can see why the author of Matthew put them all in one place, and invented the Sermon on the Mount. What we do not find is any apocalyptic expectation of the return of Christ, or some future coming of the Kingdom of Heaven. According to Jesus, it is already here.

His disciples said to Him, When will the repose of the dead come about, and when will the new world come?

He said to them, "What you look forward to has already come, but you do not recognize it."

On another occasion his disciples said to him "When will the Kingdom come?" Jesus said: "It will not come by waiting for it. It will not be a matter of saying 'Here it is' or 'There it is.' Rather, the Kingdom of the Father is spread out upon the earth, and men do not see it."

This is perhaps the wisest and most important teaching in the whole Book of Thomas. Certainly it should refute all those who believe in the apocalypse. It is also another typical saying of the true mystic. Those who have experienced the Illumination of Fire know all the great and terrible wonder and beauty of the world, the wonder and beauty of destruction as well as the renewal the fire makes possible. What we call disasters are signs of life, in the universe, in geology, and in the course of civilizations. Thus, the world is as it should be. Of course, we can always make it better. But it is not the terrible and evil place the Gnostics taught, which is one more reason for denying that the *Book of Thomas* is Gnostic.

From the larger perspective, the advent of Christianity in the West imposed a guru-disciple tradition, a discipline of chastity, poverty, and obedience which destroyed or delayed the incipient sciences created by Western philosophy. It also smothered those distinctive Western traits of individual freedom and individual genius which only re-emerged after a thousand years of darkness. No wonder the figures in early medieval Christian art look so dour and unhappy!

Please note that this oriental guru-disciple tradition cannot be blamed on Yoshua, because, like Krishnamurti, he rejected the mantle of "Master" which his followers tried to hang around his shoulders, as the following passage will show:

Jesus said to His disciples, "Compare me to someone and tell Me whom I am like."

Simon Peter said to Him, "You are like a righteous angel." Matthew said to Him, "You are like a wise philosopher." Thomas said to Him,

"Master, my mouth is wholly incapable of saying whom You are like."

Jesus said: "I am not your master. Because you have drunk, you have become intoxicated from the bubbling spring which I have measured out."

A Kind of Autobiography

When my mother was pregnant with me, she was diagnosed with cervical cancer. Both the GP and the oncologist agreed that she must have an immediate hysterectomy, with the inevitable abortion of myself. But my mother was a stubborn and courageous woman, and still is at 81. After my birth, she was checked again for cancer. All gone. Nothing there. And to this day, nearly 60 years later, she has never had cancer. So mine was a miraculous birth. My mother only told me this when I was 57 and she was 79. I suppose she was afraid I would get a swollen ego or feel that I was somehow special or different.

In 3rd and 4th grade, I was a prodigy. I made better than A's, better than A+'s, I made 100's on my report card. I was reading high school books. Naturally, I was the teacher's pet. But I didn't have any friends. So for the next few years, I became the teacher's bane, the class clown, the class cutup. But by the time I hit 8th grade, I was back to being a prodigy, taking classes on my own that weren't offered in our tiny high school. Teachers began bringing me books from the local University library.

At 15, I read Plato's *Republic*, and became a utopian dreamer. I had always been a day-dreamer, but now my day-dreams took on more focus. I also read the Mentor classics on science and philosophy, the history of H.G. Wells, and the popularizations of 20th Century science by George Gamow. I scored off the scale on the only IQ test I ever had (it only went to 140). I was a National

Merit Scholar and an NDEA Title IV Fellow, scoring in the 98.6th percentile (of those taking the test) on the GREs.

At 19, I got the idea of making a science of utopia. And I pursued this dream, despite uniform rejection and discouragement from all my professors, all my colleagues, and all my family. As Edison said, genius is 2 percent inspiration, and 98 percent persistence. Or at least, that is what he meant. It took me 30 years of working on the problem, off and on, before I finally solved it. My solution is found in the Science of Civilization.

But let us backtrack to the beginning. I sound like an egghead. I was, but I was also a mystic. That had completely different roots.

I grew up on a primitive farm, without electricity, central heat, or indoor plumbing. We drank water with a pail that we all used, drinking water out of a bucket, which I carried from the well down by the barn. We didn't heat the whole house, only the living room, with a wood burning stove. I carried the wood into the house each night. I went to school in a little town (pop. 300), and neither the school nor any of the houses had indoor plumbing.

Thus, knocking over outhouses was one of our pranks on Halloween night, along with letting a cow into the school house, shooting out the few streetlights with BB guns, and throwing eggs into or on the cars of anyone we had a grudge against. We also built barricades down mainstreet, with hay bales or huge empty oil drums. This kind of hooliganism was traditional and tolerated.

I am not complaining. I am exulting. It was a wonderful life, vanished now from the American scene. There was nothing more cozy than to sit on one side of my mother, my older brother on the other, while the stove reached a red heat, and the kerosene lanterns put out a soft golden glow, and the wind howled around the cornices, while my mother read us books. This is my fondest memory of childhood.

Do you remember the laconic Plainsman of the movies, played by Gary Cooper? This is authentic. Country people are comfortable with silence. It is considered rude to break another's reverie. So I was always free to go inward, to my luminous daydreams, or outward, to immerse myself in the south wind that blew over my bed, with its memories of South Seas, and the moonlight beaming down. Indescribable feelings filled me with longing and nostalgia, for what I did not know. I was living a certain mystical path, that of "carrying wood and water," and did not know it. I assumed everyone had these wonderfully luminous experiences, but that it was like sex, something no one talked about. I loved solitude in nature so much that I always volunteered for the really boring jobs, like plowing or herding cows.

I could enter the luminous world of the nature mystic, or the collective unconscious. Even that wasn't enough for me. I would get on my bicycle and ride round and round the yard (not the lawn, but a barren area between barns and corral). This must have seemed eccentric, but not by word or gesture was it discouraged. When the hands are busy, the mind is free, and can go where it will. Often it will roam the realm of Genius, Oceanic Consciousness, also known as the collective unconscious. Other times one will merge with the wind, the sky, the trees, mountains or surf.

This is the essence of meditation, at least of the "carrying wood and water" school of mysticism. One must spend many thousands of hours in Oceanic consciousness (advanced daydreaming) and many thousands of hours immersed in the mood-feelings of nature before one is ready for the Illumination of Fire, which I experienced at age 31. This is also known as Cosmic Consciousness. In that sense, there is a path, which one may follow accidentally, as I did, or deliberately, in which case we call it "carrying wood and water." The hero must first survive the trip through the "dark wood," which for me was alcoholism and toxic psychosis. Later one finds a Mentor. Mine was a mild mannered soft spoken linguist named Bill Coates. He introduced me to the classics of psychical research and mysticism (two quite different topics). Only then was I ready for my transcendental encounter with the ONE, where I saw, as one recognizes a face, all of space and time, fit into a single pattern. This is the divine purpose, that runs through all things. It is the meaning of life. In the New Tarot, it is represented by the Mother. There is no single word for it in English.

Speaking of the New Tarot, I spent most of my thirties studying it and doing mandalas and deciphering the alphabet of symbolic elements.

This is not a conventional autobiography. I am only including the things that were most important in my development as a mystic and philosopher and scientist. And most of these were interior and private experiences.

When I was a Freshman in college, I saw the three norns, deciders of fate in Nordic mythology. Divinity always comes in threes. There are three judges in the Chinese underworld that decide your next lifetime, and under hypnotic regression, people can remember having to go before the three judges, during the in-between life. But back to the three norns. They looked like three respectable middle-aged ladies, sitting there at my desk or standing around it, looking at me as if to say "So this is the One?" I blinked my eyes and they were gone. This was an apparitional experience, so I can say from my own experience that apparitions are just as real as ordinary reality. It is a different sort of reality.

When I was ten, in the summer of 1950, I saw a UFO, in full daylight, at close range (about 200 feet) and had it under continuous observation for what seemed like a long time, but may have been a minute or two. Nobody in my family believes this story. I don't blame them. They weren't there. Everyone but me was either in the house or the barn. My chores took me outside to feed the hogs and calves and gather eggs and carry up a pail of water, and bring in an armload or two of firewood (in winter). I was standing there, looking at nothing in particular, facing West, where the sun had just set. But it was still full light, as summer evenings usually are.

Coming up over the tallest trees on the creek that lay downhill about a hundred yards to the West was a pitted sphere, covered with a flame-like greenish aura. It came silently about 25 mph, due East, at a constant height. Overhead it made an instantaneous right-angled turn without banking or slowing down and went off due South at the same leisurely pace. After that I always knew the textbooks were wrong, but I kept that to myself. I kept a lot of things to myself.

In high school, at Monica's birthday party in Perry, I saw table-tipping. It was late autumn, the house was overheated, there wasn't room to dance, and we were too young to drink. What I'm trying to say is that the party was getting boring, we were getting sleepy, and thinking about leaving. Besides, both the Principal and the Superintendent were present. That might seem strange, but it was a small school, and informal, and they were often involved in our social activities. Indeed, it was the Principal who "called" our square dances. And he was the one who suggested that we do table-tipping. Junior Riddle is what we called him. He was also the girls basketball coach. Thank you Junior Riddle, wherever you are. And you were right about me. I didn't know everything, and not everything can be learned from books. Sometimes I think he arranged this exercise just to deflate my intellectual arrogance, the sin of pride. He succeeded.

It was a perfectly ordinary card table, with folding legs. I helped set it up. It certainly had no invisible wires. We were too poor in the fifties to buy the gadgets of illusionists, even had we known about them.

Junior Riddle sat six people at three sides of the table, leaving one side free. Fingers lightly resting, thumbs to thumbs and little fingers to little fingers, making a kind of three sided circuit. One by one those at the table said in a solemn voice, "Rise, Table, Rise." Time slowed to a stop. We had been there forever, waiting for the table to rise. In clock time, it may have been 30 to 45 minutes. Or it may have been much less. We were in our own bubble of time.

After an eternity had passed, the table did rise, or at least the free end rose, tilting back on the other two legs. It rose a good foot off the floor, and stayed there. Junior Riddle did not seem at all surprised. I'm sure our mouths were hanging open. He suggested we ask it questions, and give it a code, such as one tap for yes, two for no. In the excitement of the moment, we couldn't think of any really significant questions to ask. Like is there life after death? Is there a God? Is there meaning to life? No, we asked how many dollar bills were in Ted's wallet. Three said the table. Ted checked, and there were three dollar bills. We asked it if we were going to win an upcoming basketball game against Red Rock (see the movie "Hoosiers" and you will know what basketball means to countless small towns across the midwest). One tap for yes, two for no. It very slowly tapped once, then stopped, in the up position. By how many points? Three, it said. In fact, we lost by about 20 points. We asked it how many days until Christmas. It very rapidly tapped 25 times. We asked one another, "Is that right?" No one knew. In fact, it was wrong, as I found out when I got home and checked a calendar. But it didn't matter whether it was right or wrong. What mattered was that it was a clear case of psycho-kinesis. I know. I was the skeptic, looking under the table to see if someone was lifting it with a foot, passing my hand over the table checking for invisible threads, checking fingers to see if everyone was resting their hands lightly on the table. They were. It is possible to pull a card table, but this requires pressing down hard, inverting the last digit, and turning the joint white.

About half the high-school (total number of students: 50) were at the party. We all believed it. The other half were totally skeptical. So I don't expect you to believe it either. But I knew. Once again, I learned that the textbooks were wrong, or at least incomplete.

The course of my life was set by the books I read at 15. History, science and philosophy. I knew I didn't want to do history, but I was always torn between science and philosophy. In the end, I did both. And my on-line books have some contributions to science (mostly theoretical) and some contributions to philosophy. My invention of the science of Utopian Analysis made good use of my love of history, for it was in the political experiments of history that I found all the data I needed.

I took a bachelor's degree in Physics, and a Ph.D. in philosophy. But that didn't mean I had lost any interest in physics. I stayed with it via *Scientific American*, which I have read ever since my Senior year in high school. Also, when I was about 30, I had a chance to take undergraduate quantum mechanics again, just for fun. Once again, I had found a Mentor, an old professor who told us many tales out of school, many personal things about the great figures of the 1920s. And I really learned quantum mechanics, although I never learned the math beyond the undergraduate level.

When I was a professor of philosophy at the University of Southern California, a friend of mine was a physicist, who happened to be from India. We two bachelors often went out to dinner at the one India Restaurant in LA. Once when we were talking about quantum mechanics, he said rather vehemently that he wished he didn't have to constantly crank out equations. The paradoxes of quantum mechanics obviously bothered him. What he wanted was about twenty years just to contemplate the meaning of the equations. He never had that luxury. But I did. And I eventually realized that de Broglie's 1923 approach frees quantum mechanics from paradox. I also have an idea about quantum gravity, and another about the consequences of antiparticles having anti-gravity. That is the sum total of my contribution to existing sciences.

My philosophical contributions consist in the founding of sciences, for that is the point and function of Western philosophy, as well as its crowning glory and only accomplishment. It took me 30 years to learn how to distinguish the essence from the accidental in existing science, and learn how to apply the essence of scientific method (which makes no assumptions) to other problems and other realms of experience. That sounds very dry and abstract, but there is nothing dry and abstract about my books. Do you want to know about free will? Beautiful cities? Capital punishment? The meaning of life? It is all here.

There was a time when I thought I was supposed to start a new religion. There was a time when I thought I was supposed to be a guru. Fortunately, I came to my senses and realized that I could hardly pursue a path which I have explicitly rejected, for good and sufficient reasons, as I have both of those. No, if you are impressed with my writings, don't try to become my disciple, and don't start a religion in my name. Start or continue one of the three sciences I have either created, altered or renewed. The one I created, taking up where Hobbes and Locke left off 300 years ago, is Utopian Analysis, the science of civilization. This science will never come into full existence unless their are followers, people who become Utopian Analysts and publish their work. A science is a communal affair, continuous from generation to generation. So if you wish to be my follower, follow me in this.

There already exists a science of Psychical Research, journals, Ph.D.s, and the various SPRs (Societies for Psychical Research). But this science had bogged down, come to a complete stop, under the attacks of the *"Skeptical Inquirer,"* and its psi-cops, but for internal reasons as well. So I have re-founded the science on the work of Shafica Karagulla, someone unknown to the SPRs. I am in no way rejecting the excellent and rigorous work of Prof. Ian Stevenson, or G.N.M. Tyrrell, or any of the other pioneers of the original SPR. Indeed, I bow down to them, as the great pioneers of the subject. I hold Hobbes and Locke in the same respect. What I have done is kicked out "Parapsychology" with its roots in psychology, two pseudo-sciences if I ever saw one, and re-focused on the investigation of spontaneous phenomena, as advocated by Prof. Ian Stevenson.

Dr. Shafica Karagulla's work shows that the mind and the body are completely different things, made of different substances. It is also evident from the HSP observations that the mind has no EM interactions. This is confirmed by the NDE data, and the reincarnation data. So we simply re-define Psychical

Research as "the rigorous study, using scientific method, of rare and spontaneous events or talents, which shed light on the mind, a real entity quite different from the body, and in no way created by the body." Of course, one must understand scientific method, and people coming into this field from psychology obviously do not understand scientific method.

The other thing which has brought Psychical Research to a dead stop is the absence of a theory of the mind as a natural object. For this, one must understand 20th Century physics, as well as 20th Century Psychical Research. This may be a bold thing to say, but I believe I am the first person to understand both. Theory is extremely important, as any student of the history of science knows. So if you wish to be a follower, follow me in this: do the scientific tests of my theory of the mind as a natural object. Revive the newly re-defined Psychical Research and spread it to every university. Fight off the psi-cops with the tools I have given you.

The media should not accept the Psi-cop's claims to be experts on Psi or UFOs, when the Psi-cops have never tried to reproduce a single study of psychical phenomena or of UFOs. They reject them for the same reason Galileo's Paduan colleagues rejected his discoveries—because they just couldn't believe such things were possible.

Finally, we come to the scientific study of mystical and symbolic experiences of mankind, which I define as the science of metaphysics. People have tried to create such a science before, which go under such names as Theosophy or Thanatology. And among mystics and students of symbolic revelations, probably none but me think that scientific method has any place at this bounteous table. But I say, unless the real discoveries of metaphysics are grounded in scientific method, they are like dust in the wind. They will make no permanent contribution to the knowledge of mankind. These experiences are reproducible, which is the first requirement of science. And one can be a scientist and a mystic, using the universal language of Jungian symbolism rather than calculus. I am that person. So if you wish to follow me, follow me in this: help to make metaphysics a science. And do so with full involvement in symbolism and the mystical path, not standing back and viewing mystics like lab rats. Be your own experiment. Study the alphabet of symbolic elements and learn to interpret mandalas and other symbolic expressions, such as *The Word of One*, on-line at members.aol.com/miletus1/toc.htm. Learn the New Tarot. Become a Seeker. The day that happens, the world will have changed.

The Alphabet of Symbolic Elements

Dictionaries of symbols are useless, just as dictionaries of sentences are useless. A person may write many books without ever repeating a single sentence. A single symbol may contain several sentences of information. But an alphabet of the hundred or so most common symbolic elements provide the necessary "primer" that will make it possible for anyone to learn the language. Elements are things like color, number, orientation, species and gesture.

For me the new tarot is a Rosetta stone for deciphering the meaning of symbolic elements. I spent seven years working to understand the meaning of just twenty-two major arcana, but having achieved that, in the manner of a Jung or a Campbell, I can then go back and use it to figure out the universal meaning of each symbolic element. Fortunately, each major symbolic element recurs many times in the new tarot. Sometimes there will be several instances in the same Book. The Nameless One refers to each card as a book, and I will do likewise, for there is a book's worth of wisdom in each.

What follows is a brief dictionary of some of the most common symbolic elements:

We begin with colors. Green is the color of chlorophyll, the means of fixing solar energy for the use of all other life. In symbolic terms green is similarly a fixing or capturing of portable energy, usually in the form of money. A strong yellow is sunlight, and by association, the creative energies that make life possible. Red is blood or a flushed face, and by association, emotion, drive, motivation. Purple is the rare dye reserved in ancient times for the emperor's family, and by association is authority. Gray is ashes, and by association, death, destruction, desolation (which may be of an emotional rather than literal kind).

Blue is the color of a newborn at the instant of crowning, and at the cyanotic instant of death. Blue is the door to birth and death and therefore means renewal. That is why the flesh of the Renewer is blue in the new tarot. The flesh of Osiris, the Egyptian god of the afterlife, is also blue. A color partway between blue and purple combines renewal and authority, which suggests healing, and in particular the profession of healing. A pale yellow is more of an illumination color, the color of the aura of the teacher, for instance. Brown is earth or wood or shit and thus a building material or basis or foundation or fertilizer for other growth. The meaning of white seems to derive from white paint, which when mixed with any other color, ceases to be white. Thus white is pure and innocent, untouched by experience, virginal and ignorant.

The colors of twilight suggest the twilight of life, and the metaphysical contemplation and wisdom that is appropriate to that stage of life. Black is the ultimate darkness, so we must consider the meaning of the spectrum of light to dark. Light is illumination, visibility and clarity, while dark is ignorance and stoppage. Orange refers to the illumination of fire, and the discovery of the meaning of life in meeting challenges, and undergoing renewal.

We shall next look at numbers. When interpreting mandalas, we count the numbers of things. We have five physical senses, and five digits on our hands. When our limbs are fully extended (as in the jumping jack exercise), we make a five pointed star, with head and limbs forming five extremities. There are also five major inhabited continents on earth in the present epoch: North and South America, Europe, Asia and Africa. Five relates to our physical existence, associated with a well-rounded life in-the-body, using our senses and our limbs to their fullest. There are five jewels in the central crown of the Royal Maze and five courses of stones on the well of life in the Renewer.

There are four directions, four winds and four dimensions in our earthly plane. Quaternity has always meant wholeness and completeness on the earthly plane.

Trinity has always meant wholeness and completeness on a spiritual plane. Gods always come in threes. There is Brahma the creator, Shiva the destroyer, and Krishna the preserver, or the Father, Son and Holy Ghost. There are three pillars of the kabbala. There are three handles on the chalice of the well of life in the Book of the Renewer. If we drink from the well of life in the Renewer, we may fulfill the divine purpose by grasping the handle of creation, the handle of destruction, or the handle of preservation. All may equally serve growth and creation. This is a hard lesson, and shows us that the divine or sacred goal does not always agree with earthly morality or values.

Two is polarity. Polar opposites are the two ends or extremes of the same thing, and cannot exist without each other. Male cannot exist without female, and the north pole of a magnet implies the existence of a south pole. Two are the polar opposites on the axis of ONE. There is nonetheless always tension and opposition, if not downright war, between the dualities of polar opposites.

The meanings of all other numbers can be derived from the meanings of two, three, four and five, by adding, multiplying or taking them to a power of themselves. Eight of something shows the polarizing effects of two combined with the earthly whole of four. The symbolic meaning is materialism and greed, or some sort of polarizing earthiness. Ten shows the polarizing effects of two combined with the body number five, suggesting the misuse of technology and the corrupting effects of luxury. However, in some contexts, ten refers to the ten forms of Samadhi. That is the meaning of the ten fruit on the Tree of life in the Garden of the Renewer. Six shows the polarizing effects of two combined with the higher trinity, and thus suggests the sacred dance of Shiva carried to fanatical excess, to martyrdom or asceticism.

Seven is the additive, twelve the multiplicative, combination of three and four. Both seven and twelve have always been considered lucky numbers, the combination of the earthly and the spiritual whole. There are seven spiritual paths and seven rays of light piercing the clouds over the Renewer. There were three parts to the holy trinity, four books of gospels, twelve disciples and seven seals on the book of revelation.

These numbers constantly recur in sacred contexts, as do their combinations and powers such as nine and sixteen. Sixteen is a quaternity of quaternities, and nine is the trinity of trinities. This is like a redoubling or intensification of the original symbolic meaning. Thus, nine is the holy of holies.

The figure eight (i.e. the image or sign) should not be confused with the quantity eight. The shape of a figure eight is a moebius strip, and means infinity, i.e. the unending, since one can trace around and around the figure, going from loop to loop, inside to outside, without end. To avoid confusion with the number, the "unending" symbol is shown laid on its side.

Small rational numbers such as two-thirds or five-ninths also have distinctive symbolic meanings as elements. Small rational numbers are harmonies, a discovery made by the ancient Greek philosopher Pythagoras. Each harmony has its own feel, some good, some bad. The first twenty-one intervals of our modern equal tempered scale includes just about all the possible small whole numbered ratios, though they are not all exact. By fine-tuning, one can emphasize some harmonies at the expense of others. More on this in the chapter on mandalas, where we shall consider mandala music. But this suggests that we may need to consider ratios when interpreting mandalas.

Species of animals or plants or natural objects are also

symbolic elements. The meaning of species elements is sometimes surprising. For instance, a serpent means "initiatory experience."

This is hardly our free association with snakes. There are two strands to the symbolic meaning of serpents, with the context bringing out one or the other or both. On the one hand, serpents are chthonic, of-the-earth. They come out of the ground, and have the temperature and feel of earth.

The other association is with the penis, which is also cool to the touch, and similar in shape. (Freud was not the first to notice this!). It is not the penis, per se, which conveys the symbolic meaning. It is the first act of sex, which forever changes one. After sex, one is no longer a child, and can never go back to the childhood frame of reference. Before sex, it is impossible to fully understand adult love.

Sex is an initiation, and thus stands for all initiatory experiences that forever change a person. And this ties back to the chthonic thread of meaning, for the experiences of the nature mystic or the shaman are also initiatory and transforming experiences which prepare the novice for further steps down the path. And it is because of this large and complex freight of symbolic meaning that serpents occur frequently in symbolism. There are probably a dozen of them in the new tarot. There are three just in the Book of the Deliverer. Of course, the Deliverer is about the illumination of fire, the ultimate initiation. An initiation is not necessarily a ritual; it is any experience which changes the novice to an initiate.

Symbolism is never conventional. It is only what is unusual or unconventional that conveys symbolic meaning. One unconventional context is the hooded eagle on the shoulder of the Changer. He is hooded and jessied like a falcon, but he is not a falcon.

He is an eagle, the universal predator, the only creature that takes its prey from land, sea or air. The universal predator has always suggested the power of government, which is why governments have always instinctively liked that symbolism. To be hooded and jessied means to be domesticated, brought under control, tamed.

The symbolic meaning of a species is always associated with something unusual, unique or exaggerated in that species. For instance, sheep are the most completely useful kind of domestic animal, providing fiber, milk, cheese, and meat. They also have the strongest herd instinct. Sheep always want to go where the herd is going. This has always suggested the mass of ordinary people.

Wolves hunt in packs, cooperating with each other to prey on the sheep, thus wolves are the dominant elite of every society. Hawks soar, endlessly and effortlessly born on the wind, and thus suggest all that is soaring and windborne and all-seeing (Horus). Egrets and other large fishing birds are at home in two realms, the world of air and of water, plunging into the depths of the latter to pluck out a denizen of the watery deeps (an inspiration). This suggests the role of the creative genius (Thoth), who is also at home in two realms, the airy world of everyday action, and the inner, floating world of the collective unconscious, source of inspiration. That is why Imhotep, a great genius of the early Pyramid age in Egypt (inventor of writing and of the pyramids), was later deified as an Ibis-headed god.

Bluebirds hold the curtain of invisibility and the tools of illusion on the stage of the Actor, while playing a more positive role in the Victorious One, the modern warrior, who has unhooked the lions from his chariot. The blue birds keep the wolves at bay with a transparent curtain. Blue birds play a similar role in Disney movies, so we must have struck a deep vein of symbolic meaning here. Do not think of these as the familiar species "bluebirds." Think of this as the combination of two symbolic elements, "blue," and "bird." Blue is renewal, bird is flight, escape, uncaged, free in the ocean of air. Thus, the blue bird plays a liberating role. They appear at happy moments in Disney movies, to aid the hero or heroine in the moment of triumph.

The four elements of nature all have symbolic meaning. Water always suggests the dreaming, floating world of genius, the daydreamer. Air is the normal workaday world of thought and action, often suggested by windblown sails, hair, clouds, or clothing. Fire is the illumination of fire with its suggestion of the necessity of challenges, which may destroy as well as warm. Stone is a building material, suggested by wood or brown colors. Spark stars suggest the sudden flash of inspiration.

Orientation is always symbolically important. Left handed is yin, the receptive, passive, accepting, nurturing, maternal, feminine, lateral-thinking. Right handed is yang, the aggressive, initiating, driving, deciding, single-focused. Above is heaven, the spiritual, and below is earth, the physical. In the new tarot, orientation is always figured from the point of view of the figure, not from our point of view, and this may be generally true of symbols.

Conventional clothing means nothing. In the new tarot, the standard figure is nude, to show that all is revealed. The cloak of the Renewer implies something hidden. Only the Speaker's feet are covered, isolated from the "ground" (social convention) he walks on.

The four suits of the New Tarot are all symbolic. The four suits are the amphisbaena (a serpent with a head on both ends, much used in Aztec symbolism), stones, curved blades, and pears. Pears are distinctive in several ways. All the other trees in the orchard die after 15-20 years, while this is just when pears begin fruiting. All other orchard fruits are picked in summer, with crab apples the last, in September. But Pears are picked in the fall. Furthermore, the fruit continues to ripen after picked, if stored properly, until it becomes absolutely delicious about Christmastime. All this suggest things which take a long time to mature. For instance, Civilizations have their "second religiousness" in late maturity, and this is their final fruition. Do not confuse the original spirituality with the dried up religion it may become after thousands of years. Curved blades can be propellers, or scimitars. If a scimitar, then it suggests a decisive action, cutting time into a before and after. As a propeller, it suggests action, progress, motion. Stones are good for building. Some stones are jewels and good for wearing. Some are precious gems. Some are crystals, and may store psionic energy, or "huna." The serpent suggests initiation, and the rhythm of the dance, the to-and-fro of life and death. Why initiation? Well, Freud was not the first to notice the similarity between a serpent and the penis, which associates with sex, especially the first initiation of the virgin, which stands for every experience which is initiatory. Sex forever changes one from a child to an adult, and one cannot go back. The same is true of other truly initiatory experiences. But I have already talked about serpents.

This completes my brief dictionary of symbolic elements. A symbol can combine elements from different categories, in every conceivable way, forming images of things that have never existed in reality.

I will close this chapter with a few examples of the interpretations of mandalas done by my students. It often takes thirty minutes to an hour to interpret a mandala. I must find some quiet time. I try turning it this way and that, for the higher Self may have created a mandala upside down or side-ways to the individual making it. I look at it from various distances, and in various lights. I take my time, and let the interpretation come to me.

I begin by looking for recognizable objects. These are seldom drawn in a conventional way. For instance, a house may be a Picasso house, showing multiple perspectives at once, with distortions, and it may show the interior simultaneously with the exterior. Usually the mandala maker can help the interpreter identify vaguely drawn objects. They may "just know" that this vaguely bird-like figure is a vulture.

On a circular field of pale yellow there are four fields of gray outlined in purple. Thus, we have authority confining ashes and death. This suggested to me the emergency room environment, where the authority is provided by the doctors, because I knew the woman who made the mandala was an emergency room nurse. This scene of power and death is embedded in a field of light and learning. Red outlines a yellow center in these fields of gray.

Red also outlines a region central to the mandala, which is done in a color intermediate between blue and purple, a kind of royal blue, which is often associated with the healer. Thus, the center of this individual is the desire to heal. The red of passion encloses and bounds this healing field, as well as the life-energies (yellow) in the midst of the fields of desolation and authority. I suspect a certain unconscious rebelliousness against the power, greed and carelessness of her superiors, the doctors, who often could not be found to give her permission to do what she knew must be done. She is a natural healer somewhat out of tune with our hierarchical system of medicine.

The mandala of a very quiet student that I did not know very well, surprisingly revealed him to be a man well balanced between metaphysical and physical knowledge, a very lucky man, destined to have a happy life. His mandala was that of a domestic room with a large stained glass window, illuminating a beautiful and comfortable interior. The window was round, with seven rings and sixteen radii. Seven is a good number, representing a balance or combination of an earthly whole (quaternity) and a sacred whole (trinity). The quaternity aspect is emphasized with the number sixteen, quaternity squared. The individual segments formed by the intersection of the radial lines and circles are alternatively colored in a strong orange and a light reddish violet (a twilight color). Orange is the color of fire and of the illumination of fire. It is in the illumination of fire that we see the pattern of life, the necessity of challenges to inspire creativity.

The delicate twilight colors are seen in the sky at sunset and are otherwise rare in nature. In the twilight of life, we turn to thoughts of the eternal issues, to metaphysics and mysticism. This man had made metaphysics central to his approach to life.

I hope I have shown it is possible for anyone to learn to interpret mandalas, sacred art, mythology or symbolic dreams, though it is clearly an entirely new way of thinking in the time of Heroic Materialism, and it may take years of study to master something like the New Tarot. First memorize the symbolic elements, since they retain their meaning in all contexts. Remember the four steps for deciphering elements not in my dictionary. Remember that it is not possible to translate symbolic meaning into "plain English," and even the interpretation will be metaphorical. However we approach the goal of spiritual evolution, mastering symbolism is a necessary skill, just as learning the calculus is a necessary skill for the physicist.

And what does all this have to do with going to the stars? A knowledge of symbolism makes the Inner Journey possible, a reflection through the looking glass of the Outer Journey. We must first go in to the Soul before we can go out to the stars. By the way, I learned the symbolic elements by studying the New Tarot. It took me seven years. Each element occurs many times. For instance, there are three different kinds of serpent, just in the Book of the Deliverer. Every element always has the same meaning. And each book had to make a consistent meaning. That's how I figured it out.

Mandalas in Music and Architecture

I use the word "mandala" in its Western, Jungian sense. Jung essentially regarded any meaningful doodle as a mandala, and so do I. My chief contribution to the subject is to extend the mandala technique to all media.

Mandalas create themselves. Anyone may use the mandala technique to create beautiful works which express the high metaphysics found in New Age Revelations. What is original is my extension of the mandala technique to music, dance, drama, architecture, and cloth.

Mandala making is simultaneously a meditation technique, a divination and revelation technique, and a way to tap the hidden aesthetic potential in all of us. And it can be used for ceremonial Magick. To do Magick, first express your intentions symbolically with a layout of Tarot cards, then do the mandalas, for paintings, music, clothing or banners, and finally, do the mandala for the drama of the ceremony itself.

This can be a major group project.

A Buddhist mandala is a circle in a square, or a square in a circle, made in a divine trance. They have a center point perspective, rather than a horizon line and vanishing point. They also have symmetry in powers-of-two, i.e. bilateral, quadripartite, etc. C. G. Jung regarded any combination of circle and square as a mandala, even if the circle was sitting perched on top of the square. A Gothic cathedral rose window, a Renaissance church, and Bach's improvised polyphony are all mandalas.

Mandalas can be defined procedurally, as any work of art which creates itself, without prior plan or design or theme, simply following the impulses of the inner self. If this improvisational procedure results in a creation with symbolic meaning, then the result is a mandala. So we have two definitions of the mandala, one in terms of form, and the other in terms of process, and it is impossible to settle exclusively on one definition or the other. In every artistic medium, we shall find some version of the circle and the square, and some form of improvisation.

It is miraculous to me, someone who cannot draw a straight line, that in the unconscious process of making the mandala, something strange and beautiful and filled with symbolic meaning unfolds, in a style like nothing I've ever seen before. And all mandalas are that way. Not only does everyone have their own style, but each mandala has its own style. As for their meaning, it varies enormously.

The last mandala I did turned out to be African shields and masks (when looked at from a distance in a sufficiently dim light). This meant I was hiding behind shields and masks and not opening up emotionally to a female friend who was visiting me at the time.

In the mandalas of groups I have run, a troubled marriage stands out in one mandala, something that individual had never mentioned. In the mandala of an emergency room nurse, pride of the healer and resentment of authority was evident. One very quiet man, who had not said two words the entire semester, created the most beautiful mandala, expressing a life perfectly balanced between spiritual and domestic values. I envied him, and his wife, and told him so. A mandala can be a window into the soul, whether the mandala maker wishes or not.

There are a number of books on mandalas, but none that relate to this chapter, since they are the works either of artists or of therapists. If an artist chooses to imitate the style of a mandala, the result may be beautiful, but can it be a revelation? And how can the mandala create itself if we must follow some Indian guru's teaching in our procedure?

Remember, the Western Path rejects all gurus, guru-disciple traditions and cults. The Western Path progresses by a series of geniuses, who may be very imperfect as human beings. Indeed, we almost expect them to be a little cracked, or at least odd. But this is OK. It is easier to be a genius than it is to be a genuine guru, who is required to be a divine person, as well as possessing divine powers, knowledge and wisdom. This is such a difficult requirement that the intelligentsia of India regard gurus and swamis as frauds, or at least, self-deluded, along with their followers.

The higher arts of Western civilization have come to an end in the 20th Century. Architecture has ceased to be an art, and is merely the engineering of giant boxes. Somewhere between dadaism and minimalism, painting became an elaborate con game, played for fun and profit by the critics with their artspeak, and the collectors hoping for a tidy return. The Emperor is naked, and it is only our own lack of courage that prevents it from being shouted from the rooftops. If it looks like junk or sounds like noise, trust your senses.

And, of course, no professional musical organization can make a living performing 20th Century works. The larger the organization, the more conservative their repertoire. Symphony orchestras confine themselves to boring, bombastic blasts by Beethoven, Brahms and Bruckner. They are lovely the first time, loathsome the twentieth time.

The mandala technique offers a path to renewal of the higher arts, which have the power to transport participants beyond the mundane material world. It is part of a New Age, a golden age, a Renaissance of the Spirit. Go in Beauty. Live in harmony.

Painting: The first rule for making mandalas is that there are no rules. Having said that, we can at least give a few hints for making drawn mandalas. Use a sheet of typing paper for each mandala, taped with masking tape to a hard surface, which can withstand the point of the compass. Get out all your kindergarten art supplies, compasses (for making arcs), small squares, or plastic triangles with a right angle, rulers, liquid crayola, wax crayola, colored pencils, poster paints, regular pencils and erasers. Let the mandala create itself.

Take a break occasionally and get a fresh look at what is being created. At that point one may have a "gestalt" experience, as random lines and blotches suddenly come together as a recognizable object. Work to increase the recognizability, while eliminating superfluous lines.

Some people primarily improvise with compass and square, first in pencil, with much erasing, adding colors in later. Others do it free hand in color with no erasure, and who can say which is the better mandala? If there is a rule to making mandalas, it is to let it create itself. Do not attempt any preconceived design.

Twentieth century painting has had a liberating influence on mandala makers. A house in a mandala may be a Picasso house, showing multiple perspectives at once. We are not stuck with a horizon line and a vanishing point, or realistic portrayal of objects. Objects may be symbolic doodles, like the elements in Navaho sand paintings. Anything is possible. It might be best to stop reading at this point and go make a drawn mandala.

Interpreting mandalas is far more difficult than making them, and may take overnight. Yet it is essential, because of the revelations contained therein. Everyone can be their own source of revelation. It is not necessary to run after trance channellers or gurus. In the groups I've run, no one could interpret mandalas but me. But, of course, they did not have the benefit of "The Alphabet of Symbolism," or years of study. Try turning it this way or that, and looking at it at various distances, in various lights. Take your time. Sleep on it.

In the morning, a sudden gestalt experience may occur, just as a person is suddenly recognized at a distance. Or it may remain a doodle.

The revelation may be highly personal, instant psychoanalysis, or it may contain high metaphysical themes. How do we know it is true? If it is highly personal and the mandala maker recognizes the truth of it, fine.

If it contains universal metaphysical themes, then we expect reproducibility, in the sense that we expect to find the same themes in everyone's metaphysical mandalas, and the same themes in mystical experience. This is the beginning of the science of metaphysics.

In music, we make a distinction between the creation of a piece and the performance of the piece. In fact, the same distinction now arises in sculpture, where the artist may do a small scale sculpture in clay and at the shop it will be reproduced on any scale in marble or bronze. I apply this same distinction to all the arts, even if the creator and the performer are one and the same person. The creation and the performance remain separate and distinct acts. A drawn mandala is made on a piece of cheap typing paper, held down to a hard board with masking tape. While creating a mandala, we don't worry about staying within the lines. Mandalas can be quite sloppy in the creation. But having recognized the elements and interpreted them, why not create a polished work of art?

I have never seen an ugly mandala. But try to imagine it done on canvas or watercolor paper in a larger size, carefully painted in acrylics, oil, or watercolor. An artist could be hired to do this. That is the performance of the piece, suitable for framing and hanging on the walls of your house.

Architecture: Similarly, mandala architecture may be created in small scale in clay or plaster. Architects, engineers and a crew of builders will be required to turn the model into a real building. Creation and performance. There are new tools, such as finite element computer programs, that can be used to escape the box, and have been used by Frank Gehry to create the Guggenheim Museum at Bilbao and his other spectacular (and not rectangular) buildings.

The architects of the Renaissance, Bramante especially, created mandala buildings with central perspective and power of two symmetry, usually quadripartite, with a dome on top to circumscribe the square with a circle. If I understand their methods correctly, they began by making the intersection of two arcs, known as the mandorla. Mandorlas determined the long axis. Without changing the arc of the compass, other dimensions were set by using various points along the mandorla as the point of the compass.

So the formal elements of the circle and the square certainly exist in architecture. But I know of no one who has attempted to introduce the mandala improvisation process into architecture. The creation stage could be done in a medium like clay or plaster. Make power-of-two forms and use them to create porticos and niches. The way to make a circular dome is to mount that part of the model on a potter's wheel and let the hands form whatever shape feels right. The "performance" of the mandala in an actual building is more of a challenge. Mandala architectural creations tend to have rounded shapes.

Current building materials and building techniques do not favor curved shapes. 20th Century building, both domestic and commercial, places the emphasis on the plumb and the square.

All 20th Century building components are linear and flat. Everything from two-by-fours to I-beams to plywood panels to doors and windows are designed for rectilinear construction on the plumb and the square. How to break out of this? If we insist on curved walls, they can be made with bricks, used not as a facade but as load-bearing walls. It's not customary, but it can be done.

Make arches and domes from bricks or building stones, with a specially shaped keystone. It's an old technique, reaching back to Gothic cathedrals and Roman basilicas and the co-existing Persian civilization. Study earlier styles of architecture for their construction techniques.

For a twentieth Century approach to curved shapes, particularly in large public buildings, we could use custom made curved trusses. A truss is two flat plates separated by a continuous zigzag of flat plates welded together. Trusses provide maximum strength and stiffness for a given tonnage of steel. A custom truss can be made by first bending the top and bottom plates to a curved line, and then welding in the continuous pieces of zigzag bracing between the top and bottom plates. Finite element computer programs can determine the load-bearing strength of this truss for a given strength and weight of steel.

As for the surface of the building, we could imitate the Persians and use brightly colored ceramic tile. Even dull and subdued colored tile is an improvement over the gray and colorless buildings of the 20th Century.

The symbolic interpretation of buildings is very much like that of music, oddly enough. A great building has a certain rhythmic pattern, in the power-of-two symmetries, and in repeated elements, such as domes.

Some of the most beautiful buildings in the world are mandala buildings, including Gothic Cathedrals, the Orthodox Cathedrals in Moscow, the Taj Mahal and other great works of Islamic architecture. The circle on the square, bright colors, and symbolic meaning are all there.

Poetry: Mandala poetry tends to produce epigrams, almost like Haiku, or short passages. The Sayings of Thales are mandala poetry. I simply left myself open to phrases floating up from the unconscious, writing them down on envelopes or any scrap of paper. They often made no sense at first. But with minor editing, they became epigrams, enigmatic but meaningful. Such mandala epigrams become the lyrics for mandala music.

Music: The "square" in music is the measure, which is subdivided by powers-of-two durations of sound or silence, i.e., whole notes, half notes, quarter notes, eighth notes, sixteenth notes and so forth, where the basic unit is set by the tempo and the time signature. A circle in music is any repeated passage or theme, from the simple tune and chorus, to theme and variation in classical music.

Western music has always had the circle and the square, but before the invention of MIDI keyboard-synthesizers and personal computers, we had no tools for the improvisational mandala process.

Computer memory or hard disk memory is the equivalent of the sheet of paper, allowing one to capture and examine the mandala, erasing some, adding more. By pre-defining the tempo and time-signature, the MIDI software will transform inexact durations into powers-of-two notes within measures. That is the equivalent of the square. The editing software provides the equivalent of eraser and compass, with repetition of passages you like, and deletion of those you don't.

I do not play any instrument, but with practice, my "fingers" learned harmonious combinations and phrases that pleased me. Like mandalas in other media, the results are unusual and unlike traditional music. Relax and let the fingers create the music. Forget about the formal rules of composition, in case you know any. Silence the memory of generations of piano teachers which keep saying "don't pound on the piano!" Pound away. The result will not be noise; it will amaze you with its strange beauty. Better yet, open up the piano and create directly on the strings. Select passages for repetition (the circle). A simple song only requires two musical phrases, one for the melody and the other for the refrain, which are then repeated two or three times. The melody itself may be no more than several repetitions of a simple motif, with a few variations.

But can it be interpreted? Do musical mandalas carry or express a symbolic meaning? Indeed they do, and this was a fact well known to the ancient Greeks, but has been more or less forgotten since.

Can't we just enjoy a piece of music, and not worry about its meaning? Of course, but if music is your medium, it may also be your path to revelation. Symbolic meaning lies in the harmonies, rhythms and color. To prove to yourself that this is true, go to a piano (or any keyboard) and find middle C or any C. We'll call this note 1. Staying entirely on the white keys, first play CD together, i.e. C, the first note, and the second note lying next to it. You have now played the interval known in conventional musical theory as a second. Play CE, i.e. notes one and three on the white keys, and you have played a third. In similar fashion, try each combination of C with the white keys to the right, to play the second, the third, the fourth, the fifth, the sixth, the seventh, and the eighth. The eighth is somehow the same as note one, because it is an octave, resulting in a doubling of the frequency of note one. This is the classic eight note diatonic scale in the key of C, which just uses the white keys on a piano. Do this up and down the keyboard, from one C to another.

Now as you repeatedly sound these intervals pay close attention to your emotions. Don't each of these intervals have a different "feel?" Aren't the second and the seventh intervals dissonant, i.e. unpleasant, jarring? This is not to say that dissonance is bad and should not be used. Sometimes it expresses exactly what we are feeling. The fifth and sixth (favored in early medieval music) have a sacred, holy, unearthly sound compared to the fourth and third. The consonant intervals are the third, fourth, fifth, and sixth. And this is not surprising from Pythagorean theory, because the ratio of the two notes that make up a Third is always 5:4, anywhere on the scale. The Fourth is 4:3. The Fifth is 3:2. And the Sixth is 9:5. Pythagoras discovered this 2500 years ago, giving rise to a new word, "rational." We may use either the frequency or the wavelength of each note to demonstrate this "rationality" of harmony.

Pythagoras transformed Greek civilization, because suddenly everything had to obey rational numbers. The elements of a statue were so many "thumb" units. The proportions of buildings had to be rational numbers.

The modern well-tempered scale is a geometric series of frequencies. All geometric series have the property that the same interval always produces the same ratio. The particular frequencies chosen for this scale allow almost all small numbered ratios in the first 21 intervals of the scale. But there are a few ratios not found, i.e. a few "lost chords" which are never heard in Western music, such as 6:7. And many of the chords are not exact. However, they don't improve with exactness.

The symbolic meaning of rational numbers can be determined from the symbolic meanings of each of the two component numbers, the denominator and numerator, using our alphabet of symbolism. For instance, we know that five is worldly and secular, while four is the earthly whole, the four winds of the compass, and divinity is always expressed in threes. Thus, we expect the Third (5:4 ratio) to be common in popular and secular music, especially in a non-religious age, and so it is.

Divinity always comes in threes, so the combination of divinity and the earthly whole (the Fourth, 4:3) is holy (wholeness). The same can be said for the Sixth (9:5), since nine is the trinity squared, and five is worldly and secular. We find both intervals in Medieval and Renaissance music.

The most purely religious or sacred interval is the Fifth, which shows the first entry of the holy trinity into the world of duality (3:2). And in early medieval music, only the fifth was permitted as a harmony, although dissonance was allowed. Later the Sixth was also allowed, but by the 14th Century, when the religious orders had become quite secularized, all of the consonant intervals were freely used, i.e. the Third, Fourth, Fifth, and Sixth, while dissonance was avoided.

In the paragraph above, I have used the word "interval" the same way as the musicians, basing it on the eight tone diatonic scale. However, there are a lot more possibilities on the chromatic (twelve tone) scale, especially if we consider intervals wider than an octave. So for the purpose of mandala making, we will use Chromatic Intervals (CI), using all the black and white keys. CI one is any key played with the black or white key next to it. And so forth. What follows is a portion of the dictionary of symbolic elements which I put here rather than in the alphabet chapter. Remember, symbolic meaning cannot be translated into English.

My "meanings" are hints, only. The mandala musician should study these intervals for herself.

CI one and two are dissonant. CI three has a ratio of 5:6 and has a feeling of tension, worry, or competition. CI four has a ratio of 4:5. This is the ever popular Third. Its mood is voluptuous, sensual, earthy, hot.

CI five has a ratio of 3:4 and has a Renaissance feel, a sacred, holistic feel. I like this interval, which musicians know as the Fourth. CI six is dissonant. CI seven is known to musicians as the Fifth, and has a ratio of 2:3. This is a harmony of grandeur and has an even more sacred feeling than interval five. This is my favorite harmony. It is always uplifting and makes me think of the creation of oceans and galaxies. It is the music of the gods.

CI eight is dissonant. CI nine has a ratio of 3:5 and suggests the hero, going to extremes, whether it be extremes of creation, destruction, or maintenance of the status quo. CI ten is the musician's Sixth (5:9) and is the hero of the mystical path, so this is another religious or spiritual interval. CI eleven is the Seventh and has a ratio of 7:13, the sound of the wizard or occultist. CI twelve has a ratio of 1:2, which is the octave, the same note.

CI thirteen has a ratio of 7:15 and is disharmony on a higher level than interval one. CI fourteen has a ratio of 4:9 and has an air of disquiet. It is transhuman and alien. CI fifteen has a ratio of 3:7 and is somewhat strange, middle-eastern & metaphysical. CI sixteen has a ratio of 2:5 and has a feel of sickness, recovery, and renewal. CI seventeen has a ratio of 3:8 and suggests wrong directions and fanaticism.

CI eighteen (5:14), is ominous and threatening. CI nineteen (1:3) is the wholy trinity. Very nice. CI twenty (4:13) is brooding and relentless. CI twenty-one (3:10) suggests cosmos and cosmology. Some chords might sound better if they were exact ratios, and, in fact, piano tuners do not stick strictly to the geometric series, thereby "sweetening" some harmonies, at the expense of other intervals.

Deciphering the symbolic meaning of a melody requires

determining the chromatic intervals in the melody and looking them up in the paragraphs above. Given the symbolic meaning in each individual step in the melody and in each chord, try to put it all together. See it as a whole. It is a little like seeing the meaning of a tarot spread as a whole.

Symbolic meaning in music depends on three things: the harmonies, the rhythms, and the colors or timbres of the instruments.

Boogie-woogie has a very different feel from reggae, and a military march or Royal fanfare is very different from a waltz or rhumba. The symbolic meaning of a rhythm depends on the ways we can move to it. Is it dance-able? Is there a discernible rhythm?

I have no dictionary for rhythms, beyond saying that it is determined by the kind of dance that goes with that rhythm. I also have no dictionary for the colors in music. Clearly there is a difference in the mood of plainsong and Italian opera, and a difference between brass and reed, and between organ, harpsichord and piano. Each musician will have to find his own way of thinking about these differences. So much for music.

Dance: Let us now consider dance in its own right. In Western culture, we do not find mandala characteristics in the "high-culture" classical traditions of dance, designer clothing or drama. We find them in the folk traditions. I refer to square dancing, quilt making and popular festivals such as Carnival.

It is quite easy to find the "square" and the "circle" in square dancing. In traditional western square dancing, the entire room is organized into many squares, each of which has four couples, who start by facing inward towards a center point for that square. Sometimes they dance as four couples, spatially arranged as a square, as in "swing-your-partner." Each square periodically forms a circle, as in "all join hands" or a moving circle, as in "allemande left, right and left hands." Sometimes there are "formation" calls such as "Texas Star, ladies to the middle," in which the ladies join all four left hands in the middle of the square.

The improvisational element comes from the caller, who can put the various moves known to the group together in any order. The equivalent of the "sheet of paper" is a list of the calls. In other words, it is easy to reproduce a dance, or modify it.

Please don't think that square dancing is just for older folks, where the women wear countless petticoats and everyone dresses alike. When I was in high school (admittedly a small country high school in the Oklahoma prairie), square dance parties were our favorite form of entertainment, and we just wore blue jeans and our normal school clothing.

Any music that has a rhythm can be used for square dancing. Try it with rock and roll. Try it with the sound track of the movie "Trainspotting." Folk arts have advantages and disadvantages. One disadvantage is that tradition can become rather fixed and inflexible.

A square dance club can improvise further by inventing new steps or "formations." Clog dancing is one form of square dancing, which differs from other square dancing only in the kind of "step" used. Don't let existing forms of square dancing inhibit your imagination. All that is essential is the circle and the square, dancers maintaining physical contact with one another, the caller to introduce an improvisational element, and all dancers making the same moves at the same time, so no one feels self-conscious.

Mandala making is never self-conscious. Self-consciousness is put aside, along with deliberate design, in order to reach a level of instinct and feeling. In square dancing, no thought is required on the part of the dancers. Mandala dancing becomes an expression of the collective self. It is also important that mandala making in any medium be something anyone can do. It takes a lot of skill and practice to do some of the more showy moves of either ballroom or rock and roll dancing, as well as a total lack of inhibition. In ballroom or rock and roll, the dancer must learn the dance moves ahead of time and practice them. Many people do not have that opportunity. Most shy and awkward people do not dance ballroom or rock and roll; however, they have no difficulty with square dancing.

The basic moves and steps are easy, and since everyone in the room is doing exactly the same thing at the same time, there is none of that fear that everyone is watching the dancer make a fool of himself, which inflict some of us on the dance floor. The square dancer doesn't have to be inventive. He or she only has to listen to the caller.

Cloth: The second folk art is quilting. It has all the elements of the mandala, including the circle, the square and improvisation. Quilting has to do with clothing only in the sense that the medium is cloth. The traditional quilt is something put on the bed, or if it is a rare and expensive antique, on the wall. However, it can just as easily be sewn onto jackets, skirts, pants, bags or robes, and this is often done by quilters.

The quilting technique can be used to make banners or flags by sewing the pieces together with a layer of black paper to provide reinforcement. In this case, there is no "quilting," a term which refers to the stuffing in the middle layer of a quilt, adding bulk and warmth.

While today quilts are regarded as works of art, traditionally they were a frugal way of making use of worn-out, castoff or outgrown clothing. Indeed, the improvisational part mostly comes in the selection of colors and designs of cloth. Quilting was also a communal activity. I am not a quilter myself, but my grandmother was.

The formal elements of quilting make use of both the "circle" (repeated elements, many small pieces cut to the same pattern) and the "square," i.e. power-of-two relationships between lengths. I know a few of the many primary patterns in quilting, used to make each block. One block can be sewn onto a robe or jacket or purse. Many blocks sewn together form the top level of a quilt. The stitching that holds all three layers of a quilt has its own separate beauty and pattern.

One primary pattern is the "monkey wrench." Start with four small squares of two contrasting fabrics. Sew these together to make a larger square. Then begin adding right triangles, alternating the same two contrasting fabrics. The hypotenuse of the triangle is sewn to the edge of the previous square. In this way a sequence of circumscribing and rotated squares is made, as the square grows larger.

Some designs are created by repeated folding of freezer paper. A single pattern is cut out of the folded paper, which when unfolded provides a block pattern with 4-fold or 8-fold central symmetry. It is then ironed onto the cloth to provide a pattern for cutting.

Drama: The third folk art is drama or procession. Mandala drama has nothing to do with performance on a stage for an audience. All mandala-making is participatory. Mandala dramas are the traditional folk processionals and rituals of Carnival or other religious days still practiced in the Latin nations, and in Japan and India. The Western and non-Western "Carnivals" are surprisingly similar, tapping the universal patterns of the collective unconscious.

Mandala drama involves creating masks, costumes, floats, or objects carried, either individually or by a group of participants, putting on makeup or costumes to lose one's ordinary self, and dancing, drumming, raving wildly through the streets all night long. Usually these events have a religious or mythological basis. Sometimes the final act is to burn the large figures, accompanied by fireworks. One is acutely aware of the fact that this country was founded by Puritans, since the only Carnival here is in the predominately French and Catholic portions of the country, e.g. Louisiana.

Our Carnivals are nothing compared to the extravagance in other countries. We must lose our inhibitions, get in touch with metaphysical and mythological themes, and learn to express. Ex-Puritans will have to consciously re-invent Carnival, or processionals celebrating New Year's or the Fourth of July. Like square dancing, processional is a mandala of the collective unconscious of the group. Processionals or dramas are also part of mandala magick.

When it comes to both dancing and drama, our Puritan roots show. American culture has many roots, which is our strength, even if at times it threatens to split us into many warring tribes. Rock and roll springs from African-American and Irish roots in our culture. The New Age movement of the 1960s is unimaginable without rock and roll. Despite the excesses (especially with drugs) and the absurdities of the New Age, some real change began in the sixties.

A true New Age will be a tapestry with threads from every culture, including that of the First Nations. The Navaho still have elaborate festivals which last for days, which involve making the elaborate paintings of colored sand which are certainly mandalas. Why can't we claim some of those rites and make them our own? Would the Navaho object? I do not know. I can only say the mandala philosophy combined with our varied ancestry offers us a richness of cultural possibilities.

We can even mine our European roots for folk rituals, which are still practiced in small towns in Spain, Portugal, Italy and Mexico. We now have many immigrants from the Far East, so why not mine our East Indian, Japanese and Chinese roots as well?

Have fun. Lose your self in the greater Self. Tap the deeper roots of consciousness, and express ONE in motion.

My Meditation Practices

Knowing that I am an illuminati, many people ask me about my meditation practices, and assume that I am "visualizing a lotus in my third chakra" or sitting zazen for 5 hours a day, or something similar. I don't, of course. Furthermore, we know that such practices are not the only route to mystical states, (if indeed they even ARE paths to mystical states) because there are natural mystics in every time and place, and surely they all hadn't just stumbled onto esoteric practices such as "one-pointed consciousness."

I, too, am a natural mystic. That is to say, I wasn't consciously following any set of practices and had no teacher when I experienced the illumination of fire and the lesser mystical states that lead up to it. However, in examining my own life, I can see that there was a path that I was following by "accident." It is a path in the sense that spending a lot of time in certain lesser mystical states prepares one for the illumination of fire.

The two lesser states are "day-dreaming" and "being in a receptive state" while experiencing solitude in nature. Probably almost everyone has experienced these states. For instance, when do you get your best ideas? While washing dishes? Commuting to work? On your daily walk? I'll bet it is while doing something comfortably monotonous, which one can do without paying attention, thus letting the mind roam free. And isn't it a glowing, luminous kind of state, a minor state of ecstasy? Those are the marks of a mystical experience.

Thus, the meditation practice I advocate is just the opposite of the popular Buddhist types of meditation. Do not sit still. Do not concentrate on anything. The day-dreaming state is the very opposite of concentration. It is only when mind and soul are free that they can wander into other realms of consciousness. Concentration will never work.

Nature mysticism becomes possible when one has spent a lot of time day-dreaming. So day-dreaming is the first step on the path, nature mysticism is the second, and the illumination of fire the third. I found the endless sighing wind of the prairie the most conducive for communion. For others, it might be the endless crashing of waves on a seashore. Or the sighing of trees in a forest. Again the signs of communion are a glowing, luminous, somewhat ecstatic state of mind. One absorbs the mood of the place. However, if you think the wind, or the mountains or the sea speaks to you, you are hallucinating. Symbolism or verbal thoughts are quite absent in the consciousness of nature. So my second piece of advice on meditation is to spend a lot of time in solitude in nature. Don't concentrate. Don't think. Just absorb the mood of the place, or the wind, or the sea.

Clearly, the most important requirement for most people who wish to become mystics, is a change in lifestyle. Get far away from cities or towns. Learn to enjoy solitude (this is another mark of the mystic, who is never bored with his or her own company). Find yourself some simple tasks which you can do automatically. "Carrying wood and water," is what the Taoist mystics called this path. And, as a child, I did carry wood and water, since we had a wood burning stove and no running water. The pump was a good hundred yards from the house. It is difficult to find such conditions today.

The person who is constantly worried about something, constantly scheming about something, will never become a mystic. Don't worry. Don't hurry. And that too, requires a change in lifestyle. The people least likely to ever know an ecstatic moment are those driven and harried workaholics whose goal only seems to be the accumulation of things.

By contrast, the mystic is always trying to get rid of the accumulation of things. Possession works both ways. Do I own the car, or does it own me? Do I own the house, or does it own me? If you want to know how it is physically possible to pursue the ecstasy of the mystic, read the chapter on "The Seeker."

The Seeker

"There is One only. You are that One . . . Each droplet of the ocean is totally individual from all others, yet they make one body of water. Each is the ocean. You are the ocean. Even in the depths, there are no levels . . . That which appears to be a diminishing of the Self is in reality a greater realization of the Self. The ocean has been dumped into one who says "I have been thrown into the sea.""

This is from *The Word of One,* ed. Sharpe & Cooke, Tarnhelm Press, Lakemont, GA 1975. This is what I call the revelation of the nameless one, for the source of these ouija readings (1962-63, Carmel, John Cooke, Rosalind Sharpe and others) never identified itself except as a silver dollar, which is literally true, since they used a homemade ouija, redrawn for each session, with a symbol in the middle. They used a silver dollar for the planchette. The Word of One is on-line at members.aol.com/miletus1/toc.htm.

There is ONE only, and you are it! And so am I, and so is every thing that has consciousness, including the soul of the rocks, trees and storms. Somehow the ONE gave rise to separate islands of consciousness, which we call souls. Somehow the ONE gave rise to mind and matter, and set the drama of the universe into motion. Mind, in turn gave rise to apparitional realities of the astral planes. But these are secondary realities, which will not exist forever. A spirit (mind+soul) may exist through countless incarnations, perhaps for millions of years, but it is not forever.

The universe may last for billions of years, but someday it will come to an end, how I do not know. The only true and eternal reality is ONE. From it we came, and to it we will return.

This is a radical idea for modern Western scientific humankind. So how do we know it is true? I believe it because I have found so much else that is true in the Revelation of the Nameless One. It contains the new ecological ethics, saying "Thou shalt walk away from the pile of bones and return to the garden of Eden, where all animals are tame." In the Book of the Deliverer, it perfectly describes the Illumination of Fire and the path to it. This is worth explaining a little bit, because the path of meditation which I followed, and which is depicted in the Deliverer, is quite different from those schools of meditation which we have inherited from the ancient and decrepit cultures of the East. You will never reach the Illumination of Fire following the path of Buddhism or Hinduism as they exist today. So that is another radical idea, rejecting everything that is chic in today's New Age culture.

"The Deliverer is the name of the Book-Strength. Its meaning is: that which is to come to each . . . She is not the Deliverer— nor is he. The flame is." In the book of the Deliverer, a man stands in the flames and consumes a cup of flames, which inflames him from the inside. And, indeed, during the Illumination of Fire, I felt filled and surrounded by the orange light of fire, and I wondered for a moment if the building were on fire.

The illumination of fire is the supreme initiation, and in symbolism, initiation is indicated by serpents. There are serpents of fire forming the infinity sign overhead, and a large, golden, serpent with blue forked tongue faces the figures on stage right, emerging from a black box. The tongue is the main sense organ for serpents, and blue means renewal.

Let me give you more details of this book. A lion stands behind a seated woman facing us, in the nude. The lion's forepaws rest on her shoulders. She warms her hands at a cauldron of fire. A nude man, stage left from their point of view, holds a cup of fire with both hands and drinks, burning the grass around his feet.

and lighting his center. The figures are serene and attractive. In the background is the ocean.

The ocean and the golden serpent represent other mystical states which one must find before one is ready for the Illumination of Fire. Thus, there is a path, in that some steps must be taken before others are possible. The golden serpent with the blue tongue represents nature mysticism, which opens and renews our inner senses, opening us to other mystical states. "Bathing in the waters" is another mystical state, an immersion in the collective unconscious of mankind. This is the root of genius. I was a natural mystic, like Richard Bucke. I followed this path because I enjoyed it, because it came natural, not because I was seeking mystical experience, or had even heard of such a thing.

The essence of this path is many years of solitude in nature, with work or some activity (it can be no more than walking) to keep the body occupied. The mind is then free to wander where it will. It is only when one has no worries, no problems to occupy the mind, and some monotonous task which can be done without attention—it is only then that the mind is free. And that is the essence of this path of meditation—to free the mind to roam happily where it will, immersing itself in a trance-like state. I was fortunate in that no one ever squelched my day-dreaming. I could not get enough of it. Farm chores provided lots of it. I always preferred the most monotonous tasks, like plowing (with a tractor) or herding cows. But I wanted more, so I rode my bike around and round the farm yard, for hours in the summer heat. But no one stopped me. No one said "that's weird." For that I thank my parents, parents I chose for this and other reasons. I have heard this path called "carrying wood and water," as in the saying "before Enlightenment, carry wood and water; after Enlightenment, carry wood and water." Remember, this is the absolute opposite of all the popular forms of meditation imported from the East, all of which require concentrating on an image, or a mantra, or ones navel. The state of wood-and-water meditation is the very opposite of concentration. Don't forget that! This is all important.

Now suppose one wished to consciously follow this path to the Illumination of Fire, which reveals a pattern running through all things, the meaning of life, the Divine Purpose. Well, you have to seek solitude in nature, and lots of monotonous activities to keep the body occupied. Grinding corn for instance, to make flour for tortillas. Unfortunately, the kind of primitive farm I grew up on no longer exists, not even in the Third World.

One problem: how can you afford to leave the world behind, and live for years in the deserts or mountains without a job? It can be done, if one chooses to live on a sufficiently primitive level. Simplicity of life is not asceticism; it is merely the way we can buy our freedom from the economic and social system, and leave the world behind. That has always been the goal of the seeker. In what follows, I describe such a life of simplicity in a fictional format. And it naturally creates many meditation opportunities.

The Life of the Seeker: The time is the mid twenty-first century. A line of walkers is seen in the distance, carrying heavy backpacks through the trackless desert. As they approach a low range of rugged mountains, they follow an invisible trail, known only to themselves. Finally they come to a secluded valley, exactly like many others. No sign that humans have ever come this way. But the leader of the group pushes on a large rock and it sinks into the ground, revealing a small opening to a cave. The group begins to unpack their loads, which seem to consist mostly in large burlap sacks full of grain or beans. As the sacks are passed into the small cave and stored, one of the group changes into a loose flowing robe of unbleached cotton. He seems to be some sort of acolyte. The leader unpacks a small pump and takes the acolyte down to the mouth of the small canyon, where it opens to the desert. Moving several rocks reveals openings to underground storage tanks, designed to store the runoff from the small watershed during the rare summer downpours. Each tank is made from a fifty gallon trash can. There are ten in all, and they are all nearly full.

The leader speaks to the acolyte: "There are other Seekers about a mile up this spur. We'll let them know you are here. Someone should be down to visit you in a few days. You are set for a year."

The group soon departs. The acolyte is left alone. He begins to make an inventory of his meager possessions. 500 gallons of water, and one small dry cave. A solar stove, in sections. Two cotton robes, and two woolen robes, one pair of homemade boots, and one pair of homemade clogs (wooden soles and rope straps), plus materials to repair them. Plus the set of conventional backpacking clothes worn in, which he (or she) will wash and carefully pack away until the year is up. His food for a year consists in six bushels of corn, one of red beans, a bushel of soy beans, and a peck of mung beans. There is also a two gallon can of black strap molasses, a very long winding string of chilis, a five pound brick of tea, a one-gallon container of dried non-dairy creamer (his only source of fat), a pound of salt and a large jar of powdered snuff. There is one sack of limes and another of cabbages. These last two items will be occasionally replenished by visitors. It is considered polite to bring a sack of each when you visit a Seeker in the wilderness. Total cost for food, fifty dollars in Twentieth Century equivalents, more or less.

Inside the cave, hollowed out of rock, are a large stone metate with a smooth grinding stone, and a large stone mortar and pestle. Nestled together are a large stack of small plastic buckets, and another stack of nested lightweight steel pans. There are also empty five gallon buckets that were once grease buckets. They contain a roll of small trash sacks with twisties and rolls of toilet paper. The metal buckets have metal lids which can be dogged down. There are also a few empty one gallon plastic milk jugs with lids. His or her personal backpack contains all personal items, such as books and paper. Also a string hammock and a sleeping bag.

The day is early still, so he begins work on food preparation, though his own pack contains ready-to-eat food for several days.

A Seeker spends much of his day on food preparation. It is good work-meditation. The Seeker takes two plastic buckets and pumps them full of water from one of the underground storage containers. From now on he is on water rationing, and he must monitor his usage carefully. It rains on average but once a year in the desert and it is September, so he cannot count on rain again for a year.

He first sets up his mung bean sprouter. Chinese bean sprouts are sprouted mung beans, and it will take several days to get his first crop. These are his principal source of C and B vitamins, once his limes and cabbages run out. He grinds up a small piece of limestone rock on the metate and adds it to water and a large double handful of corn in one of the plastic buckets. Corn is the staple food of the Seeker. In another bucket he puts a handful of red beans to soak. In another bucket, a handful of soy beans. The soy will be used to make tofu, and the red beans will be boiled and refried. It will be the following day before any of this will be ready. One of his plastic containers is oblong and shallow. He fills this with loose soil and plants his packet of Swiss Chard. This will be his only fresh vegetables for a year. This one time only he uses some of his precious fresh water on his "garden." Later on, the garden will get all waste water, after it has been used for as many purposes as possible.

Metal nuts have been inserted into the rocks outside, though you would have to look closely to see them. To these he screws hooks, which will support his hammock. For much of the year, he can sleep out-of-doors, though in winter it can get quite cold in the desert. He also unpacks his solar stove. This is a double parabola, with a black tube at the focus. The solar stove is a long trough-like apparatus, with a table-like extension to the black tube at one end. Once heated up, molten sodium flows through the apparatus, heating the cooking surface. He puts on a teakettle. There should be just enough sunlight left to make a pot of tea.

After a few days, his routine is something like this. He gets up at dawn, goes to the toilet (nothing more than an area of sand some distance away, where everything is carefully buried), and makes a cold breakfast of tofu, corn mash grits, bean sprouts and lime juice. He will probably also have some cold polenta with molasses. He dips his bean sprouts, which he will do several times a day, takes his corn out of soak and mashes it into grits in the mortar. He then spreads it out to dry.

Some of it he adds to his sour mash, his chief source of vitamin B-12 (also occasionally of small amounts of grain alcohol, used to preserve various desert medicinals). Then he goes for a long walk.

An hour or so later, when the sun is high enough, he will make some tea, and begin to make tofu. The soaked soy beans are mashed up and boiled. The resulting soy milk is then curdled with lime juice and allowed to set. The red beans are put on the solar stove to boil and he begins to grind corn flour on the metate. After several hours work, he has ground a prodigious pile of fine corn flour, some of which is used to make tortillas. It is now about noon, time for the principal meal. He first cooks up an enormous pile of tortillas, then mashes and refries the red beans. He soaks one of the chilis in hot water, and mashes it up to make a fiery hot sauce. Now dinner is served. Some might find it monotonous. It mostly consists in many bean-mash and bean sprout enchiladas, flavored with hot sauce. The corn and beans complement one another in their amino acids to provide complete protein, complex carbohydrates and very little fat. Perhaps he will also have some cubes of tofu lightly fried. And perhaps he will have a bowl of corn meal mush with creamer. A few minutes cooking of corn meal and salt is sufficient to make the make the mush. A little non-dairy creamer in water produces a rich "milk."

The evening meal will be much the same, except that he will also cook up a large pan of polenta and make some ginger and cabbage soup, as long as he has cabbages and ginger. Once his Swiss chard is producing well he may occasionally have a small salad, flavored with lime juice and herbs from the desert. Or perhaps a small mess of greens.

His mineral requirements are slight. The tofu provides

calcium, the molasses provides various trace minerals such as copper and selenium, and cooking on an iron griddle provides traces of iron. A man will lose almost no iron, except from bleeding. In fact, a man can easily develop a toxic buildup of iron if he takes those all-in-one supplements. So he doesn't. Too expensive, anyway. Women Seekers may bring a small bottle of iron supplement pills, taken occasionally. An adult not engaged in heavy manual labor in the hot sun can survive quite well on a pound of solid dry food and a gallon of water a day. He requires no refrigerator or freezer. Dry grain and beans will keep quite well for a year if kept dry and away from rodents and weevils. That is the purpose of the grease cans. Bulk grain and beans also have the virtue of being incredibly cheap if one pays the commodity prices which farmers receive. Indeed, it is this which makes it possible for a Seeker to "live on nothing," without working and without begging. Any American can come up with fifty dollars a year for an indefinite number of years.

The frugal life of the Seeker buys him time and solitude in nature, and freedom from the worries and responsibilities of civilization. It is true that he spends many hours a day in monotonous and repetitive work required by his food preparation. But this is perfect for inducing the meditative state of mind which begins with day-dreaming and ends in oceanic consciousness, one of the ten mystical states. Being alone, away from the rattle and noise of technology and towns, he is free to immerse himself in nature. And nature in the desert is quite fascinating, with a varied plant and animal life and a very clear atmosphere. Far from cities, the night time sky is brilliant.

This may be a good place, for those who wish it, to experiment with natural entheogens, such as Peyote. Aldous Huxley has the theory that the brain acts as a reducing valve on experience, letting in only what is necessary for the organism's survival. Entheogens throw open the gates. Aldous Huxley used mescaline, which is the active ingredient in peyote, and his primary experience was the immanence of divinity in all things. This is something that cannot be rationalized, or explained, only experienced. In truth, it would probably be better to use pure mescaline than eating Peyote, which always induces vomiting. There are many other natural entheogens. Two that are found in cowlots are jimson weed and purple nightshade. Toltec shamans used various parts of the jimson weed, while some of those who follow the Craft used purple nightshade, with its little lantern blossoms. In the cowlot on the farm where I grew up, very few things would grow. Jimson weed, purple nightshade, milkweed, and cockleburs.

The Seeker also has his exercises designed to develop wizard powers. This is a full time job (but not one that pays well!), so the life of the Seeker buys him the time to practice. There is also study and even conversation. His solitude is not complete. There are caves all through these mountains, and for each there is a small watershed which has been tapped for a 500 gallon water supply. Every mile or so, there may be found Seekers, both men and women. And they do visit one another, and congregate periodically. Seekers are not required to be celibate, nor are they required to abstain from alcohol, tobacco, peyote, jimson weed or magic mushrooms. Not that such use is encouraged. Most Seekers are naturally abstemious and some are even celibate. It all depends on what they are trying to accomplish. The apparent asceticism of their life is merely a consequence of the simple life, not an end in itself. It is the way they buy freedom and time.

Since the desert Seekers never take baths or do laundry, you might imagine that they would smell! Not so, however. They sponge bath with a wash cloth once a day and after performing the necessary ablutions. Seekers alternate robes each day, shaking the other one out and leaving it to air out on a line. With a little caution, one can stay clean without taking baths or doing laundry, which are not forbidden, of course, but merely impractical given the water rationing. Of course, Seekers of both sexes begin their period of solitude by cutting off all their hair, so shampoo is not required. Occasional clipping will keep it short. This is simply done to save water.

Some Seekers find power and wisdom, through practice, meditation, and mystical experience. Some return to the world as an accomplished Deliverer. But most love the desert life so much that it is hard for them to leave. In some cases, the power and wisdom of such individuals becomes so great that the world comes to them, rather than vice versa.

There are others who never take up the life of the Seeker full time, but escape to the desert now and then, for a month or so, just to refresh their senses and revitalize their energies. Others find their mission in life to be the pack mules and cave diggers and cistern builders, who make it possible for Seekers to live on nothing.

Once the Seeker experiences the beauty of an absolutely unspoiled landscape and the joy of a rich inner life, he can only pity the poor city dweller and his life of noise and confusion, trapped in the rat-race, surrounded by the mass produced thoughts and entertainments pandered by those of low thought and brutalized spirit.

No one could have predicted such a development in the hi-tech world of the Twentieth Century, but these desert hermits are increasingly regarded as the leading edge of mankind, the most advanced and creative souls on the planet. Odd to think that their freedom from things was once regarded as a perverse sort of self-denial. They have merely learned that possessions possess their possessors. Most people work for their things; the things do not work for them.

Now the scene shifts. It is night and winter in the city. We enter a large building at the outskirts of town, with a magnificent view towards some distant mountains. It is a building that seems to turn its back on the works of man, with its high stone walls without windows facing the city, and its darkness. For there are no electric lights in or about this building. Inside, in the great hall, a roaring wood fire crackles in a huge fireplace. Around on rugs or crude wooden furniture are many of the inhabitants, laughing and talking. There are tapestries on the walls, and curtains over stairway doors and hallways, to cut down on drafts. It is all very medieval looking, for there are no signs of modern technology, in the building or on the inhabitants, who are all dressed in long and loose woolen cloaks and felt slippers. You are given such attire when you enter the mandalium on a visit or a retreat. The only heat is the single fireplace in the great hall, and charcoal braziers people carry to their cells. Yes, that is how they refer to the rooms given to guests and permanent residents alike. They are small rooms, with hand-hewn wooden furniture, a kerosene lamp, and a hammock. They are not unlike the caves of the Seekers in size and furnishing. The building is set around a courtyard with fountains, trees and gardens. It is a lovely place in summer, but winter is when you can catch the Seekers at home. For this is where they live, in places like this, when they are not up in the hills or out on the desert. And when Seekers travel from city to city, they stay in the local mandalium. Not that a Seeker is forbidden to ride in a vehicle or enjoy modern conveniences if they wish. The austerity of this place is freely chosen, to stay close to nature and its moods. Everything is stone and ceramic tile in this place. The furniture (what little there is of it) is massive and unpadded. It is all built for the ages, and constructed by hand from green wood, patiently carved in the old way out of logs cut by the carver.

    Visitors are always welcome. Visitors prepare their own food, and the food is the same that Seekers eat in their caves and desert camps. This is no hotel, but it is a kind of refuge, a quiet and contemplative place, with a rule of silence. The rule is that you do not disturb the reverie of another unless he or she indicates that you may do so. Here is where you come if you are interested in the wisdom or power of the Seekers. While they will never interfere in the evolution of another, and never offer advice or information unasked, they are always willing to share what they have, and help those in need, if they believe that is consistent with the evolution of the one in need.

In the winter there are often "mandala concerts." Seekers and guests alike may create mandala music, dance, poetry, drama, masks and costumes, and mandala painting. This is not done for an audience. All must participate. It is because of the mandala sessions that this place is called a mandalium. It is contrary to new age morality to impose a belief on another, so there is nothing here that quite corresponds to the classes of universities, the services and sermons of religion, or the guru and his flock of disciples. Still, this seems a holy place, full of learning, and visitors leave feeling renewed.

Conclusion: Does it seem we have wandered a long way from Interstellar Travel? That is because you expected it to be about machinery, when it really is all about psi powers, which can only be developed by a species which is spiritually advanced. So we first learned some of the main facts discovered by Psychical Research, and looked at a theory which could advance that subject greatly, if it is ever tested. An evolved society is one that has taken care of its social problems, and thus we had to go into utopian analysis in some detail. Finally, we come to matters of soul and divinity. I told you that jumping lightyears requires both physics and mystics.

So what is the point of this book? That the evolution of interstellar travel reflects the evolution of spiritually advanced societies. Evolution is usually gradual. Yet, it may also develop by jumps. One such jump was the invention of scientific method in the 17th Century. Since then, scientific method has expanded its scope by a series of smaller jumps, to many other subjects, from economics to geology and biology. In this book, I shall expand the range of scientific method to new territory. In psychical research and Ufology, there are true scientists, but there are also crackpots. Before now, scientific method has never been applied to ideology or religious faith. There have been many attempts, such as Marxism, Christian Science, and Scientology, all failures. It is by no means obvious how to apply scientific method to a new subject, but I have done so in this book, and you will have to judge if I have done so correctly. One thing I am sure of. Knowledge is more evolved than ideology or articles of faith, which only provide excuses for riots and wars.

Scientific method is not restricted to any particular realm of experience, or any particular question. I am confident that we are close to a great revolution in human thought, one which will be brought about by the final defeat of reduction. A single fact can collapse a mountain of sophistry. That fact could arise from a test of the Prana-pump, which would give scientists the first "produce on demand" Psi phenomena. It is "produce on demand" because we have no conscious control over it. Whoever performs this test will win the Nobel Prize. No takers so far.

It is not all dragon-slaying in this book. There is a new age dawning. I put that in small caps, since I merely mean that with a new worldview, and new sciences, and a new spirituality with its own new aesthetics . . . life will change, dramatically. As David Spangler says ". . . the New Age is not a new religion . . . . Christianity is like a great cathedral . . . . By contrast, the New Age is more like a flea market or a county fair, a collection of differently colored and designed booths spread around a meadow." (Ferguson, p. 80). New age people are by no means all alike. They are involved in everything from Goddess Spirituality, to Reincarnation, to Shamanism, to Ecofeminism. Indeed, Spangler lists 40 quite different things that New Agers are involved in, and this is not a complete list (Ferguson, p. 81). But one thing we all say is "I am spiritual, but not religious."

This is our common theme, the rejection of all religions, including the religion of reduction. Another common theme is the search for spirituality in numerous different ways. This could really change Western Civilization. However, there can be no higher spirituality so long as the ideal of liberty is ignored, and sellers of harmless marijuana or entheogens are treated more harshly than murderers. We will never get control of global population so long as the US opposes population control. And why does it do that? Because the Republicans are under the control of the religious right. So social change is a high priority for me, and perhaps the first change needed is a change in our form of government, so it cannot be hijacked by special interest groups. I do not think that other kinds of spiritual evolution can proceed very far until we return to the great libertarian ideals of the Enlightenment. For one thing, the mental part of spiritual evolution is likely to take centuries, perhaps millennia, yet at the present moment, the mere survival of the species until the year 2100 CE is in doubt. So those problems come first. I shall call these problems "utopian" rather than spiritual.

I hope to contribute to the search for spirituality proper, in various ways. One is to point out to the general public some of the genuine scientific classics in psychical research and Ufology. Another contribution is an alphabet of symbolic elements, making it possible for everyone to learn the language of symbolism, since spiritual truths can best be expressed in art, music and architecture. Significant aesthetics, such as classical music, capable of lifting the spirit to exalted states, has more or less vanished under the Heroic Materialism of the 20th Century. Let's start all over again, with mandalas. I have extended the mandala concept and technique to all media.

If we wish to bring about a new age, what should we be doing? All the many things we New Agers are already doing. Working to get medicinal marijuana legalized. Participating in sacred dance or drumming. Working on alternative energy sources. Learning meditation. And a thousand other things. Beyond that, we need to form a community. It is only as a community that we can really change things.

What do we New Age people have in common? More than anything, it is a rejection of the cold and heartless worldview of reduction, and an affirmation of everything opposite. That means we believe in the sacred earth, and the independent existence of mind and soul. And in free-will. We are not soul-less automatons, and neither is a butterfly, a liverwort, or a fungus. Even bacteria display animacy, which no machine ever has or will. We find divinity in mystical states, and sometimes in psychedelic experience. After taking Mescalin, the active ingredient in peyote, Aldous Huxley "saw" the immanence of divinity in all things. And that too is something new age people generally accept. The world is alive and sacred. Everything has a soul. These are the things we believe in, but we don't intend to make it into a religion.

I want to suggest a subtle way we can identify ourselves to one another, without being noticed by the fundamentalist Christians or the reductionist and materialist followers of the religion of science. The early Christians had the same problem. They wanted to identify themselves to one another, to develop a sense of community, yet not call attention to themselves from the Roman Authorities or the powerful Pagan Priests.

One way they did it was to draw a simple fish-like symbol in one continuous line. It is really just a loop with each end of the line extended, to suggest the tail of a fish, without finishing the end of the tail. The uninitiated would regard it as just a doodle. Often, this was drawn in the dust, to see if ones companions were Christians or not. The early Christians gradually developed a complex cryptography. One common sign was the Chi-Rho, which looks like a capital X with the letter P drawn vertically through the center. The Rho sign is like a "P" with the top part shrunk to little more than a knob. Being Greek letters rather than Latin, the Romans might not recognize them as letters, and their significance would be unknown.

I suggest we new Agers do the same thing. We need to create a sense of community. There are a lot more of us than we know. Our next door neighbors might be new Agers, and we wouldn't know it, unless they were fairly blatant. One way we can do this is with clothing and jewelry, both for men and women. New age jewelry is made of silver or copper, seldom of gold. It uses semi-precious stones, polished but not shaped. Examples will be found on PyramidCollection.com. New age stones are seldom cut and faceted like diamonds and emeralds. Usually they are cabochons, often of irregular shape. Minerals that naturally form crystals are left in that form.

In the Pyramid catalog, there is a lot of marvelous new age clothing for women, but I don't see much for men except for some T-shirts. There is a pair of T-shirts, each having one half of the Taoist Tai Chi symbol. This would be meaningless to religious people, but new Agers would recognize it. We also need some way of marking our houses and our cars. A bumper sticker that said "I am a witch" might be a bit too blatant. But what about an inconspicuous Chinese ideograph for Wisdom? In the Pyramid catalog, there is a box of 20 wood backed rubber stamps of Chinese characters, and a red inkpad. Again, meaningless to the masses, but capable of identifying one new Ager to another.

So let us create a loose community, where we live, and in the world at large, committed to our numerous immediate causes, united in working for spiritual evolution, however we might separately define that.

I wish to conclude with some quotes from the book *The Word of One*. I shall not comment on them. You either get it or you won't. Symbolic revelation from the depths of Self is part of empirical metaphysics, so long as one can verify the content by experience. This particular revelation was given to a group of Seekers in the winter of 1962-63 in Carmel, California. The transcript of these sessions make up the book *The Word of One*. Each of the participants was given new names. John Star Cooke, the leader of the group, was named "Legion," while the second in command so to speak, Rosalind Sharpe, was named "Gayla." Material was received with a home made Ouija board, created anew for each session, using a silver dollar as the planchette. The source of this material never gave itself a name, so they referred to the source as "WE," assuming that this revelation somehow came from their own deeper selves. The Doer is one of the Books revealed, and is a seven year old boy, holding an unrolled scroll to be read. He is flanked by a white horse rearing on a human skull, and a black horse, loosely held by a ribbon. A beautifully figured Sun is high overhead. This is the new version of the Sun card. Mother is another book, and represents creativity. She is the new version of the High Priestess.

"ONE is all .... Deny not ONE while you live. The world is full of those who say they seek ONE. How is it that seekers always blind themselves first to their surroundings? Until they remove the film, they seek in vain. Do you wish a word of comfort? There is none. Do you wish a better road? There is none. Do you wish a Savior? There is none. For you, there is only ONE. You will make that do." p. 385.

"There is a stirring felt in sleeping regions. Great must be the full awaking. Neither din nor force shall accomplish this. The awakened One arises. The sleeping one sleeps. There is an arouser but he wakes not up."—p. 170.

"Over all lies a mantle of fog through which the sun is coming—the son is coming .... The breath of life is in your hands, the spark of death, also. Quicken the new birth and fan the spark that the passing past is laid at rest. Desire above all things the Sun."

"The Rosetta stone is rolled away. A burden is lifted. A free soul flies onward. Yellow eyes, unblinking, number the years."—p. 171.

"The siren bell has rung. Its penetration has entered but not emerged. Therefore its vibration continues its wonders to perform ... The market place is a-thrive. Strange beads and salt are vended. Buyers there are none. A pitcher of water reflects the sun. The thirst is mighty but the sun is reflected undisturbed. Maggots will grow if the pitcher is not emptied."

"Children parentless seek the Mother. She is busy begetting the Sun. He is now with the world. His cord is severed. He will soon speak. He will speak of the Mother."

"Fairy frost at the windows betoken good fortune. Magic are the times now, Magickal are the happenings. The Doer has been activated."

"The juice of memory rises. When it spills will be the time of reversal. It is coming. Be ye prepared. Mighty shall be the roar, violent the rending, joyous the release." p. 164

"Great will be the transformation now while nothing visible appears to happen—yet the New Man will stand naked in glory. Tis a promise seen dimly now." p. 112

"LEGION: Is the Great Event Imminent?

WE: Yes.

GAYLA: How imminent?"

At this point a sudden wind whipped open the heavy door beside the group and night air rushed into the room.

"WE: Take a breath. It has taken place . . . ." p. 413.

Bibliography

Arndt, M. et al. (1999) *Letters to Nature*, vol 401, October 14, 1999 pg 680.

―――― (1989). *Traffic Congestion; A Toolbox for Alleviating Traffic Congestion*. Washington, DC: Institute of Transportation Engineers.

―――― . (1991). *Abortion: Opposing Viewpoints*. San Diego, CA: Greenhaven Press.

Albert, David Z. (1994). Bohm's Alternative to Quantum Mechanics. *Scientific American* 270, #5, May, 1994. p. 58 ff.

Alexander, C., Neis, H., Anninou, A. and King, I. (1977). *A Pattern Language*. New York: Oxford University Press.

Auerbach, Jerolds. (1983). *Justice Without Law?* New York: Oxford University Press.

Black, David. (1986). *The Plague Years: A Chronicle of AIDS, the Epidemic of our Times*. New York: Simon & Schuster.

Blackmore, S. (1988). Do We Need a New Psychical Research? *Journal of the Society for Psychical Research*, 55, 49 ff.

Blackmore, S. (1993). *Dying to Live*. Buffalo: Prometheus.

Bockris, John. (1975). *Energy, The Solar Hydrogen Alternative*. New York: Wiley.

Boutros-Ghali, Boutros. (1992). *An Agenda For Peace*. New York: United Nations.

Brennan, Barbara Ann. (1993, 1994). *Hands of Light, Light Emerging*.

Broadbent, Geoffrey. (1990). *Emerging Concepts in Urban Space Design*. New York: Van Nostrand.

Cappon, D. (1971). "Mental Health and High Rise." *Canadian Public Health Association*, April.

Corso, Col. Philip J. (1997). *The Day After Roswell*. New York: Pocket.

Crowe, Timothy D. (1991). *Crime Prevention Through Environmental Design*.

Edwards, Frank. (1966). *Flying Saucers—Serious Business*. Secaucus: Citadel Press.

Eisenbud, Jules, M.D. (1967). *The World of Ted Serios*, New York: William Morrow.

Fanning, D. M. (1967). "Families in Flats." *British Medical Journal*, November, No. 198.

Ferguson, Duncan S. (1993), Editor. *New Age Spirituality*, Louisville: John Knox Press.

Figgie, Harold. (1992). *Bankruptcy 1995: The Coming Collapse of America and How to Stop It*. Boston: Little, Brown.

Fisher, Helen. (1994). *Anatomy of Love: The Mysteries of Mating, Marriage, and Why We Stray*. New York: Fawcett Columbine.

Fishman, Robert. (1989). *Urban Utopias in the Twentieth Century*. Cambridge: MIT Press.

Friedman and Berliner. (1992). *Crash At Corona*, New York: Paragon House.

Gallion, A. & Eisner, S. (1986). *The Urban Pattern*. New York: Van Nostrand Reinhold.

Gardner, Martin (1966). *Dermo-Optical Perception: A Peek Down the Nose*. Science. 152:1108.

Halpern, Paul. (1992). *Cosmic Wormholes; The Search for Interstellar Shortcuts*. New York: Dutton.

Herbert, Nick. (1988). *Faster Than Light; Superluminal Loopholes in Physics*. New York: New American Library.

Howard, Philip K. (1994). *The Death of Common Sense; How Law is Suffocating America*. New York: Random House.

Jacobs, J. (1961). *The Death and Life of Great American Cities: The Failure of Town Planning*. New York: Random House.

Karagulla, S. (1967). *Breakthrough to Creativity; Your Higher Sense Perception*. Los Angeles: DeVorss & Co., Inc.

Kelsey, Denys and Grant, Joan (1967). *Many Lifetimes*. New York: Doubleday.
Kilbourne, E. (1988). *Influenza*. New York: Plenum.
Krauss, Lawrence. (1995). *The Physics of Star Trek*. New York: BasicBooks.
Krier, L. (1987). "Atlantis, Tenerife." *Architectural Design*, 58.
Kuhn, T. S. (1962). *The Structure of Scientific Revolutions*. Chicago: University of Chicago Press.
Lazare, Daniel. (1996). *The Frozen Republic; How the Constitution Is Paralyzing Democracy*. New York: Harcourt Brace & Company.
Leakey, Richard, and Lewin, Roger. (1995). *The Sixth Extinction; Patterns of Life and the Future of Mankind*. New York: Doubleday.
Le Corbusier. (1967). *The Radiant City*. London: Faber.
Lerner, Eric. (1991). *The Big Bang Never Happened*. New York: Times Books.
Lynch, Kevin. (1981). *Good City Form*. Cambridge: MIT Press.
Macklin, John. (1965). *Strange Destinies*. New York: Ace.
Mallove, Eugene and Matloff, Gregory. (1989). *The Starflight Handbook; A Pioneer's Guide to Interstellar Travel*. New York: Wiley.
Marx, Doug. (1990). *The Homeless*. Vero Beach, Fl: Rourke Corp.
Mitchell, J.L. (1981). *Out-Of-Body Experiences, A Handbook*. Jefferson, North Carolina: McFarland & Company.
Monroe, Robert. (1971). *Journeys Out of the Body*, New York: Doubleday.
Moody, R. (1975). *Life After Life*. St. Simons Island, Georgia, USA: Mockingbird Press.
Morris, R. (1993). *Cosmic Questions*. New York: Wiley.
Morville, J. (1969). *Borne Brug af Friarsaler*. SBI: Denmark.
Newman, O. (1972). *Defensible Space: People and Design in the Violent City*. New York: Macmillan.
Ostrander, S. & Schroeder, L. (1970). *Psychic Discoveries Behind the Iron Curtain*. Englewood Cliffs, New Jersey: Prentice-Hall, Inc.

Penrose, Roger. (1990). *The Emperor's New Mind*. Oxford University Press.
Powers, Robert. (1981). *The Coattails of God; The Ultimate Spaceflight—The Trip to the Stars*. New York: Warner.
Rabinovitch, J. and Leitman, J. (March, 1996). "Urban Planning in Curitiba," *Scientific American*. SA: New York.
Randles, Jenny. (1997). *Alien Contact; The First Fifty Years*. New York: Sterling Publishing Co, Inc.
Ring, K. (1982). *Life at Death*. New York: Quill.
Rivenburg, Roy. (March 24, 1995). "Blinded by the Light?" Los Angeles: *LA Times*.
Rojansky, V. (1938). *Introductory Quantum Mechanics*. Englewood Cliffs, New Jersey: Prentice-Hall, Inc.
Rucker, Rudy. (1982). *Mind and Infinity*. New York: Bantam.
Sabom, M.B. (1982). *Recollections at Death*. London: Gorgi.
Sagan, Carl. (1986). *Contact*. New York: Simon & Schuster.
Sagan, Carl. (1997). *The Demon-Haunted World*. New York: Ballantine.
Smylie, D.E., and Mansinha, L. (December 1971). "The Rotation of the Earth," vol. 225, #6, *Scientific American*, pp. 80-88.
Spence, Gerry. (1989). *With Justice For None: Destroying an American Myth*. New York: Times Books.
Stenger, Victor J. (1990). *Physics and Psychics*. Buffalo, NY: Prometheus Press.
Stevenson, I. (1966). *Twenty Cases Suggestive of Reincarnation*. New York: American Society for Psychical Research.
Sutherland, Cherie. (1992). *Reborn In The Light; Life After Near-Death Experiences*. New York: Bantam.
Tipler, Frank J. (1994). *The Physics of Immortality*. NY: Doubleday.
Twining, H. LaV. (1915). *The Physical Theory of the Soul*, Westgate, CA.: Press of the Pacific Veteran.
Tyrrell, G.N.M. (1953). *Apparitions*. London: The Society for Psychical Research.
Vaughan, A. (1970). Poltergeist Investigations in Germany. *Psychic*, April.

Watson, Lyall (1973). Matter and Magic. *Supernature*. Garden City: publisher unknown.

Wesselman, Hank (1995). *Spiritwalker; Messages from the Future*. New York: Bantam.

Wilber, Ken. (1984). *Quantum Questions; Mystical Writings of the World's Great Physicists*. Boston: Shambhala.

Wilson, William H. (1989). *The City Beautiful Movement*. Baltimore: Johns Hopkins University Press. The 19th century Park and Boulevard system which gave us Central Park in NYC.

Winters, Randolph. (1994). *The Pleiadian Mission; A Time of Awareness*. Yorba Linda: The Pleiades Project.

Wolf, Fred Alan. (1989). *Taking the Quantum Leap*, New York: Harper & Row.

Printed in the United States
6133